Humor at the Speed of Life

Ned Hickson

To Steve and Cathy,
Thank you for reading
and your humor
Ned Hickson

Port Hole Publications
Florence, Oregon

Ned Hickson is an award winning syndicated humor columnnist. This, his first book, is a compilation of columns, most of which were published by the *Siuslaw News* in Florence, Oregon. Reissued by permission.

ISBN- 13: 978-0-9892608-3-1
ISBN-10: 0-9892608-3-6

Cover by Ned Hickson; image courtesy

Published by Port Hole Publications
179 Laurel St. - Suite D
Florence, Oregon 97439
Website: portholepublications.com

Dedicated to

My wife, Alicia, whose love, beauty and laughter are
constant inspirations;
My mom, Susan, who helped me understand the
importance of humor in life;
My children, Elyse, Connor, Jake and Elizabeth, who keep me
grounded in youthful truth;
My grandmother, Nonnie, who showed that humor,
like wine, only gets better with age;
And my readers — every single one of you.

This Just In...

After 15 years as a humor columnist, it finally hit me. And by that I mean my editor's stapler. She had been threatening to throw it since 2004, when I first discovered the secret candy drawer she had cleverly labeled: Extra Work for Reporters. For the past nine years she had been warning me, "If you don't stay out of my candy drawer, I am going to set this thing for 'stun' and *hurl* it at you!"

As I sat there, blurry-eyed and rubbing the back of my head, I came to an important and potentially life-changing realization:

I really need to publish this book now, before she gets a new stapler.

Once my editor replenished her candy stash, there was a good chance another direct hit would result in serious brain damage, ending my career as a journalist and leaving me to write for daytime television. The truth is, readers have been asking me for years to compile a book of columns. As one reader from Gwynette, GA., wrote in, "If you ever come here for a book signing, you better have pastries or something." When you receive that kind of validation from readers, you don't want to let them down. With that in mind — and a week's worth of medical leave — I began sifting through more than a decade's worth of columns written since I began here at Siuslaw News in 1998. Many of the columns in this book appeared long before syndication; a few never saw publication at all (for good reason?); and at least one got published only because my editor was on vacation.

You'll find this book has been divided into six sections, making it easy to find columns tailored to meet your specific reading needs. For example, let's say you're looking for Three Good Reasons to Avoid Any Monkey With a Pet Chihuahua. That would obviously be a hard-hitting news story, and therefore is in the section: **This is Why I Became a Journalist** (I meant that as a question).

Or let's say you want to know if today's tougher tax Llws will let you depreciate your ostrich?

If you answered **Social Trends** (and other frightening anomalies) for $100 then you are absolutely correct!

But you really need to cut back on the Jeopardy! watching.

Other sections in this book include:

Parenting Is as Easy as One, Two... Scream
(My fountain of knowledge on parenting is an open ~~bar~~ book.)

Why Is the Dog Wearing Cowboy Boots?
(They say pets help us live longer. "They" haven't met my dog)

Women Are From Venus and Men Won't Ask for Directions
(Observations and insights that have gotten me into trouble)

Inspirational Holiday Columns That proved life threatening
(Hey, even the NRA fears the National Fruitcake Lovers Society)

So, brace yourself.

In the pages that follow, you will find what represents my body of work as a humor columnist.

My apologies in advance for not getting to the gym more often...

—Ned

Florence, Oregon
Nov. 16, 2013

This is why I became a journalist

(I meant that as a question)

Snoring is sure sign of a seasoned journalist

Every journalist has a routine. For example, I always write my column early in the morning. The earlier the better. That's because, generally speaking, I'm not awake yet. Sure, I may be drinking coffee and typing, but if you were to monitor my brain activity, it would register somewhere between an earthworm and the average American watching *Dancing With the Stars*.

Admittedly, my brain doesn't open for business until about 10 a.m. By then, I've been at the keyboard for three or four hours with no real memory of what I've been writing. I assure my editor this unique quirk is the sign of a seasoned professional.

And he assures me the reason we need to keep replacing my keyboard is because, at least once a month, he finds me face down, drooling on the return key. That may be true, but I tend to do my best work under pressure. And there's nothing like the pressure of trying to finish a column before saliva short-circuits your keyboard. In addition to a lack of cognizance, I also prefer writing early in the morning because there aren't any distractions, like... oh, I don't know... say, being blinded by a crazed fly.

The truth is, this column was going to be a stunning piece of social commentary. I had planned to utilize all the tools I've acquired as a columnist (namely, spell-check and the "delete" button, assuming it hasn't been drooled on) to discuss a little-known but steadily growing segment of the voting population:

Chihuahuas who have mistakenly been issued voter registration cards in Florida.

Anyone who has written Pulitzer Prize-winning material will tell you it takes an incredible amount of concentration and skill to produce work of such significance.

I know.

As a recipient of the Putziler Prize for "Most Consistent Use of Spelling Errors" in 1999, I was, quite literally, only a few scrambled letters away from a Pulitzer myself. In keeping with that standard, I should've been able to finish my Chihuahua column in spite of being the unwitting target of a psychopathic fly. I have no excuse other than to say, before this experience, I would've never considered sealing up my cubicle and installing an air-lock door complete with retinal scanner and emergency fly swatter.

It actually started out like any other annoying man-Vs-fly situation.

Fly lands on hand.

Hand shoos fly away.

Then, and without warning:

Fly attacks eyeball.

Things immediately moved into the realm of Alfred Hitchcock Presents, complete with — I must admit — screaming that would've frightened Janet Leigh. In all fairness, I now had only ONE good eye, which limited my peripheral vision and put me at a distinct disadvantage to the fly which, as we all know, has enough eyes to see in all directions at once, including behind, which is the direction I happened to be running from.

Yes, I probably should've stood my ground.

And if he hadn't blinded my other eye, I probably would have. However, as I stood there swinging blindly at the fly with a rolled up magazine, I realized two important things precisely in this order:

1) I looked like a Star Wars fanatic pretending to be in Jedi training.

2) Someone could walk through the door at any minute.

Because of this, the Pulitzer Prize committee will have to wait. In the meantime, I still have a chance at another Putziler, depending on how I spelled Chihuahua.

Cosmetic surgery — boldly taking us where no one in their right mind has gone before

Today, we will be talking about an important milestone in the field of cosmetic surgery. Why? Because on my desk this morning was a press release with the following headline:

At long Last! *Buttocks Enhancement* Surgery available in U.S.!

So, as you can see, I really had no choice.

Especially since, as a professional courtesy, one of my fellow journalists had taken the time to write "Urgent!" across the top. (And, yes—these are the kinds of things that regularly cross my desk.)

As you might expect, buttocks enhancement surgery is just like other cosmetic procedures in that the sole purpose is to improve the physical attributes of a person. This is accomplished by either enlarging or reducing the size of said attribute.

Which can be singular or plural.

And we'll just leave it at that.

In this case, however, we're talking about enlarging the buttocks. While many people, such as myself, prefer to achieve this naturally through a program of rigorous eating and lack of exercise, there are others who don't want to wait for the holidays for a larger rear. For these people there is Dr. Mark Jewell, vice-president of the National Aesthetic Society, which is currently offering this procedure here in the U.S.

According to the press release, buttocks enhancement surgery has actually been popular in South America for many years.

Ah, yes — South America! We may not have indoor plumbing, but just look at our butts.

The enhancement process itself can take place three ways. The first is to inject fat directly into the gluteus muscles, which may SOUND gross, but...

Okay, yeah — it's actually pretty gross.

The second is to go with plastic implants that are inserted directly behind the gluteus muscles. This technique, according to Dr. Jewell, is supposed to look the most natural.

That is, as long as you don't plan on going swimming.

If you do, the natural buoyancy of the plastic implants will add a whole new meaning to the term "bottoms-up." It's because of this that you can expect to see an increase in the number of pool injuries, particularly those caused by large children leaping onto what they thought was a wayward floatation device.

The final option is for the surgeon to make an incision directly in the skin surrounding the buttocks, and then stretch it up much like a face lift. The main difference being, of course, that too many of these, and you'll permanently suffer from the world's worst wedgie.

This brings us to our next segment: Face transplants.

This is exactly what it sounds like — surgically replacing someone's entire face all at one time. This is obviously a vast improvement over replacing someone's face over the course of many years, which, as you know, was first pioneered by Michael Jackson.

According to a report in Britain's *The Daily News*, plastic surgeon Peter Butler says he plans to carry out a full-face transplant as early as next April. Butler says the experiment will be performed at London's "Royal Free Hospital." Which is the perfect place since, if something goes wrong, his patient will be royally...

Well, you know.

Butler, however, isn't the only surgeon vying to perform the first successful face transplant. According to a recent article in the journal Medicine, there are at least three other teams of surgeons around the world working on techniques that will allow facial skin, muscles, blood vessels and nerves to be removed from a corpse and attached to someone other than Ted Koppel.

As you can see, we have a lot to look forward to when it comes to the future of cosmetic surgery. Yet, I'd suggest against going in for buttocks enhancement surgery and a face transplant all at once.

Unless you're willing to risk finding out that hindsight really is 20/20.

Science links obesity to fat, lazy microbes

Scientists at Cornell University have created a device capable of measuring the weight of a single cell. This is big news because it moves us beyond the limits of sub-gram measurements "nano," "pico" and "femto," and into an exciting new realm of measurements known as "zeppo," "harpo" and "groucho." This could eventually lead to the smallest and least-known unit of measure, "shempo."

Many of you are probably wondering how useful this information really is when it seems most things — cars, houses, Americans in general — are actually getting bigger. Personally, I see no benefit in being able to describe my weight as "a little over 70 trillion harpo-grams." And I can tell you no husband wants to be around when his wife discovers, after eating that extra helping of potato salad this July Fourth, that she not only gained back the 17 trillion zeppo-grams she'd lost, but also put on an extra two billion grouchos.

It doesn't matter that all of this adds up to less than a single uncooked lima bean; what matters is that I make the potato salad, and will therefore be held responsible.

As Cornell University scientists explained, this new system of measurement is a tremendous breakthrough because it allows them to weigh things that had previously been too small for anyone to actually care about. To help you appreciate this advancement, I will attempt to explain the science behind the discovery. Being that this is a family newspaper, I should warn you that I will be referring to "oscillating cantilevers" and "sextillions." Rest assured that these are completely innocuous words, especially since I have no idea what they mean.

And once again, being that this is a family newspaper, I will refrain from guessing.

According to scientists, their discovery was made by using "tiny oscillating cantilevers" to detect a change in the mass of something as small as one "sextillion." This is equal to one-thousandth of a femtogram, or put in more practical terms, roughly the size of one bacterium nostril.

Why is this important?

Because, as far as I know, this is the first time anyone has actually used the term "bacterium nostril" in a newspaper column.

The bigger question, of course, is how this new ability to weigh microorganisms will affect you and me, the general nose-breathing public? With our nation's obesity problem in mind, I am using this technology to launch my own weight loss program. Unlike other programs, mine strikes at the heart of our obesity issue by placing blame where it belongs: squarely on the shoulders of big fat microbes, which constantly hang all over us, therefore making us appear to weigh more than we actually do.

The "Nedkins Micro Diet" is actually in bookstores right now, so look for it on the shelves. You'll have to look hard, though.

It's pretty small.

Three good reasons to avoid any monkey with a pet Chihuahua

As a journalist, I'm trained to recognize even the most subtle signs of trouble:

A misspoken word.
A reluctant glance.
A gang of monkeys destroying a library.

Thanks to my training and experience — and several highlighted newspaper clippings sent in by concerned readers — I have painstakingly pieced together what I, as a member of the conservative media, believe is undeniable evidence that animals are planning to take over the world. We will begin in eastern India, where scores of monkeys have swamped a college in Darjeeling, which, until recently, had taken great pride in its school slogan:

Loreto College — Unlimited tea and monkey-free!

"That has all changed now," said one student, who refused to be identified out of fear of reprisal. "They interrupt my classes, steal my lunch, hassle me and the other students. It's like junior high school all over again."

According to the article, which was first reported by the *Indo-Asian News Service* and sent to me by Norman Buckner of Kalamazoo, Mich., the biggest problem is that the monkeys have no fear of humans. This in spite of repeated threats by angry school officials to "fail each and every student without an opposable thumb."

As unsettling as that article was, it wasn't until reading this next piece from *The Register-Guard* in Eugene, Ore., that I began to consider canceling my PETA membership. This story was frightening for two reasons. First, because it involves rats (which, as many of you know, I would gladly recall from Earth, given the proper authority). And second, because the thought of rats popping up in any toilet within 100-miles of my home has caused me to consider switching to a full-time liquid diet.

According to an article sent in by Tammy Ruger of Creswell, Ore., a Eugene woman heard splashing in her toilet one night and, after lifting the lid, was startled to find ...

You guessed it!

A monkey!

Okay, not really. It was a rat, which had apparently been a pearl diver at some point in its life, because that's the only explanation I have for this phenomenon. The woman, who asked not to be identified for fear of reprisal, said that she immediately dropped the lid, called the city's Public Works Department, and was told that she wasn't alone, and that "...rats were everywhere, emerging from the sewers by the thousands and consuming people in SLOBBERING, RABID HORDES!"

This was followed by screaming, laughter and a dial tone.

Later, Public Works officials admitted that, like many larger cities, Eugene's sewers have rats, and that they can sometimes scurry up a pipe and into someone's toilet bowl, leaving residents "a little shaken." Or, in the case of one humor columnist who asked not to be identified for fear of reprisal, too traumatized to sit on anything other than a hammock.

Our final piece of the puzzle comes from Doreen Kimble of Santa Clara, Calif., who called my attention to an incident in which hawks — specially trained to keep pigeons from doing what pigeons do on visitors to the New York Public Library — were grounded after one swooped down on an unsuspecting Chihuahua.

The dog's owner, who asked not to be identified for fear of reprisal, said that the falconer believes the Chihuahua was mistaken for a rat, a notion that the dog owner deems ridiculous.

And I have to agree.

According to the report, they weren't even anywhere near the bathroom.

Forget meteors; giant rabbits world's biggest threat

As a journalist, I'm trained to recognize even the most subtle signs of trouble.

A misspoken word.

A reluctant glance.

A horde of slobbering rabbits.

Thanks to my training and experience — and several highlighted newspaper clippings sent in by concerned readers — I have painstakingly pieced together what I, as a member of the conservative media, believe is undeniable evidence that rabbits are planning to take over the world.

How? By radiating themselves and producing offspring roughly the size of Volkswagen Beetles. You're probably thinking this could never happen.

At least not outside of New Jersey.

But at this very moment, according to a recent BBC report, rabbits living near a nuclear plant in Caithness, Scotland are under surveillance after EPA officials discovered what they described as "bunnies hopping in and out of solid waste pits." In addition, investigators found rabbit feces that, for months, had been mistaken for "small piles of Trix cereal."

According to the report, the UK Atomic Energy Authority has been told to use any means necessary to fix the problem and keep rabbits from burrowing into the waste pits. Some biologists, like Dr. Yam Higginsworth, warn it may already be too late. "In my opinion, come spring, the surrounding woods will be littered with rabbit pellets the size of basketballs," Higginsworth predicted. "From an ecological standpoint, this is not good."

The parliament of neighboring England has demanded the Scots formally present a plan for dealing with the threat before the Queen's scheduled annual holiday in the Scottish Highlands this October.

"Suffice it to say, the Queen of England will not vacation anywhere there is a chance — however remote — she will have to fight a giant rabbit," warned a stone-faced Tony Blair, who added: "However, I'm sad to say Charles and Camilla's tickets are non-refundable."

In a statement issued from the White House, President Bush expressed his concern, as well as his willingness to discuss how best to deal with the problem, based on his past experience dealing with, "What he still believes were giant jack-o-lopes," said White House Press Secretary Scott McClellan. When asked if there was any evidence to support the President's claim, McClellan said there wasn't, but that the CIA was in the process of obtaining a postcard from Texas depicting a man riding a jack-o-lope on the high plains.

In an awkward moment, one member of the press corps asked if a 25-cent postcard was really enough evidence to justify the President's claim, to which McClellan retorted, "Are you new here?"

Residents of Scotland see the world's escalating concern over the threat of giant, frequently fornicating radioactive rabbits as unfounded. As one man outside of a pub in Edinburgh put it, "I've been seeing giant rabbits around here for years."

On Monday, the first draft of Scotland's plan is expected to be completed.

"We have every confidence that Scotland will devise a comprehensive, effective plan to deal with this situation," said Blair. "But even if they don't, we're still sending Charles and Camilla."

For flu sufferers, things are about to get messy

Today, in an unprecedented move, I am joining hundreds of other columnists around the nation who will be addressing the flu vaccination crisis while simultaneously wiping "Influenza blowback" from their computer monitors. For those unfamiliar with this term, here's how it might be used on an episode of CSI:

"Well, judging from the chew marks on this Robitussin safety cap, and the presence of oozing and gelatinous Influenza blowback on his computer monitor, I'd say our suspect has the flu. [Cut to lightening-quick journey through mucus-filled nasal cavity.] Chances are, he's still in the area. Maybe even in this very room."

"Ahhh-CHOO!"

"Gesundheit. By the way, which investigation team did you say you're from?"

While national attention remains on the shortage of flu vaccine, health department officials say, as a result of the vaccine crisis, we are now facing what was once unthinkable.

"The nation's supply of facial tissue has become dangerously low," warned Dr. Julie Gerberding, head of the federal Centers for Disease Control in Atlanta. "If we're not careful, many Americans will be left using standard bathroom tissue during the peak of flu season."

This warning prompted an emergency meeting on Capitol Hill where top health officials were questioned about the oversight. However, the session was unexpectedly cut short when committee members were forced to evacuate after Senator Ted Kennedy sneezed. A photographer who was seated directly in front of the senator is reported to be in stable condition at a nearby psychiatric hospital.

Senator Kennedy later released a statement saying, although unfortunate, the incident illustrates an important point, "Which is, regardless of what you might have heard, my face does not get any larger when I sneeze. As I've said before, my face getting any larger is — and will remain — a physical impossibility."

According to health officials, the current crisis began when Chinese regulators unexpectedly shut down tissue manufacturer Bung Corp. last Tuesday after it was discovered that millions of boxes bound for the U.S. had been printed without the necessary safety instructions required by the Consumer Products Safety Commission.

Clark T. Randt, America's ambassador to China, immediately flew to the factory where he demonstrated, before a panel of regulators, that he was capable of using the instruction-less tissue without injury. In spite of multiple demonstrations, including one in which Randt, bound by Chinese finger cuffs, was forced to blow his nose with the help of a blindfolded aid, Chinese regulators remained unconvinced. As a result, 43 million boxes of tissue once bound for the U.S. has been shipped to France where, according to one French official, "It will be stuffed into jackets and used as body armor."

Faced with the impending shortage, the CDC introduced a nationwide "voluntary rationing" system yesterday to ensure that supplies of tissue would meet the needs of high-risk users in the months ahead.

"The bottom line is, don't blow your nose until absolutely necessary," advised Dr. Gerberding. "This is a time of crisis. I think, as Americans, we should all be willing to overlook a few snot bubbles."

As a responsible member of the media, I plan to do my part by blowing my nose as little as possible until this crisis passes. For those of you planning to attend any of my speaking engagements in the near future, let me apologize in advance to anyone seated in the front row.

At a newspaper, every roll is crucial

There are few things that can bring a newspaper to a halt when it is facing a deadline. In fact, aside from a natural catastrophe or a critically important breaking news story (Example: Anything related to *Dancing with the Stars*), nothing stands in the way of our commitment, as journalists, to ensure that the power of the press continues — unless, of course, the unthinkable happens, and we run out of toilet paper in both employee restrooms.

As professionals, this is a scenario we train for. We know how to recognize a potential "situation" that could leave us vulnerable and without back-up. Yet, as we learned today, all it takes is a momentary lapse in resoluteness for things to escalate into a full-blown crisis.

"Has anyone seen Bill?" (Note: The names in this dramatic re-enactment have been changed to protect the innocent, such as myself, from being physically assaulted by "Bill.") A cursory sweep of the newsroom lead to an exhaustive search of the front office, sales room, break area, composition department and, eventually, the restrooms.

Total elapsed time: 1 minutes, 30 seconds.

(We're a small paper.)

Being that we are seasoned journalists capable of recognizing the most subtle signs of trouble, and given the fact that the news department is within six feet of the bathrooms, we quickly deduced that a toilet brush being jammed repeatedly under the doorframe meant a potential situation was brewing. And due to the respect I've gained from my peers in the news department, coupled with the fact that I was standing closest to the door, I was asked to investigate.

After talking with "Bill" and confirming that the adjacent restroom and storage area were, indeed, also without toilet paper, it became clear that our doomsday scenario had developed into the "perfect storm."

I explained the situation to our publisher, who looked grim as he gathered us around his desk. "You're positive a roll didn't fall behind one of the commodes."

I shook my head.

"What about the medicine cabinets?" he blurted. "Maybe somebody stuffed one in there. Or above one of the ceiling tiles?!"

Our editor put a steady hand on his shoulder. "This isn't helping, and the clock is ticking."

Everyone exchanged uneasy glances. We knew "Bill" had been sitting there for a good 20 minutes.

Completely alone. Except for the scrub brush, and what must have been a difficult decision to use it as a signal for help.

"What about paper towels?" someone asked.

"We switched to those stupid hand driers, remember?"

The frustration was tangible.

"Maybe Bill could turn around and aim his ..."

A unanimous look of disgust immediately squelched my idea.

"Sorry," I muttered. "I just feel so helpless."

"What about asking if anyone has some tissue, or a handkerchief they don't want anymore?" someone suggested.

Our publisher put his fist down. "I'm responsible for the safety of everyone in this building. I can't risk starting a panic!"

And so it went.

Out of respect for "Bill," I can't divulge exactly how he was rescued. What I CAN tell you is he drew on his journalistic experience to get out of a tight spot. In a completely unrelated matter, if anyone has an extra phone book, please bring it by the office.

Ours seems to be missing the "Government" pages.

Overcome your fear of flying by getting totally Flugtagged

It's been 100 years since the Wright Brothers proved that manned flight was possible. This eventually led to the very first commercial flight and the discovery of something just as important in man's pursuit of the sky:

The air-sickness bag.

You may not think this was an important discovery, but trust me: Anyone who has sat next to me during a flight on anything other than a coin-operated spaceship will tell you the only thing more important than the discovery of the air-sickness bag itself is discovering how to get rid of it once it's been used. For me, problems generally begin once we've reached our cruising altitude. This is when — for reasons I don't quite understand — all pilots are trained to address their passengers by informing them exactly how high they are and how fast they're going. I DON'T WANT to know these things. If I did, I wouldn't be curled up in a fetal position with my thumbs in my ears and an air-sickness bag pinched between my knees.

I went to school.

I learned about Sir Isaac Newton.

I know there is a fundamental law of physics that says: Everything that goes up must have at least one intoxicated pilot.

That's the only thing running through my mind while the flight attendant is trying to explain that there are more air-sickness bags available, and to please stop vomiting into the seat pocket. While there are plenty of books out there aimed at helping people overcome their phobias, I've always believed in facing things head-on. So when I got an invitation to attend the next Red Bull "Flugtag" in Long Beach, Calif., I immediately said to myself, *Why am I being invited to a swingers convention?*

I quickly discovered that "flugtag" has nothing to do with any type of disciplinary action between masked strangers, but is actually a German word meaning "flying day." The more I read about the event, the more I realized that HERE was something that could help me conquer my fear of flying by joining a group of people who purposely fly their planes off of the Long Beach Pier and into the ocean.

I should mention that these planes are completely human-powered and rarely fly more than 20 feet, mostly because, aerodynamically speaking, it's hard to get liftoff when your aircraft is shaped like a giant cheese wedge, basketball shoe, or flying monkey.

Clearly, this event is more about entertainment than it is about flying. Though the longest distance ever recorded at a Red Bull Flugtag was only 195 feet, it's still farther than most planes at Hooters Airlines ever traveled.

After giving it a lot of thought, I've decided to try to attend this year's flugtag in August. I say try because, in order to make it there and back again before my deadline, I'd need to....

You guessed it!

Take a plane.

As you can see, this creates a bit of a conundrum. Then again, it may be just what I need to force me out of my comfort zone.

And everyone else out of theirs, if I can't find an air-sickness bag.

Ear lobes and unemployment: It's National Good Posture Month again

Hey, straighten up because this is National Good Posture Month!

I discovered this, of course, while slouched so far over my computer keyboard that the curvature of my spine resembled a bell graph. On the screen was the news headline "Are You a Sloucher?" and a warning from the American Chiropractic Association explaining that, aside from alcohol and the invention of the reclinable chair, slouching is THE leading cause of bad posture in America — and the main reason why taverns have stools instead of La-Z-Boys.

According to the ACA, bad posture is most prevalent when we are standing, sitting or lying down. On behalf of the ACA, I urge you to stop doing these things immediately! It may sound tough, but it can be done through sheer determination, planning, and the purchase of a $300,000 anti-gravity chamber. Unfortunately, for many of us, the anti-gravity chamber isn't really an option. This is because 1) our fear of confined spaces is greater than our fear of slouching, and 2) sheer determination and planning has left us with less than $30 in our bank account.

This means finding other, less expensive options when it comes to improving posture. The first step in this process is to determine if we actually HAVE bad posture. To do this, the ACA suggests having someone — such as a co-worker who doesn't mind losing their job — watch you throughout the day to see if the center of your ear stays over the center of your shoulders as you work. Studies show that, for every inch your ear extends beyond the center of your shoulders, it takes 10 percent more effort for neck muscles to support the head.

I should also mention that, for every hour your friend spends staring at your ear lobes, the more uncomfortable you're going to feel the next time you two get together for a beer.

If, after the experiment, you determine that you are, indeed, a sloucher, then the next step is to begin practicing better posture habits. One of the easiest ways to do this is to have your newly-unemployed co-worker follow you around with a bull horn yelling "straighten up, sloucher!" This is not only an effective way to ensure good posture for yourself, it's also a good anger-management tool for your friend between job interviews. However, while this is an effective option, it can also be a really annoying one, especially if you're caught slouching in a high-profile place — such as the mens' room at a hockey game. If that happens, trust me: Bad posture will be the least of your problems.

Finally, as we enter into National Good Posture Month, remember to keep your back straight, your chin up, and your ears toward the center of your shoulders. Let me know how it goes.

I'll be the one with the bull horn.

Setting things straight with the American Chiropractic Association

We all make mistakes. The difference is, when you make one, you probably don't get contacted by someone from the American Chiropractic Association in Arlington, Virginia.

Or maybe you do.

In which case you may want to consider folding up this newspaper right now and going in for an adjustment.

But, unless you mistakenly informed readers that September was "National Correct Posture Month" when, in fact, we're all free to slouch until May, I'm guessing you've never gotten an e-mail from Angela Kargus, Communications and Public Relations Manager for the ACA.

There are two things I know about Angela:

1) She is very nice.

2) She probably has excellent posture.

I also know she read my column a couple of weeks ago. As Angela pointed out, it proclaimed "National Correct Posture Month" in the wrong month, and provided recommendations on how to avoid slouching that Angela informed me were outdated.

It's true. Even as a trained professional, I somehow overlooked the more recent recommendations made specifically for today's slouching public. Because of this, I'd like to apologize. Particularly to those of you who, based on my recommendation, are being followed around by someone with a bullhorn yelling "SLOUCHER!" whenever you slump your shoulders.

I think Angela and I would agree you should stop this immediately because, to be quite honest, it's possible you have more important issues to deal with than posture.

Not that posture isn't important. It's EXTREMELY important.

In fact, I'm posturing right now.

My point is, as a journalist, there's nothing more important than credibility. Except for maybe having Spellcheck. That's why when we in the news media make a mistake, we hold our heads high. We step forward. And we admit, through an error in judgement, we hired Dan Rather as a fact checker. However, this wasn't the case when it came to the errors in my "slouching" column. No. I'm taking the burden of that mistake squarely on my shoulders.

First, because I have no one to blame but myself. And second because, thanks to the ACA website, I now have the name of a good chiropractor. Though I have not gone to him yet, his nickname "Dr. Thunder Thumbs" certainly has me intrigued. So intrigued that I haven't slouched in nearly a week — and that includes while sleeping or using the commode, which I often do simultaneously.

My wife has actually been seeing a chiropractor for a few years now and, along with the many health benefits she enjoys as a result of chiropractic medicine, our marriage has also benefited since, on a regular basis, she is reminded that her pain in the neck is being caused by something other than me.

I would like to say that even though I was wrong about "National Correct Posture Month," October really is National Spinal Health Month.

Honest.

On a side note, it also happens to be Auto Battery Safety Month. My suggestion is to actively participate in both by combining the two and hooking a pair of jumper cables to your...

On second thought, I'm going to check and make sure this idea meets the approval of both the United Spinal Association and someone from Die Hard.

That said, I'd like to thank Angela and the ACA for straightening me out on the whole posture thing.

Naked News broadcast viewed as too cheeky by some

(**Warning:** At all costs, the following information must NOT fall into the hands of Geraldo Rivera.)

According to an ad in the *Toronto Star* newspaper, the producers of the cable TV show *Naked News,* they are seeking anchors for their daily internet news program. For those of you who've never heard of this program, let me take just a moment to explain it:

They report the news, and they're naked.

That's pretty much it.

And for most men, that's explanation enough, which is why the website now averages 6 million viewers per month. Now, before we go on, I'd like to clarify that I happened upon this website completely by accident, while innocently searching for information about naked "gnus," which, as you may or may not know, is the tragic plight of African wildebeests suffering from premature baldness. While painstakingly gathering this sad information, I accidentally went from reading about an entire herd of hairless antelope in Botswana, to watching as a naked weatherman pointed to three developing storms at the same time — in Seattle, Maine, and the Gulf of Mexico.

I will not explain precisely how how he did this.

However, in my haste to leave the website, I accidentally switched over to the "All-Female" broadcast team. It was at this point that my journalistic integrity kicked in, and I felt an obligation to you, the reader, to investigate until I discovered the bitter truth.

Or at least until my editor discovered what I was doing.

As a result of this investigation, I learned that, just like *CNN* and other major news channels, *Naked News* offers in-depth coverage of events from all around the world.

I also learned that I am easily distracted from this coverage.

For those of you who are wondering how you can become a reporter for this cutting-edge news organization (or, at the very least, what the organization's dating policy is), you'll be happy to know that, according to the audition requirements listed on the *Naked News* website, no broadcasting experience is necessary!

That's right! There's no need to let your lack of experience stop you from realizing your dream of standing buck naked in front of a TelePrompter.

I didn't.

Which is why I now work for a newspaper.

This isn't to say that any thoughts I had of becoming a part of the *Naked News* movement have been put on the shelf. In fact, I am actually naked right now.

Which is why I'm currently looking for a job in radio.

Chewing the fat in a giant Wienermobile

After more than a decade of working in the high-pressure environment of our newsroom, where at any given moment you could find yourself surrounded by as many as two other journalists all typing at once, it takes a lot to get our adrenaline pumping. In fact, we have been at the epicenter of the national spotlight three times here in Florence. Sure, two occasions came after being singled out as having the nation's highest rate of ... (yawn) ... retirees.

But the third time involved REAL explosives.

And a dead whale.

And quite possibly an unlicensed demolitions expert going through a divorce. This would explain using half a ton of dynamite to dispose of a rotting whale carcass that washed ashore, and how one onlooker literally chewed the fat after being struck by a piece if flying whale blubber.

Hey, it was 1970! Whales didn't have the safety features they have today! Even experts, with their fancy calculations for trajectory, explosive force, velocity, alcohol content, etc., couldn't have anticipated a piece of whale fat, roughly the size of a Volkswagen Beetle, taking out an actual Volkswagen Beetle. Because we are subjected to this kind of tension-filled atmosphere on a regular basis, last week, when the 27-foot-long Oscar Mayer Wienermobile rolled into town, we met it with the kind objectivity you'd expect from seasoned journalists who laugh in the face of high-velocity whale fat:

We immediately leaped from our chairs and simultaneously wedged ourselves in the doorway so tightly we had to be dislodged with a copy machine.

This left our editor with the difficult task of deciding who would cover this assignment. After taking into account experience, dedication and overall proximity to the door, she chose me to cover the giant Wienermobile. I have to admit, after seeing the size and scope of this story, I began to feel a little inadequate.

However, Wienermobile driver "Lots-of-Ketchup" Lisa assured me this reaction was very common.

She then took me on a tour of the Wienermobile, which can seat eight comfortably, or as many as 26 uncomfortably, depending on how strictly the seatbelt law is enforced in your area, particularly when it involves people riding on top of a 27-foot-long hot dog.

I know what you're thinking:

How can I get a job like THAT?!?

OK, maybe it was just me.

But according to the Oscar Mayer Wienermobile website (www.hotdoggerblog.com), any college graduate who is "outgoing, creative, friendly, and who has an appetite for adventure" can be a candidate. Having a good driving record also helps because, according to Lisa, in spite of its naturally aerodynamic design, handling a wiener of these proportions on the open road, and even proper waxing and buffing, takes practice, which is why drivers must attend special classes at "Hot Dog High," and why, coincidentally, I am moving on to the next paragraph as quickly as possible, while this is still a family-friendly column.

I would like to thank Lisa and the folks at Oscar Mayer for including us on their national tour. I'd also like to thank them for avoiding fatty fillers in their hot dogs; the last time something 27 feet long and full of fat came to Florence, the results were explosive.

Investigating the latest crisis: Flamin' Hot Cheeto addiction

Being a journalist can be dangerous. Especially when it involves middle schoolers and their snack food. I knew this when I approached my editor, who can also be dangerous, particularly when her candy drawer is found empty, even though she keeps it locked with a key hidden in a folder labeled Extra Work for Reporters. In spite of this danger, I asked if I could go undercover to investigate what *Fox News* reported as "a growing crisis in schools across the country — and we're pretty sure that country is somewhere in the U.S."

What I'm talking about, of course, is the growing crisis of Flamin' Hot Cheetos addiction. According to an article in the Chicago Tribune, a teacher in New Mexico wants to ban Flamin' Hot Cheetos from school due to the snack's complete lack of nutritional value and its addictive nature.

"But Twinkies are fine," she added.

As a result, other school districts in New Mexico, as well as California, have initiated their own bans on the snack, in some cases confiscating any Cheetos found on students and consuming them on the spot.

"It's for their own good," said a teacher who conducts locker checks with the help of her dog Nacho, a 30-pound Cheeto-sniffing Chihuahua. "Back when he could walk, Chester couldn't sneak up on kids because of his nails and heavy panting. Now he has a Hoveround; problem solved."

My editor, recognizing the risks involved with my being emersed in the underworld of middle school Cheeto addicts for an entire day, expressed her concern with a supportive shoulder squeeze.

"Better make it a month," she said. "In another state."

"But I ..."

"Fine, a week in town. Now get out."

With my editor's support, I began my investigation. This meant creating a disguise to avoid suspicion, which I did by wearing glasses, a bow tie and sweater vest. As I discovered, this allowed me to blend seamlessly with any school administrator who has been transported through time from 1950. After just a few days of following orange Cheeto smears, "rapping" with kids and "keeping it real," I gained their trust. So much so that I was given a special nickname:

"Mr. Narc."

Ironically, it was my rapidly growing "street cred" that brought me to the attention of school administrators, who began to question my validity after checking the visitor sign-in sheet and discovering no one named Mr. Narc. This effectively ended my investigation, which had been leading me toward the teachers lounge where, according to my informants, staff members secretly keep a giant flat screen TV, an ice cream bar, video games, have private concerts from One Direction, travel through hidden tunnels to their classrooms, and enjoy an endless supply of Flamin' Hot Cheetos.

I can't prove any of this, of course. Any more than my editor can prove I stole her candy.

Unless she's reading this.

I wonder what schools are like in Idaho?

What says 'thirsty' better than a sweaty humor columnist?

As I'm sure you can imagine, being a humor columnist I am constantly working up a sweat. In fact, I can already feel perspiration forming. By the end of this paragraph, I will be a drippy, sweat-stained mess. Most people don't know it can take hours to finish a column. The reason has nothing to do with procrastination, writer's block, or even the ability to *Google* Sophia Vergara; many of us humor columnists simply become too sweaty to operate our keyboards without sliding off and potentially endangering ourselves and others.

Newsrooms everywhere understand this, which is why we are often placed in special cubicles that are either refrigerated or, at the very least, equipped with a drain pan.

Yet, somehow, beverage companies continue to overlook us as potential thirst-quenching icons when developing trendy ad campaigns. Chances are, you'll never see a commercial featuring a humor columnist at a keyboard with green Gatorade streaming out of every pore in his body. Or witness a humor columnist emerge from a droplet of Propel fitness water and do a back flip out of an office chair (which we often do, by the way, sometimes for no reason at all). That's because our segment of the beverage-buying market is considered too small to worry about, even though, as analysts have shown, it is a powerful one, at least in terms of odor.

According to the advertising people I spoke with, the key is finding a beverage product that fits the humor columnist profile; something that seamlessly combines beverage consumption and sweaty writing; something that speaks to millions of thirsty consumers and tells them:

Hey, what you really want is a beverage that tastes funny.

I had given up on finding such a beverage until this past week, when I opened a package containing what has to be the strangest soda concept since New Coke. In this case, we're talking about quenching your thirst with the crisp, refreshing taste of "Broccoli Rice Casserole."

Or "Salmon Pate'." Or my personal favorite, "Brussels Sprout."

Apparently, the folks at Jones Soda Co., who produce these flavors as part of a limited-edition "Holiday Pack" each year, are aggressively targeting a niche market known in the advertising world as the "gagging consumer." This became clear during an impromptu taste test I held here in our newsroom, where all ten of my test subjects preferred drinking these sodas over, say...

The taste of bile.

I knew right away I'd found my product. Who better than a humor columnist to promote a beverage that is marginally preferred over stomach juice? I immediately contacted Diana Turner at Jones Soda Co. and informed her of my availability.

I then called her back and explained I meant as an advertising icon.

After careful consideration that seemed to go on forever but lasted closer to four seconds, I was told that the goal of the "Holiday Pack" was to raise $150,000 for children's charities, and that paying for a "beverage icon" would mean less money for those charities.

I told her I was cheap.

She said every dollar counts.

I agreed to do it for free.

She asked me to please stop calling her.

As it stands, I still haven't become a beverage icon, and it doesn't look like I'll become one anytime soon. Until then, I'll just have to quench my thirst for becoming a promotional figurehead by consuming these extra bottles of "Turkey and Gravy" soda.

That's if I can hold onto them with these sweaty hands.

Becoming Canadian could lead to a strained Molson muscle

Today we will be talking about Canada.

Why?

Because aside from the many similarities we share with Canadians, such as celebrating our independence day the very same weekend, and our historic bi-lateral agreement banning any future above-ground testing of Nadya Suleman's reproductive system, I have been offered an official Canadian citizenship starting at 12 a.m. on Jan. 1.

OK, so my citizenship will only last 24 hours.

Possibly less, depending on how I pronounce the word "Poutine" (which, from what I understand, is a French word meaning "clogged artery"). However, if all goes well, I will get to spend an entire day as a real Canadian, eating nothing but Tim Horton's Donuts, chewing purple gum that tastes like soap, and stretching my Molson muscle (which I swear only sounds inappropriate for a family newspaper).

Undoubtedly there are readers in the U.S. who are surprised, possibly even outraged, by my willingness to become a Canadian citizen. Rest assured this decision came after many hours of soul searching, and the realization that with my free Canadian health coverage — and access to a high performance vehicle — I could potentially see more medical specialists in 24 hours than I've seen in the past 15 years on my HMO. I could use a different dermatologist for each mole on my body! This is a vast improvement over my current health plan, which only covers moles large enough to be claimed as a dependent.

And even then, only until it reaches age 18.

You may be wondering how the offer of a 24-hour citizenship came aboot (that's not a typo; it's Canadian phonetics). As much as I'd like to tell you it's a direct result of the impact my column has had on the Canadian people, the truth is it has more to do with a friend at the *Rimbey Review* in Alberta, who offered me this one-day citizenship. This is in exchange for a monthly shipment of Kraft Macaroni & Cheese from the U.S. which, by not being subject to Canada's "Goods and Services Tax," will save him an estimated $3,000 a year.

At least in U.S. dollars.

I'm not sure what that equals in Canadian currency because it's measured in millimeters.

Or kilograms.

Or some type of denomination meant to confuse U.S. tourists — thousands of whom are arrested each year for driving 120 mph through downtown Edmonton. These are the same people who arrive in Alberta in late July dressed in polar fleece because they think there's a 50-degree temperature drop between the U.S. and Canadian border. To be honest, free medical coverage wasn't my only motivation for becoming a Canadian citizen. I'm more interested in seeing attractions like the giant Ukrainian Easter egg in Vegreville, Alberta, which stands an amazing nine meters tall!

According to my calculations, if this were an actual egg, it would have to be laid by a chicken roughly the size of Rita McNeil.

Or, in standard U.S. measurements, one-in-five people leaving McDonald's.

As you can tell, I'm excited about my 24-hour Canadian citizenship. To make the most of it I plan to see as much of Alberta as possible, beginning with a quick trip through Edmonton, and continuing on to Rimbey and Vegreville. Of course, that's assuming I don't get arrested for speeding, or worse — get hospitalized by a non-French-speaking woman after striking up a conversation about her "Poutine."

Hey, at least I'll have health coverage.

Shooting a country music video? Avoid the Black-Eyed Four-Step

Admittedly, being a humor columnist has its privileges:

Complimentary full-body waxes.

Unsolicited fruitcake.

Tickets to the World Toilet Expo.

The list goes on.

However, occasionally I'm invited to be part of something really cool that doesn't require shaving my entire body or sitting on a giant, revolving commode that burps. In this case, I'm talking about being on the set during the making of a music video for country singer Adam Marshall. According to Adam and his producer, after reading some of my columns, they thought it would be fun to have me write about the making of their music video, *Cowboy Hat*. As an added bonus, they created a part just for me, in which I play the pivotal role of "Crowd Member" who, according to the script: Could be replaced by a coat rack if necessary.

The truth is, I've been a fan of country music for years and probably would've pursued my own career if things had turned out differently, and my musical talent had extended beyond being able to perform the drum solo from "Wipeout" on my inner thighs. Because of this, I had to settle for the only record deal I could get, which is a generous contract entitling me to 15 free CDs, as long as I agree to buy one John Tesh album sometime before I die.

Because I have no experience in front of the camera (not counting the occasional home video, where, in most cases, I'm either choking on a bratwurst or trying to pull an appendage out of something), I'm not sure how I'm going to do when it's time to start shooting. Chances are, the director's command for "ACTION!" will then be followed by someone screaming "MEDIC!"

My son has spent the last few days helping ease my fear of cameras by sporadically leaping out of closets or from behind furniture with our video camera rolling. He insisted this process would eventually cause me to build a resistance to my fear. But so far, all we have is about 90 minutes of footage with me screaming from various places throughout our home — kitchen, tool shed, crawl space under the house. I'm not sure what he thought was going to happen when he surprised me in the bathroom, but once I stood up and started running for the door, we were both screaming. Even if this doesn't work, it won't be a total loss because, after we get this thing edited and add some music, I think we'll have a good chance of finding a distributor at Sundance.

In some respect, I suppose my son's idea has worked; as long he isn't allowed anywhere near a camera on the set, I'll be just fine.

The other thing I have to worry about is dancing. This is a music video, after all, and a good portion of it takes place in a country bar with Adam Marshall singing. I'm assuming this will lead to dancing. Possibly even to the Cotton-Eyed Joe or Texas Two-Step. Or, in my case, a dance I created while living in Texas called the Black-Eyed Four-Step, wherein I would accidentally step on the feet of various women throughout floor and get punched in the eye by their boyfriends. I should mention that I was always completely sober and, in each case, had started out dancing with my wife before getting disoriented by my own boot scootin' boogey.

So, when the video airs in April, don't be surprised if I've been replaced by a coat rack.

Especially once they've seen my rendition of "Wipeout."

Behind every country star is a good soda wrangler

As I mentioned several weeks ago, I was invited to participate in a music video by country singer Adam Marshall, whose single *Cowboy Hat* was released last week. Though I haven't actually seen the finished video yet, I can tell you the music is great, that everyone in it is attractive, and they can all dance really well. Which is why I can say, with some certainty, I am not in the final cut.

Yes, I met Adam Marshall. Yes, I was wearing a cowboy hat and boots.

And yes, I did get so nervous dancing with a "Coyote Ugly" girl that I forgot things like my name, and how to utilize my central nervous system. In my own defense, I didn't realize "Coyote Ugly" was a euphemism for someone at a singles bar who is highly attractive; at least not until I stepped forward to meet my dance partner and politely introduced myself as "Wowwy." That was pretty much the extent of our small talk, which there is a lot of during a video shoot. That's because for every minute the cameras were rolling, there was at least an hour of preparation time for things like make-up, lighting, sound checks and administering first-aid to my dance partner. However, the majority of our preparation time was spent on "blocking," which is when the director decides where the "talent" will be in each shot. As it turned out, the director involved me in this crucial decision-making process several times, often by suggesting, "Someone please move Ned, he's blocking the talent again."

On the second day of shooting, after recognizing my inability to dance, act, or form a complete sentence in the presence of any "Coyote Ugly" girls, Adam took me aside. We discussed how I could contribute to his video in ways more suited to my particular talents. After a long discussion, we determined this would be by holding his soda between takes. I excelled at this and quickly became known to crew members as "Adam's Soda Guy." This was much better than my previous titles, "Who Is This Guy," "She Won't Dance With This Guy," and "Someone Please Hog-Tie This Guy."

In addition to the instant prestige I gained, there were also a lot of perks in being Adam's personal "soda wrangler." For example, using my authority to skip to the front of the beverage line whenever I said, "Adam needs a soda." This worked even after they took my bull horn away, and I was forced to make my announcement through a rolled-up issue of Country Weekly. I also insisted on wearing a walkie-talkie so that if we were separated, I could still meet Adam's beverage consumption needs by contacting him on a regular basis. This turned out to be a good idea since, coincidentally, we were separated more and more as the day went on. In fact, there was a frightening two-hour period where we had no contact at all.

Fortunately, everything was OK and, according to his producer, Adam had simply misplaced his walkie-talkie after throwing it into a nearby lake. Adam later explained to me that it had nothing to do with being annoyed, and that he was simply demonstrating to a crew member how, as a Marine, he had been taught to lob a grenade.

After two days of watching Adam serenade the camera with his song "Cowboy Hat," I suddenly realized there's really only one thing keeping my own dream of being a country music star from coming true:

A complete lack of talent.

Which isn't to say my dream of country stardom is completely out of reach. Who knows? There's always a chance I could make it to the stage of the Grand Ole Opry.

Even if it is just to bring Adam a soda. I'll keep my walkie-talkie handy, just in case.

First step to good golfing: Get a grip

When our editor began looking for someone to captain our Relay for Life golf team, it only made sense that she came to me first. That's because, being that I was once a sports editor, I'm naturally a great golfer. Just like I'm a great shot-put thrower, quarterback, point guard, stock-car racer, extreme skateboarder, free-style swimmer and calf roper. In fact, I sometimes wonder where I might be today had my sports career not been tragically cut short by my complete lack of athletic talent. This discovery was made as early as first grade, when, during a dodge ball game, I was knocked unconscious and rushed to the nurse's office after being hit by the ball.

Forty-seven times.

(And I should mention that recess only lasted 10 minutes in those days.)

So, when my editor asked me to captain our golf team, I of course said "Yes!"

After which I was knocked unconscious by a loose dodge ball in the newsroom. Okay, that didn't really happen, but I did agree to captain the team, which meant giving myself a crash course on golfing — beginning with golf terminology. I immediately got online for help and, thanks to the power of the Internet, found myself on an inappropriate website after typing in the first term on my list: *Mixed Foursome.*

For anyone else who might be looking to the Internet for golf-term clarifications, I'd also suggest avoiding *Scotch foursome, Shag bag,* and *Loose impediments.* While these are all legitimate golfing terms, try explaining that to your editor when she finds you doing an Internet search for the term *Double-D.*

(Which, by the way, means when a driver is used on the fairway after it has also been used to tee off — so THERE, Ms. Smarty Pants!)

After getting a handle on the game's terminology, the next thing on my list was golf etiquette. I know for a lot of people, one of the things that keeps them from actually trying golf is the fear of unintentionally doing something that, as a result of not knowing the proper etiquette, gets them clubbed to death by someone with a 9-iron. That's because, to the outside observer, things that seem to warrant a good clubbing are actually no big deal. You want to swing your club and take a six-inch gouge out of an otherwise perfect lawn?

Fine.

Want to drink a beer AND drive an electric cart through the woods?

Perfectly acceptable.

However, walk between someone's ball and a small hole in the ground, and there's a good chance you'll be found floating in a water hazard.

The thing to remember is that you will undoubtedly make some mistakes your first time on the course, and that's to be expected. What won't be expected is a hollowed-out golf club that can be loaded with tees and used as a blowgun should you need to defend yourself.

But you didn't hear that from me.

This brings us to the actual fundamentals of playing golf — which begins with finding your "natural swing." Ask any golfer the secret to doing this, and they'll tell you it's all about having the proper grip. To achieve this, simply make sure the back of your left hand, as well as the palm of your right hand, are both facing your target. Then, using the thumb of your right hand as a guide, wrap your fingers around one side, then do the same with your left while, very slowly, bringing them both back into a perfect arch so that your beer doesn't spill on the way to your mouth. After a couple of practice swigs, place your beer back in the cooler and tee-off.

This may not improve your swing much, but it will provide you with a legitimate excuse as to why you shot a 187 on a par 72 course.

And if that isn't enough, you can always claim that playing in a mixed foursome was just too darned distracting.

Let's keep American literature out of cage fighting

Like a lot of syndicated columnists, I get hundreds of emails every week. And just because, unlike other columnists, most of mine involve some type of male enhancement product, it doesn't mean I'm not occasionally inspired to do more than press the "delete" button so many times I develop a blister.

Such is the case with David Harris-Gershon.

David, who lives in Washington, DC., recently contacted me about a unique item he is auctioning off at www. mywritingfund. com.

BUT WAIT!

Before everyone jumps online, creating a massive Internet shutdown inadvertently raising the terrorist threat level to "Sea Foam," I'll save many of you valuable time by clarifying what David is not auctioning off:

1) An opportunity to purchase advertising space across his forehead, back, recently-shaved head, or buttocks.

2) Tupperware containing a hermetically preserved slice of raisin toast bearing the likeness of an individual known for brief, mysterious public sightings, such as Jesus, Elvis or Dick Cheney.

3) Anything related to Brad Pitt and Angelina Jolie.

For those still interested, the two of you should know that David's auction item is more valuable than any of those things. That's because he is offering something no one else (without unfettered access to free pharmaceutical samples) can offer you: total, unsubstantiated optimism.

...That your $100,000 investment toward his Masters degree in creative writing will usher in the next great literary voice;

...That your philanthropic gesture will make a difference in the life of a struggling writer;

And perhaps most importantly,

...That your 20 percent share in David's future earnings as a writer will make you — his sole shareholder — filthy, stinking rich.

Before we continue, there are a couple of things you should know about David:

1) He is an excellent writer. Therefore,
2) He earns his living as a cage fighter.

OK, not really. He's actually a schoolteacher. But I think we can all agree the line between these two occupations is very thin. The difference, of course, is that he would make a lot more money as a cage fighter, even one with a name like "Language Hammer," whose unique fighting style included shaking hands, then immediately curling into a fetal position around his thesaurus while shouting descriptive, one-word insults from between his tightly-clenched thighs.

I can tell you after exchanging e-mails with him and visiting his website, David would never be a cage fighter. That's because, in addition to being a man of principle who loves his family too much to sacrifice his integrity, he doesn't really have the thighs to withstand that kind of punishment.

What he does have is a natural gift for writing about life in a way that is simultaneously personal and universal. His story "Sense of Direction," which was published in the *Colorado Review*, is a touching and witty journey through his family's past, set in the context of getting lost with his wife while re-visiting his home town of Marietta, GA. It's a wonderfully told and insightful piece that had particular relevance for me since, as many of you know, I get lost on a regular basis. As a University of Georgia graduate with an English degree, David has supported his family for the last seven years by doing the unthinkable:

Attempting to educate teenagers.

He would now like to pursue his Masters degree in creative writing full time and become a unique voice in American literature. And by that I don't mean the voice that has to keep telling students to stop drawing body parts on their textbooks. Being a family man with a second child on the way, David came up with the idea of holding an auction as a way to avoid strapping his family with a large debt. The minimum bid amount of $100,000 covers his tuition — with the winner receiving 20 percent of his future earnings as a writer.

Even if you don't have enough to cover the minimum bid amount, visit his website and cheer him on. If you DO have $100,000 to help cultivate a great literary voice, enter a bid.

If nothing else, it'll be worth it just to keep "Language Hammer" out of the ring.

When it comes to risqué photos, try to avoid flashing anyone

At this very moment, as you sit drinking your morning coffee and reading the paper, I am taking pictures of naked senior citizens. I should point out that 1) they are aware that their pictures are being taken because 2) they asked me to do it after 3) taking one look at me and realizing they had nothing to be embarrassed about. The photos are for a goofy calendar that will be sold to raise funds for a pool in Mapleton, Ore. You should also know that the photos will not actually show anything controversial because all private areas will be covered by a strategically positioned prop, such as an AARP card.

The idea came from Nancy Walker, who reads the column and, after finding out that I'm also a photo buff (Ha! Buff!), approached me about taking the calendar pictures. Why? Because — as Nancy put it — she and her friends feel they know me well enough through my column that being around me with little or no clothing is "no big deal." Naturally, I found this very flattering, and, at the same time, a little disappointing. Especially when you consider that I've been sending free copies of my column to the Playboy Mansion for years and have yet to receive the same vote of confidence.

I did receive an actual letter once, sent by registered mail and signed by Hugh Hefner himself, that said, and I quote:

Please stop writing to us.
You're scaring the girls.
— Hef

Being that this is a pool fund-raiser, we naturally chose the pool as our backdrop. And, being a professional, let me just say that back-drop is a word that I plan to use very carefully. Because they understood the complexity of today's shoot, Nancy and her friends prepared for it by meticulously practicing their poses ahead of time and working out the details. As I discovered, these details included getting a few husbands to participate! That's right! I'm using exclamation points because they were very excited about this!

I am not!

However, I am also a mature adult. Besides, the husbands' level of excitement about this project remains to be seen. And I'd prefer that it stay that way.

To help my subjects feel a little more comfortable, and because I understand the importance of ABSOLUTE TRUST in a situation like this, I briefly considered the idea of taking all of today's photos while being completely — you guessed it:

Intoxicated.

Just kidding. I actually thought about doing it in the buff. But I felt no need to embarrass the older men who, since retiring, have frittered away their time by going to the gym twice as often as I do.

Keeping in mind that the goal in all of this is to create a goofy — yet tasteful — calendar that people will want to buy and potentially even hang up somewhere in their home or office, it goes without saying that I will not be appearing anywhere in it. I know this comes as a big disappointment for those of you who....

Okay, so no one is actually going to be disappointed by this.

That's perfectly okay; the last thing I want is for anyone to get excited.

Evidence suggests connection between nacho-flavored Doritos, crazed squirrels

Several years ago while visiting the Grand Canyon, my chance to enjoy one of the world's greatest natural wonders was marred by an unprovoked squirrel attack. Anyone who's been there can tell you that the park is completely over run by hordes of crazed, hyperactive squirrels. It's gotten so bad that the park service installed coin-operated food dispensers, the idea being that tourists could feed the squirrels while remaining blissfully unaware that the pellets were, in effect, simply a diversion meant to save their lives.

The problem is that the squirrels are now SICK of these pellets, which tourists still purchase, but now hurl directly at the squirrels while fleeing back to their cars. In most cases, they never get to see the Grand Canyon at all, choosing instead to escape by turning their windshield wipers on high and dislodging enough squirrels to navigate their way into the nearest Sequoia patch.

(Movie note: *Thelma & Louise* originally ended with them eluding the police, then tragically plunging into the Grand Canyon in a hail of gun fire, food pellets and flailing squirrels.)

I bring this up because of an e-mail I received from Janet Blevons of Ashland, Ore., who sent me an *Associated Press* news story headlined:

Squirrel Terrorizes Town

According to the article, residents of Knutsford, England are living in fear following several attacks from "a rogue squirrel" that is apparently attracted to (and who isn't) nacho-flavored Doritos.

"It's very unusual behavior," said a British zoologist, who didn't specify whether he was referring to the attacks or the rodent's choice in snack food.

What is clear is something I've known since that fateful day at the Grand Canyon—which is that squirrels can't be trusted.

And I'm not the only one who feels this way. Students at the University of Washington have created a website called scareysquirrel.org, which records attacks from what students say is "a well-organized gang of squirrels" wearing

tiny leather jackets with *No Fear* stitched on the back. And, just like in Knutsford, these squirrels have an affinity for nacho-flavored Doritos.

I know what you're thinking:

As long as I stay away from Doritos, I won't become a victim.

I'd like to say yes. But the fact is, I'd probably be sued by Frito-Lay. Besides, there were no taco chips involved when a wet squirrel leaped into a 10,000-volt power station in France, knocking out electricity to 5,000 homes and causing hundreds of injuries as French residents, in a wide-spread panic, all rushed into the streets at the same time to surrender.

Scare tactic, or stupid squirrel? We'll never know for sure.

What I *do* know is that if you're serious about protecting yourself and the ones you love, then it's time to start thinking about wolf urine. That's right. For some reason, squirrels really hate this stuff. There are several ways to go about obtaining it. For the frugal-minded who refuse to pay in-store prices, there's always the option of going out and getting it yourself. Needless to say, this presents several challenges, including — but not limited to — being eaten alive.

Another option is to leave urine gathering to the professionals and simply purchase one of the many squirrel repellents now available without a 10-day waiting period. One such product is Shake-Away, which only sounds like a new weight-loss program. Actually, it's a repellent made from dried fox urine that supposedly offers 6,000 square feet of protection in each 20-ounce bottle. Since the product is all natural, it's completely non-toxic, which means it can be sprinkled around gardens, door ways, or even directly onto things you wish to protect.

Starting with nacho-flavored Doritos.

Take it from me: You can't run from static electricity

When I was a kid I had a book called Mysteries of the Unexplained that contained AMAZING BUT TRUE! stories aimed at stirring the imagination, eliciting a sense of wonder, and prolonging the bed-wetting experience by at least three years. I'd huddle beneath the covers with my flashlight and read about strange psychic phenomena documented by real scientists, physicists, private investigators, and the occasional freaked-out paranormal expert who, at the end of the story, usually abandoned his profession to become a plumber:

"Even now, after all these years, I can still feel those icy fingers whenever a cold breeze blows across my plumber's crack..."

Though the book was mostly about ghosts, aliens, strange disappearances and creepy folklore (...so stand alone in the dark, if you dare. Hold a mirror and repeat the words "Sassafras Sally." And prepare to be slapped by a pair of wet tea bags), it was spontaneous human combustion that really got to me. I think it's because, in my mind, ghosts, aliens, strange disappearance and folklore could all be avoided by exercising a little caution.

Spot an alien spaceship? Run.

Worried about Sassafras Sally? Introduce her to Chi tea.

Concerned about taking a cruise through the Bermuda Triangle? Go to Disneyland and settle for the "Pirates of the Caribbean" instead.

But burst into flames in the middle of Mrs. Frump's sixth-grade classroom, and chances are you'd be reduced to a pair of smoking sneakers long before you could acquire a hall pass and make it to a water source. Because of this fear, I mapped out the location of every fire extinguisher and water fountain at Jane Adams Elementary, and remained within eight feet of something to douse myself with throughout much of the sixth grade. Suffice it to say, except for visiting the public pool and local fire station, I missed most of my class field trips.

I'm 39 now, and, aside from "All-You-Can-Eat Frijole Night" at Juan's Cantina, I've overcome my fear of spontaneously combusting.

At least until yesterday.

That's when "Peggy" from our composition department handed me a news article about a man in Warrnambool, Australia whose clothes spontaneously built up 40,000 volts of static electricity. According to Frank Clewers, he was unaware of being a human power grid until a secretary noticed his shoes were burning a hole in the office carpet. After several awkward minutes of misinterpreting his secretary's warnings of "You're sizzling!" and "You're making my hair stand up!" as sexual innuendo, Frank realized what was happening and contacted the fire department. Fire official Henry Barton believes it was the combination of Franks' woolen shirt and synthetic nylon jacket rubbing together that created a charge "just shy of spontaneous combustion."

I'm no electrician, but had shag carpet been involved, I doubt Frank would still be alive.

After reading about this incident, I thanked "Peggy" (whom I used to like), then slowly removed my nylon coat and wool sweater, trying to generate as little friction as possible, by cutting them from my body with a pair of scissors. That's because I'm one of those people who's constantly building up small amounts of static electricity. Our cat became aware of this phenomenon after rubbing on my leg once. This was followed by a loud "pop," a blue flash, and our cat performing a hissing cartwheel.

Needless to say, thanks to "Peggy," my condition has now escalated from minor annoyance to full-blown phobia. I no longer leave the house without a copper wire running from my undershorts to the ground, and I go through at least four cans of "Cling Free" a day.

My wife, with her degree in sociology, tried forcing me to face my fear by rubbing her hands on the TV screen and then running at me in the dark. This did not work. Not only that, but now we have to replace the coffee table.

I'm sure I'll eventually overcome my fear again. In the meantime, I really need to finish mapping out the extinguishers and water sources in our office.

Be careful when picking a topic; especially if it's your nose

From time to time, a column strikes a collective nerve with readers. These readers then respond — in many cases — by calling me collect. After my column last week, it's obvious that excessive ear and nose hair has been on a lot of people's chests. And by that I mean in terms of subject matter, not actual hairs falling from men's ears and noses during the course of conversation, eating or — whatever. It seems I have become the "go-to" guy when it comes to ear and nose hair confessions.

The subject is generally brought up by wives, such as while standing in line at A&W and ordering a chili cheese dog for their husbands. One minute they're talking about the origin of the Coney dog, the next I'm being told what it's like trying to carry on a conversation with a spouse who doesn't seem to notice he has hardened Cheez Whiz in his nostril hair. This puts me in the difficult position of trying to sympathize with the wife while, at the same time and being a male myself, trying to defend his honor by saying something like, "Uh...has he tried the chicken strip basket?"

And this isn't to say the topic hasn't been brought up by men. In fact, it has come up several times — while getting gas, buying groceries, attending a funeral mass, standing at a urinal — and usually starts off with,

"Have you been talking with my wife?"

There have also been emails and letters, wherein readers feel safe describing, in frightening detail, nose and ear hair abominations they have witnessed, are married to, or are currently cultivating.

One individual even sent a photograph, which arrived by email under the heading:

Look at my nostrils!

Sure, I probably should have known better than to open it. Especially before I'd had my coffee or gotten within arm's reach of a defibrillator. As a result, I now meet once a week with a psychiatrist, who says I can begin the next phase of my recovery as soon as I'm able to look at the photo without wearing a welder's mask. I should point out this photo was intercepted by Homeland Security because agents believe this person's nose hair could be hiding a small terrorist cell.

Don't get me wrong. As a columnist, you hope to illicit a response so you know that people are reading. My thanks to all of you for your emails and letters; it's good to know you're out there.

And I'm in *here*.

Don't become the victim of an unprovoked gravy ambush

Admittedly, the closest I have been to an actual military "hot zone" was when, on a grey August day in 1977, my Cub Scout troop was deployed to sell candy on the same block as the Girl Scouts. Our prime objective was Hilltop Road, which was a critical strategic vector.

At least in terms of foot traffic.

Because our troop transport had overheated in the Carl's Jr. drive-thru, the Girl Scouts had already claimed the high ground next to a busy movie theater. Outnumbered and without tactical advantage, we implemented our most effective defensive strategy, which was to form a tight perimeter directly behind 200-pound Billy Schlependorf. This quickly turned to chaos as we were overrun by a swarm of green berets and brown knee-highs, forcing us to retreat in a hail of Thin Mints and stale marshmallows. The last thing I remember was stepping on a well-thrown "ants-on-a-log" that sent me headfirst into a three-foot-tall Darth Vader waiting in line to see *Star Wars*.

So, because of this common bond of courage under fire, it was no surprise when my friend, who is a firefighter and soldier with two tours in Iraq, confided in me that he had recently been attacked in his own kitchen — by leftover Thanksgiving gravy.

Let me set the scene:

This is SEPTEMBER.

That's right. According to my friend, who asked not to be named, and who I will respectfully refer to only as "Sean" or "Sgt. Connor" but never as "Sgt. Sean Connor," the gravy boat in question had been in the back of his refrigerator waiting to ambush him since last November.

This is not uncommon.

I actually have a Tupperwear dish with guacamole from Cinco De Mayo 2001 that became self-aware in 2009, and who I now claim on my tax return as an 11-year-old Mexican exchange student named Guaca Jole Mole.I have never been attacked by Guaca. But if that ever happens, trust me: He's out of there.

Anyway, getting back to The Great Gravy Ambush ...

While reaching for what I'm sure was a healthy snack of carrot sticks or high-fiber yogurt, "Sean's" fingers came into contact with the enemy, in the form of a harmless gravy boat filled with what he called a "dark brown, meteorite-like substance."

Being a take-charge kind of guy, and due to his reflexive hand-to-hand combat training — and because his wife had asked him to clean out the gravy boat 10 months ago — he instinctively grabbed a butter knife and plunged it into what he described in technical combat terms as a "dried gravy crevasse." It was in that moment, while locked in a struggle to dislodge the rock-like gravy, that he cut his finger on the razor-like edge of the crevasse as he forced it down the garbage disposal. Showing no mercy, he started the disposal and immediately came under heavy fire from "gravy shrapnel" flying across the kitchen.

Dropping into a low-crawl, he assessed his "tactical situation," and concluded that if the new kitchen cabinets got scratched by flying gravy debris, he should probably just keep crawling onto a busy highway.

But this is a man who has led other men into battle!

[begin exciting slow-motion action sequence]

Crouched on the floor, he took a deep breath and dove toward the countertop, gravy shrapnel whizzing past him as he simultaneously — and in mid air — scanned the row of switches, finding the disposal and slamming his injured finger down on it, effectively taking out the enemy.

Ok, so the first switch was actually the kitchen fan.

... Then the sink light. ... Then the pantry light.

The point is, it doesn't matter how many switches it took; all that matters is that the disposal switch is now painted RED.

With Thanksgiving less than two months away, I hope "Sean's" story will help prevent others from falling victim to a similar type of gravy ambush.

And hey — don't even get me started on Girl Scout cookies.

There's nothing funny about firefighting... well, mostly

As some of you may know, in addition to writing a humor column, I'm also a volunteer firefighter — a subject I have purposely avoided in my columns because, let's face it: Entering a burning structure with someone who writes about glow-in-the-dark mice isn't exactly reassuring.

For this reason, I have tried hard to separate my two pursuits. As I've discovered, this is a little like trying to separate marshmallows using a blow torch; the longer you keep at it, the more they blend together.

The truth is, once the emergency is over, firefighters are funny — which is why, after three years, many are still asking, "Why haven't you written about being a firefighter yet?"

So to all of you, I say:

You asked for it.

Before we get started, let me clarify that I set some ground rules for myself. For example, in order to preserve anonymity, I will not use names like Sean Connor, Boa Warren, Adam Borg, Tim Snapp or Bill "Single-Lay" Schlependorf. And just to clarify, a "single lay" is when a water supply line is hooked to a hydrant from an engine.

For any of you who thought otherwise, while disappointed, I think it illustrates why I should cover some basic firefighter terms before we continue — and why I might need to seek a higher class of readership. Here are some actual terms we use, in spite of how they sound, that have nothing to do with Internet searches:

Reverse lay, cross lay, double female, minute man, hard suction, straight stream and flashover lap dance.

Ok, I made that last one up just to see who was paying attention.

Apparently, everyone was.

Now that we've established some basic terminology, and potential grounds for my termination, we will quickly move on to the next subject. In fact, the quicker the better.

A lot of people have asked me why anyone would want to run into a burning building? The simple answer is that firefighters are just like anyone else: Unless we are trying to avoid going to a *Twilight* movie marathon, we don't want to run into a burning structure either. However, there is also a deeper and more complicated answer, which involves a trait all firefighters have in common:

Really cold hands and feet.

I should probably mention they also share an inherent need to respond to a crisis and help people, even if it means putting themselves at risk for the protection of others.

But mostly, we're just trying to get our hands and feet warm.

Which isn't to say the only time the engines roll is when something is on fire. Particularly for firefighters here on the Oregon coast, search and rescue emergencies such as car accidents, ATV injuries, boating accidents, lost hikers and mushroom pickers, and Bigfoot sightings by "other kinds" of mushroom pickers, account for more than half the calls we respond to. To ensure we are trained and physically capable of handling any type of emergency, such as an ATV accident involving a mushroom picker and Bigfoot, firefighters must complete a special academy designed to teach the skills they need, as well as test their physical agility and endurance.

This is accomplished through nine days of intensive hands-on training, live drills and nearly 100 hours of class time studying all seven seasons of "Rescue Me."

Ha Ha Ha! Just kidding, chief!

(On a completely unrelated note, if anyone at the station finds season five in the training room, it's mine.)

So far, we've covered basic terminology and training, which brings me to another question people often ask: What's it like being IN a fire? Well, it's sort of like if you grabbed all the dried out Christmas trees within a two-block radius, lit them on fire, then jumped in the middle wearing pot holder underwear.

[Official disclaimer: Do not do this.]

While the protective clothing we wear, called "turnouts," certainly helps, it's still fire we're talking about, which means you still feel like a Ball Park Frank. To complete the experience, crawl around on your hands and knees wearing a blindfold (since it will be too smoky to see) while carrying a 30-pound bag of dog food on your back to simulate the weight of your air pack.

To re-cap: If feeling like a blind, backpacking Ball Park Frank sounds good to you, then firefighting might be the right fit.

All kidding aside, as I mentioned earlier, I have avoided writing about being a firefighter because it's something I take seriously. However, as I've learned, sometimes its the humor that gets you through the bad stuff. When our pagers go off in the middle of the night, and we are buckled up heading to a scene with lights flashing and sirens screaming, you're never sure of what you're going to find — which is part of why we do it. The other part is knowing, every time we buckle up, we'll find people next to us in the engine who are there for the same reasons, and willing to put themselves in harm's way to help others.

The only exception to this, of course, would be if there's a glow-in-the-dark mouse involved.

Join us for in-depth Olympic coverage, live ... from Utah

As many of you know, every two years I try to convince my editor to send me to the Olympics. The closest I've come was during the winter Olympics in Utah, when I was offered gas money, thermal underwear, and a set of binoculars for watching the events "from a great spot on the third floor of a car garage not far from the Olympic Pavilion — or thereabouts."

This year is no different. Especially when you consider the games are taking place in Canada, which means there's no way I'm going to see anything from any car garage in Utah. However, it doesn't mean we won't be offering you the same in-depth coverage as the larger media outlets. It's just that ours won't include any photographs, scores, statistics, biographies or interviews with Olympians, unless you count Buddy, our vending machine repair guy, who won the Brickerville High School "Donkey Basketball Olympics" in 1987.

(To be honest, that interview is still sketchy. The last time I asked Buddy about "riding a donkey for the gold" he threw a Diet Sprite at me.)

While it's true we won't have anyone at the Olympic Games again this year, it doesn't mean we weren't able to come up with something just as exciting and informative, especially when you compare it to, say...

Staring at a grapefruit. Keeping that in mind, I'm proud to announce an in-depth look at all 15 Winter Olympic events in a special three-part series we're calling:

Fifteen Reasons to be a Summer Olympian

We will begin with The Slalom: First introduced by Germany in 1936, this event combines the speed and skill of downhill skiing with the bravery one attains from consuming large quantities of German beer. Athletes launch themselves down slopes and attain speeds of up to 120 km per hour (approximately the speed of sound) while navigating around flags, moguls, photographers, journalists, border patrols, assorted swimmers and cabana boys before crossing the finish line somewhere in Peru. Events also include the "Super-G," which combines the thrill of slalom with the danger of rap artists on skis.

Next, an event dating back to 1932 when a Swedish marksman was driven into a snow bank by a hot-dogging American skier, The Biathlon combines cross-country skiing and long-range target shooting. Endurance is the key factor as competitors race around long loops of varying lengths, stopping only occasionally to shoot at targets until, eventually, firing five shots from a seated position inside of a portable commode.

Since 1924 The Bobsleigh has been thrilling Olympic spectators with its combination of speed, technique and general lack of a steering mechanism. In both the two-man and four-man events, each athlete has a specific purpose. This begins by getting the sleigh off to as fast a start as possible before piling inside the chassis, where athletes contribute individually by grabbing their ankles and saying the Rosary. Once they cross the finish line, the brakeman goes to work by pulling on a handle that, for all intents and purposes, does absolutely nothing.

There you have it, our first installment of pre-Winter Olympic coverage. Join us next week for a look at Curling, Figure Skating, and several other exciting events, none of which can be seen from Utah.

Like speed skating, our Olympic preview continues, because we can't stop

Hello and welcome to another exciting installment of our exclusive Winter Olympics preview:

Fifteen Reasons to Be a Summer Olympian

It's a preview so exclusive even the Olympic Committee doesn't know about it. And, quite frankly, we'd like to keep it that way. That's because while the larger media outlets routinely get bogged down with boring interviews and analysis of things like the effect of wind trajectory on Bob Costas' hair, we are able to avoid all that. How? By going nowhere near the actual Olympic games. This allows us to provide you with valuable information that news sources in Torino are missing because they're too busy trying to keep their cannelloni from freezing.

Last week, we began our special preview with an in-depth look at the slalom, bobsleigh and biathlon events. For those who missed it, here's a quick re-cap: Athletes who compete in the slalom and bobsleigh are insane, and though biathlon sounds exciting, we challenge you to watch it without drooling on your arm.

OK, now that we're all caught up, we can begin this week's installment of our special Olympic coverage by taking a look at cross country skiing — which is even less exciting than the biathlon since there's no shooting involved. (At least in the biathlon you are occasionally awakened by gunfire.) In cross country skiing the only sound is the commentator, who is trying to keep himself awake by finding exciting words to describe what appears to be several people looking for the nearest ski lift. Which isn't to say there isn't plenty of excitement at the Winter Olympics. In fact, when it comes to curling, the longer you watch four people moving a large stone across the ice using nothing but brooms, the more exciting cross country skiing gets.

For those of you who are unfamiliar with the sport of curling, this competition became an official Olympic event four years ago as a replacement for ice bowling, which [Pause here for dramatic effect...] fell through at the last minute.

In curling, each team consists of four players: the Lead, who delivers the stone; the Second and Third, who sweep the ice; and the Skip, who calls out important strategy like "Sweep faster!" and "Do you think anyone's still watching?!" This continues until one team is able to place its stone closest to the center of a special target marked on the ice. Or until Bud Light pulls its corporate sponsorship.

Next we have figure skating, which gets its name from the Ukrainian phrase Ukrlegnz Kgronzmof Itzentofl, meaning "Cold ankle twist." Figure skating combines music with complex skating routines that include a series of required elements, such as the "salchow," "double axle," and the dreaded "triple latte."

This brings us to freestyle skiing, in which skiers perform jumps, flips and other thrilling acrobatic maneuvers, just like I do, except that they don't land on their heads. Continuing along that theme, we will end today's installment of our three-part Winter Olympic preview with the Nordic combined, which, as you might expect, combines skiing and large hairy men in horned helmets.

That's what you'd expect, but you would be wrong.

It actually combines the acrobatics of freestyle skiing (jumping and high speeds) with the stamina of cross country skiing (yawn), effectively re-creating how Nordic men returned home from pubs some 200 years ago.

Next week we will wrap up our special preview with a look at luge, skeleton and other Olympic events whose athletes are routinely denied medical coverage.

Let the games begin! (Before we get sued)

Hello and welcome to the final installment of our groundbreaking (at least in terms of blatant copyright infringement) three-part Winter Olympics preview:

Fifteen Reasons to Be a Summer Olympian

Today, we will be focusing on some of the most dangerous and exciting events at the winter games. Events like luge, skeleton and ski jumping. Events that require an extraordinary amount of physical and mental conditioning before an Olympic hopeful, such as myself, can compete without soiling his polymer body suit. While I've never actually trained for a spot on the U.S. Luge team per se, I experienced something very similar in the winter of 1999 when I slipped in the snow and landed on what rescuers believe was a discarded Volkswagen hubcap.

Whatever it was, I clung to it for most of my 3/4-mile descent down the "pro" slope, which I executed in perfect Olympic "supine" position — feet down and head back — except for all the screaming. In retrospect, a skin-tight polymer body suit would've helped. Especially when you consider it would've prevented me from being allowed near the slope in the first place.

Luge, as many of you know, requires athletes to ride a tiny sled feet-first down a winding ice track while exceeding speeds of 130 km per hour (U.S. conversion: really, really fast) with almost no ability to steer. Keeping that in mind, the sport of Skeleton, which is the same as Luge except that athletes are positioned on their stomachs, is often referred to as "mysterious" and "bizarre," primarily because no one understands why any person who isn't on crack would want to compete in luge while going headfirst.

This brings us to the thrilling event of ski jumping, where athletes utilize a combination of strength, speed, precision, equilibrium and concentration to soar high above the field of play before landing gracefully, after more than 100 yards of flight, on Bob Costas.

OK. That actually only happened once, in 1990, when Jim McKay told Costas about a "short cut" between the biathlon and ice hockey events. This footage was later edited into the now famous clip: "The agony of defeat."

Next, we have snowboarding, which made its Olympic debut eight years ago, thanks to the persistence of Jack Burchett, an American surfer who said he conceived the idea while — and this is a direct quote — "Looking for some action during the long winter break." In addition to snowboarding, Burchett is also credited with two other conceptions, which his lawyers flatly deny he was involved in outside of wedlock. Our next event combines balance, speed, endurance and inner thigh muscles the size of Mini Coopers to produce the fastest human-powered sport held on a flat surface: speed skating.

In this event, athletes skate around an icy track at speeds of 40 mph while simultaneously running the risk of bursting into flames due to the amount of friction generated between their enormous thigh muscles, some of which are so large they occasionally hold their own press conference.

This brings us to what is arguably the most popular Winter

Olympic sport, Ice Hockey. We say "arguably" because — Hey, we're talking about HOCKEY here! You wanna make something of it?! That's right. Hockey is by far the most physically aggressive Winter Olympic sport, as long as you don't count women's figure skating. In ice hockey, competitors with sticks chase a small puck around the rink and try to score points by slapping it past a goaltender. Whereas in women's figure skating, competitors chase and slap each other for making passes at, and attempting to score with, their favorite bartender.

And there you have it. We hope you've enjoyed our special Winter Olympics Preview. Join us again in 2010 when we'll offer an inside look at the Winter Games in Vancouver, Canada, in a special series we're calling:

How to compete like an Olympian without straining you Molson Muscle

Let the games begin!

Never had food poisoning? Thank a humor columnist

Being a journalist, I naturally have journalist friends who, whenever we get together, want to talk about (yawn) heady issues facing the nation and the world. This is done in a discussion format similar to *Meet the Press*, except that our debates are often interrupted by someone's beer foaming over. Aside from that, it's just like the show on TV. As you can imagine, our exchanges get pretty heated as each of us presents an important topic of debate.

What is our stance on Iran?

Should we overhaul Social Security?

How do we deal with North Korea?

Or, as I challenged: Why does the new Bugs Bunny look like he's been shooting steroids with Jose Canseco?

That's usually when our debate comes to a screeching halt and I'm forced, once again, to defend my journalistic integrity by explaining the value of what I do, then underscoring it by offering to pay for everyone's beer. Admittedly, I have it easy compared to other journalists who must worry about gathering "facts" and finding "sources" while I, on the other hand, can "make" things up without "leaving" my desk. Which isn't to say I'm not held to the same journalistic standards as everyone else. I can't claim, for example, that dipping your head in Frito-Lay bean dip can promote growth similar to that of a Tibet mountain yak.

If I were a less responsible journalist who tried to substantiate his claim with testimony from a yak living in, say... the San Gabriel Mountains, I could open myself up to litigation from Frito-Lay, the state of California, and, quite possibly, every bald person smelling of bean dip.

The fact is, what I do comes at great personal risk. Not just in terms of potential lawsuits, but also in terms of actual physical danger — particularly when you consider how often I mention my wife in my column. This is an occupational hazard my "real" journalist friends never have to contend with. Chances are, they'll never write a story, be lying in bed the next morning, and have a city official roll over and smack them in the head with the newspaper.

Yet, week after week, at the risk of returning home to an angry wife and total financial ruin, humor columnists like myself sit at their keyboards, surfing the net until an hour before deadline.

Why?

Because each of us REALLY AND TRULY believes we're making the world a better place by doing everything we can, as humor columnists, to stay out of the skilled-labor work force.

Let's face it, for every culinary position a humor columnist takes up, there are at least a dozen people hurling into a commode. Countless people (i.e., there's no time to count them before my deadline) owe their lives to the fact that I — and others like me — are sitting in a newsroom making stuff up. Imagine being stuck on a mountainside knowing that the person repelling down a rope to save you is the same person who, if they had a choice, would rather be writing about glow-in-the-dark mice.

Would you be willing to put your life in that person's hands? Or would you go ahead and take a chance that a giant Slip-N-Slide will suddenly sprout from the mountain? If it were me, I'd take my chances with the Slip-N-Slide. Even if it wasn't wet, and it meant sliding down half a mile of dry plastic.

The point is, we humor columnists know our place in the world. We understand the risks involved in what we do. Which is why, as a humor columnist who actually worked in the food service industry, I can say, with some authority:

You really should wash your hands after reading this.

Social trends
(And other frightening anomalies)

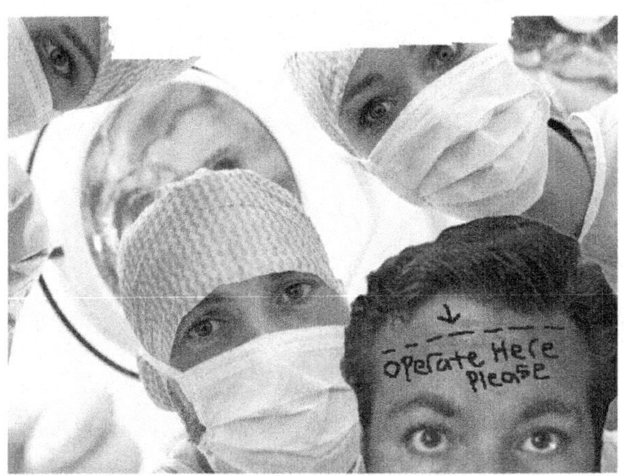

Surgery is safer when patients come with instructions

A recent study conducted by the healthcare industry shows an alarming trend in America's operating rooms. According to the study, reports of "wrong-site surgery" are on the rise. To clarify, "wrong-site surgery" occurs when a doctor operates on, say...

Your brain.

When he was supposed to operate on, say...

Your big toe.

Or someone else.

Or even someone else's big toe.

That's right; in a few cases, doctors have even operated on the wrong patient. However, the report strongly emphasizes that THIS IS VERY RARE, and only occurred when doctors didn't have the right patient to begin with...

"Let's see, according to this chart, Mrs. Freemont is 68-years-old and is here for a triple by-pass. Nurse, please shave away that thick hair on her chest, right below her Hell's Angels tattoo."

"Doctor, are you sure this is the right patient?"

"Absolutely, it says so right here on her chart."

"But this patient looks like a man."

"To the untrained eye, perhaps. But if you'll lift up her hospital gown you'll see...HOLY COW!"

"What is it, doctor?!"

"This is going to be more complicated than I thought..."

The organization that conducted the study, which was headed up by Dr. Dennis O'Leary, says there are a number of reasons "wrong-site surgery" has increased in recent years. According to Dr. O'Leary, "Doctors are busy, and people are being put to sleep before there is an opportunity to verify who they are, what procedure is going to be performed on them, and on what site."

What this means, of course, is that you should always insist on staying awake long enough to meet your surgeon, and, if at all possible, scrub in for the operation itself. For situations when that isn't possible , such as assisting with your own brain surgery, it's a good idea to write out a list of instructions that you can keep with you at all times. These instructions should include: Your name, the type of operation you'd like to have, and what part of your body you'd like it to happen on.

Here's an example:

Hello.
My name is Ned.
I'd like to have brain surgery, please.
If possible, I'd like it to happen on my head.
(Please see arrows)

You should know that the surgery which holds the greatest risk to patients is orthopedic surgery, which involves operating on the arms and legs, and therefore increases possible confusion between right and left:

"Okay, let's open up that right arm...Wait a minute. Is it supposed to be MY right, or HIS right?"

"I'm not sure, doctor."

"Let's see...if I turn this way, that would make it my right and his left — uh, right?"

"That's true, doctor, but what if it's your left."

"You're right! Let's try flipping him over, and then we can...WAIT! He's clutching some instructions..."

I should mention that out of the estimated 40 million operations performed in the U.S. last year, only 58 resulted in "wrong-site surgery." I should also mention that none of them were fatal, and that all of them happened to Michael Jackson.

As you might've guessed, the results from this study have prompted hospitals to find ways to reduce the numbers of "wrong-site" incidents that occur each year. While I've had a chance to read over some of the suggestions, I'm going to refrain from including any of them here — just to avoid stepping on any toes.

Especially if they happen to be my doctor's.

Don't worry: tougher tax laws will still let you depreciate your ostrich

It used to be that when the IRS discovered you've been claiming a child who is actually a 50-pound Labrador retriever named "Billy," everyone would have a good laugh. Not any more. The Treasury Department says it will be cracking down on "aggressive tax deductions" filed by U.S. taxpayers in order to keep the federal government from being bilked out of hundreds of millions of dollars — money that could otherwise be spent on important federal programs, such as the Government Shutdown Caribbean Getaway Fund.

As a service to our readers, several of whom are actual U.S. taxpayers, we thought we'd contact some of the brightest minds in tax law in order to clarify what we can still get away with. Unfortunately, everyone was too busy working on the Osbourne family's latest tax returns to help us so, as responsible members of the news media, we were left with only one option:

Forget taxes and talk about *The Bachelor*!

Just kidding. We rolled up our sleeves. Got on the Internet. Made phone calls. And eventually came up with some real-life tax claims you should NOT make unless you want to end up in jail, or worse, on the computer screen of a humor columnist trying to meet a deadline.

Our first example comes from Raleigh, N.C., where a man with an unsuccessful furniture-store business did what any enterprising owner would do: hire an arsonist to burn it down. After determining the fire was indeed the result of a three-piece sectional explosion which then spread to a spare gas can kept near the curtains display, the insurance company paid the man $500,000. He then dutifully reported the amount on his tax return, which also included deductions for the loss of the building, its contents, as well as a "consulting fee" of $10,000 paid to the arsonist. It's unclear whether the man actually used the term "arson consultant" on his return. The point is, if you're going to burn down your business for the insurance money, don't be stupid:

Do it in North Carolina.

Our next example involves an ostrich farmer from Louisiana, where apparently, without our knowledge, the state motto has been changed to:

We raise ostriches that could step on your state bird.

In this case, the farmer filed a claim for the depreciation of his ostrich which, as it turns out, it's perfectly legal! In fact, you can claim the depreciation of any animal used for breeding. However, it doesn't mean that if "Buster" gets out and fraternizes with the neighbor's cocker spaniel that you can claim him as a deduction.

Even if "Buster" happens to be an ostrich.

So what does all this mean to you and me, the average U.S. taxpayers? It means that if we want to claim ourselves as a tax deduction, we need to begin breeding immediately.

No. What it really means is that with tax day upon us, you only have a few weeks left to get "Billy" a social security card if you want to claim him on your taxes. And if you begin to suspect that the IRS is catching on, do what one Wyoming CPA told his client to do, and simply mark "Billy" as "deceased" on your next tax return. If they want to know what happened, just tell them the details are still sketchy.

All you know is that it involved a freak sofa explosion somewhere in North Carolina.

'Bathroom rage' could soon be clogging court system

Several years ago I came up with an idea while standing in line for the rest room, which, in this case, was actually a row of six portable toilets set up to meet the needs of approximately 8,000 men, women and children, each of whom had apparently consumed two or more 128-ounce Big Gulps in the previous 20 minutes. Necessity is the mother of invention. Which is why, as I stood waiting next to a continually running water fountain that was broadcasting every splash over the PA system, I found it necessary to occupy my thoughts with a way to speed up the public commode-using process. This was like trying to take your mind off of having surgery by watching *The Medical Channel*.

Regardless, it led to a revolutionary idea I call the "Rodeo Commode."

Like other commodes, it provides users with a private and sanitary environment in which to complete their bodily functions. However, unlike ordinary commodes, the "Rodeo Commode" allows a person just eight seconds before the doors fly open and, finished or not, they are bucked out of the stall by a hydraulic system similar to a mechanical bull — including, if necessary, spinning a full 360 degrees in order to dislodge even the most experienced riders in the "Rodeo Commode" circuit.

Unfortunately, just like my idea for an all-commercial cable channel (allowing viewers to tune in and leave the room as often as they like without worrying if they missed anything), the "Rodeo Commode" was met with skepticism by my list of potential investors — i.e., several plumbers who I know are in daily contact with pipe dope.

As it turns out, I was simply ahead of my time. I know this because of a new social phenomenon experts are calling "bathroom rage," wherein, much like "road rage," a confrontation between two strangers quickly escalates into a potentially dangerous situation.

In the rest room.

The big difference here is that you won't be traveling in excess of 60 mph while sitting on a commode. And if you are, you have a right be angry. Especially if someone cuts you off. According to the New Haven Register in Stratford, Conn., police charged Andres Diaz and Joseph Augusto with breach of peace following a confrontation in a McDonald's rest room that started when Diaz apparently "took too long." Augusto, who was waiting to use the commode, was enraged when Diaz emerged from the stall with a copy of Anna Karenina and an "Oprah's Book Club" t-shirt.

Okay, I made that last part up. But the two men did get into a fight over how long Diaz was in the bathroom after Augusto confronted him about it. That's when, according to the police report, "The two men allegedly bumped chests, then chased each other around the restaurant with their weapons — Augusto with a small pocket knife, and Diaz brandishing a McDonald's straw dispenser."

The restaurant chain refused to comment on the incident other than to say it was "unfortunate." Following the advice of its lawyers, the restaurant chain has now adopted a strict new policy of making straws "only available on request."

This, my friends, is "bathroom rage" rearing its ugly head and, in a matter of speaking, slurping out of society's collective soda cup. What if Diaz had grabbed a toilet paper dispenser instead? My point is, we could end this madness right now, before some unfortunate teenager is hired to hand out allotted squares of bath tissue.

With the help of the "Rodeo Commode," there's no reason to take "bathroom rage" sitting down.

The bigger your lips, the sexier you'll be... if you date a sucker fish

Nothing says "sexy" faster than someone with a pair of giant lips, even if that person's collagen injections have made their lips so enormously seductive that they can't actually pronounce the word "sexy," and must instead settle for calling themselves "shek-shee." The point is, big lips are no longer just a cosmetic enhancement for people less fortunate than Mick Jagger and

Angelina Jolie, whose lips are so large and incredibly sexy that they are prohibited by international law from bearing children together because, quote: *Said children could potentially upset the delicate balance between populations of humans and sucker fish.*

Though we all know that true beauty stems from inside, as any cosmetics surgeon will tell you, no one will notice unless your lips are the size of tractor tires. Which is why a new product called *City Lips* is being heralded as the newest, easiest and safest way to give you the lips you always wanted, but never dreamed you could have. At least not without surgically implanting tire stems in them and inflating your lips to 350 psi. Until now, those of us unable to afford expensive collagen injections were forced to live with the embarrassment of having normal, everyday lips. But thanks to City Lips, you can avoid the hassle and expense of collagen injections by using their patented do-it-yourself lip enlargement process!

That's right! Say goodbye to snobby surgeons telling you how much better you'd look with Julia Roberts lips when their own lips look like Phyllis Diller's. With each purchase of City Lips you'll receive one bottle of specially formulated "lip transformer" solution and a patented dual-action applicator. This applicator is a crucial part of City Lips' groundbreaking, two-step process — which starts by applying the "lip transformer" with one side of the patented applicator and then, after turning the applicator over, whacking your lips with it as many times as possible for 10 minutes.

Okay, I made that last part up. But according to City Lips, their new product has been named "Best Over-the-Counter Lip Plumper" by *Good Housekeeping*, which, as you know, recently debunked the common misconception that you could increase the size of your lips by spraying them with *Pledge* (although it will keep them shiny and smelling lemony fresh).

I'd also like to point out that after three large margaritas, trying to say "Best Over-the-Counter Lip Plumper" will at least make your feel like your lips are really huge.

I bring this up because I'm concerned about the mixed message this sends to young women. On one hand, they're seeing supermodels getting thinner and thinner. On the other hand, they're seeing those same models trip over their own lips on the runway, with nothing to break their fall except for other stumbling models, who then land in a flailing heap of inflated lips and silicone.

No more. It's time to quit pouting, pucker up, and accept each other's lips just the way they are.

Unless pouting makes your lips look fuller, of course.

Beware of dangerous, unreasonable pickles

It wasn't long ago that I found myself driving down the road with an 800-degree onion ring searing my flesh. I had just left a Burger King drive-through and, after exchanging pleasantries at the window and maintaining my composure long enough to exit the parking lot, pounced on my combo meal like a hyena at a gazelle feed — laughing and eating, laughing and eating. So, when I ripped into an enormous onion ring and felt the breading fall away into my lap, I had no one but myself to blame when my appetizer became a sizzling, onion-flavored chin strap that turned my frenzied laughing to screaming on I-5.

Though I had been branded a road-food junkie — apparent by the scarlet "O" encircling my lower lip and chin — I never once thought of calling a lawyer in an effort to seek damages against Burger King (and the Onion Growers of America) for supplying me the means with which to be an idiot. As much as I'd like to say that I reached that decision based on my moral character, it really had more to do with a recurring image of what the trial would be like.

[Insert gauzy, dream-sequence here...]

"Mr. Hickson, when you ordered your food at the drive-through, how did those combo-meal pictures make you feel."

"Angry — Tortured, really. They seemed to be taunting me. I think I might have cried a little."

(Dramatic pause by my lawyer) "So, it's safe to say that, based on the fact that you were ordering food, Burger King should have known that you were hungry enough to risk bodily harm in order to satisfy your appetite.

"I would think so."

"And yet they sent you out onto the highway with hot onion rings ANYWAY, knowing full well that you would probably try to eat them."

"Y-yes."

"And is the girl who worked the drive-up window that day here in this court room?"

"Y-yes," I say from the witness stand, and point incriminatingly to a 16-year-old wearing braces and a Viva Loca t-shirt. *"If not for my wife throwing her supersized-cup of soda in my face, I might've been scarred for life because of that girl!"*

Pandemonium breaks out.

[...Insert reality here]

The reason I bring up this painful subject is because of (another) lawsuit filed against McDonald's by an Iowa woman, Veronica Martin, who burnt herself on a hot pickle slice. According to the report, she is seeking $110,000 (apparently the going rate for garnish-burn victims) for the "physical and mental pain" caused by a pickle that fell from her burger and onto her chin. Veronica's husband, Darrin, is also suing — for $15,000 — because he says, ever since the accident, he has "been deprived of the services and consortium of his wife."

Now, I'm going to sidestep the whole hot-pickle-leads-to-lack-of-consortium thing, and just issue a hearty "thanks" to the Martins for bringing this safety issue to light for all Amercians.

That said, I'll leave you now.

All of this talk of food is making me hungry.

Over 200 hours of Olympic coverage, and still no elephant polo

Like much of the world, I will spend a good portion of the summer Olympics watching hundreds of athletes from all over the world doing things that I could do if I just had strength, speed, agility, grace and an unquenchable desire to leave the couch for anything other than more snack food. With 280 hours of Olympic programming scheduled this year, that leaves just four hours a day for things like working, eating and sleeping. With that kind of coverage, it's hard to imagine any sport that could've been overlooked.

For those of you with a weak heart (or who are simply tired of standing), I suggest you sit down before this next revelation, which is that, in spite of heavy lobbying, you will not find Unicycle Hockey, Gale-Force Kayaking or Elephant Polo among this year's Olympic competitions. Being a journalist, I wasted no time and immediately called the Olympic Committee headquarters and demanded to know the *truth*!

When I didn't get that, I went ahead and demanded *free passes*!

I didn't get that either, but was told that the FBI would be watching my home until the games were over.

Because we won't be seeing any of these events during this summer's Olympics, let me take the opportunity to introduce them to the handful of readers who might not be familiar these sports.

We'll begin with unicycle hockey, which actually has its roots in Germany — where they drink A LOT of beer. Though no one knows for sure how the sport got started, everyone agrees that beer was a crucial element. The rules of the game, and what constitutes a "foul," are pretty much the same as regular hockey — except that, in this version, plunging your hockey stick into the spokes of your opponent's unicycle is considered "a foul." Scoring is also very similar to regular hockey; players move the puck in an effort to get it past the bartender.

Needless to say, Budweiser has signed on to be a premier sponsor should this event ever make it into the Olympics.

If your sporting interest is geared toward individual events, it doesn't get any more exciting than gale-force kayaking, which is exactly what it sounds like: someone in a kayak during a hurricane. To do this requires a special kayak, something that was first developed by lifeguards in Australia as a tool for rescuing people caught in the surf. Naturally, the next step in this evolutionary process was for people to begin using these kayaks as a tool for getting caught in the surf during hurricanes and, therefore, need rescuing.

Last year alone, a total of 12 gale-force kayakers died — a number that the health department says is entirely too high. Especially when you consider nine of those deaths occurred out of the water, while driving to the beach during hurricanes.

This brings us to my personal favorite, elephant polo. To compete, you must have a mallet ($73), a polo ball ($22), and an elephant (priceless). The game takes place over two 10-minute periods called "chukkers," which is exactly what you'll feel like doing after 20 minutes of elephant riding.

The game begins with the referee tossing the ball between two opposing elephants who are positioned within a small circle.

(**Note:** The game ends if the referee doesn't leave the circle in time.)

Keep in mind that it is a foul if your elephant lies down in front of the goal in order to block it from opponents. It is also a foul if your elephant picks up the ball with his trunk. The same goes for picking-up, or lying-down on, any officials. Finally, if after two "chukkers" the game is tied, the next round will be sudden death.

Because this is a family-oriented newspaper, I can't get into the details here. But I will tell you that a gale-force kayak won't do you much good.

Newest cell phone feature is so hot you may need a fire extinguisher — Really

Technology is great.

Except when it explodes in your pants.

I've never really liked cell phones to begin with, and now that they've started self detonating, I like them even less. According to a news article sent in by Susan Grigsby of Alpharetta, Ga., Nokia has launched an investigation into why two of its cell phones recently burst into flames — a feature Nokia officials say wasn't supposed to become available until next year. As you might expect, cell phone sales have dropped slightly as a result of these incidents. That's because luxuries like instant text messaging, computer games and video imaging don't mean much if your cell phone suddenly ignites into flames, turning your morning commute into a flaming lap dance and an appearance on *The World's Wildest Police Chases*.

It would be different if exploding cell phones were an optional feature, i.e., for an extra charge, you, as a cell phone customer, had the option of detonating someone else's cell phone with the press of a button...

"Hello? That's okay — the movie just started. What? Really? No way. And what did SHE say?"

"WARNING! Detonation sequence has been initiated! Beginning countdown! Five..! Four..!"

"Hey — you mind if call you back? My phone's about to explode."

While Nokia officials are blaming defective batteries as the root cause of Exploding Cell Phone Syndrome, I have to disagree. The fact is, cell phones are simply being asked to do too much and, because of it, are having a total melt down. I've had my cell phone for five years, which by today's standards means it should be part of a traveling history exhibit for school children. However, I've kept it because 1) unlike newer phones, it's larger than a Saltine cracker and doesn't have buttons the size of Braille, and 2) it provides me with all the functions I need in a cell phone:

I can call people.

People can call me.

I can hang up on people.

That's all I'm really looking for in a cell phone. If I wanted to play video games and exchange text messages with friends, I'd just stay at work. Comparatively, the life expectancy of today's cell phones is about one year. That's assuming everything goes well and you don't go blind trying to use it, and out of sheer frustration while trying to place a call to your ophthalmologist, end up crushing it in your fist like a grape.

In most cases, this isn't covered under warranty. The same thing goes for any damage your phone might incur after accidentally triggering a gas-station explosion. That's right. According to a recent warning from AAA, static discharge from cell phones "has the potential to ignite gas vapors, although it's still safer than if your cell phone actually explodes."

Because of this danger, the National Fire Protection Association has offered a couple of tips to motorists.

The first is to avoid using cell phones, laptop computers or portable radios while refueling. And if you happen to be using them all at once, you're just asking for trouble. Be safe; at least wait until you're back on the highway. And most importantly, if a fire starts, leave the area and call someone. Unless of course that's the reason the fire started in the first place.

Florence, Oregon: Nation's best spot for retirement, exploding whales

I'm sure many of you have heard that Florence, Ore., where my family and I happen to live, has just been named THE best place to retire in the United States. I say "many of you" because, at this very moment, both roads leading into town are clogged with traffic, most of which consists of giant U-Hauls driven by white-knuckled retirees from Florida. My guess is that they were told to evacuate due to hurricane [insert most recent here], and just kept heading west until they (a) hit water again, or (b) found the brake.

An article about our ranking recently appeared in USA Today, and the Chamber of Commerce has been flooded with calls from news agencies wanting to know how it feels to be in the national spotlight, and if, due to the publicity, we expect Ben Affleck anytime soon.

The truth is, we Florentines have earned ourselves national attention twice before.

The first was in 1970 when, while attempting to dispose of a decomposing whale carcass (by utilizing a well-thought-out plan involving (1) several pints of beer at the Beachcomber Tavern and (2) a truckload of dynamite), several onlookers were slightly injured after being struck by a piece of flying blubber roughly the size of a Volkswagen Beetle.

Then in 1998, just as our tourism slogan "Stop Your Blubbering and Come To Florence" was losing steam, we were back in the national spotlight after our city-wide search for a pet monkey named "Bo-Bo" was mentioned on Paul Harvey. This led to our next tourism slogan, which I can't repeat here since, nowadays, petting someone's "lucky monkey" can mean something entirely different.

As you can imagine, being crowned this year's Magic Kingdom of retirement is very exciting for everyone.

Except, of course, for those of us who (1) actually live here and (2) are not retired. That's because we Florentines must now live up to a national image that, for the first time, doesn't include a crisis involving some type of mammal. We once had the comfort of knowing that flying blubber, while helping boost tourism, isn't an amenity most people look for in a retirement community. That has all changed. People now know we have a performing arts center, library, hospital, restaurants and, perhaps most importantly, a large supply of healthy sea mammals.

This has led to an unprecedented number of visitors, many of whom have already made arrangements to have their Lay-Z-Boy drop shipped by the end of the week. It's not that we don't welcome the boost to our local economy; we just want to make it to the bank without being struck by a Ryder truck. So, to that end, we'd like to make two things clear in order to keep the situation under control.

#1: Running past a house and throwing a wad of cash in the yard does not constitute a purchase agreement.

#2: It's NOT okay to keep circling the city in your moving truck until someone moves out.

As a community, we realize the impact national exposure will have on our small town.

Which is why, as a community, we're not above blowing up another dead whale or launching a monkey attack in order to keep things from getting out of hand.

Thank geckos for stickier tape and new action movie for Bruce Willis

It's true I sometimes make fun of scientific discoveries that, in my opinion, seem a little silly — such as genetically altering a mouse to glow in the dark. That's because I just can't see any benefit to creating a rodent with its own built-in night light. While it might make for goofy fun at the lab when all the lights are out, should one of these neon mice manage to escape and reproduce, I'll be the one stuck taking my cat to therapy twice a week.

However, from time to time, there is a scientific breakthrough so significant, so far-reaching, so groundbreaking that even I — a trained humor columnist — must stop and say:

Wow! This is quite possibly the most important scientific discovery since....

The glow-in-the-dark mouse!

(For me, the yardstick by which all modern scientific discoveries are measured.)

Thanks to researchers at Lewis and Clark University and the University of California Berkley, we are on the verge of another milestone in scientific achievement, and something that could quite possibly change the world as we know it. At least in terms of adhesiveness.

Gecko Tape.

After hearing this exciting news, you're undoubtedly thinking the same thing I was: *Ewwwww.*

But rest assured that this new tape is NOT actually made from geckos. However, it is strong enough to support the entire body weight of a full grown elephant which, apparently, is just one of its many practical applications. However, before we get to that, part of my job as a journalist is to take highly technical information and, through a rigorous process of study and research, find a way of explaining it to you, the reader, in such a way that I, the journalist, look smart. To do this, I will be using terms like *setae*, and *spatulae*, and *Van der Waal forces*. I might even include the term *proluminal crotominoids* (pronounced pro-loom-i-nal crow-tom-i-noids), which essentially means that I've run out of actual scientific terms and am now making them up.

That said, I will explain the science behind Gecko Tape. To begin with, geckos have 100 times the wall-climbing ability of spiders. Something that, back in the 1960s, nearly led Marvel Comics to pass up spiders and introduce the *Amazing Gecko-Man!* who, along with his ability to climb walls, would possess other gecko-like superpowers — such as licking his eyelids and detaching his rear end as a means of escape. (The idea was shelved after sketching just three panels of a fight between Gecko-Man! and Doctor Octigrab.)

The secret to the gecko's clinging ability lies in its toes, each of which contain microscopic setae (tiny hairs). At the tip of each setae is a spatulae (pad) that is approximately 10 millionths of an inch across, which the gecko laces with poluminal crotominoids (Super Glue) before climbing. This produces an effect called Van der Waal forces, which I haven't figured out yet, but nonetheless would be a really great name for a Bruce Willis movie.

After years of study, researchers have discovered that the combination of setae and spatulae cause electrical charges around molecules to become unbalanced, resulting in an unnatural attraction to each other, such as Brigitte Nielsen and Flava Flav. Scientists have now found a way to duplicate the gecko's setae and spatulae in order to create the most adhesive tape known to man. The next big challenge, of course, will be packaging. It's not like you can sell it in a roll like duct tape. How will you ever get it apart?

Still, when they do eventually figure it out, I'll be the first one in line. I plan to buy several rolls and leave strips of it all over the house.

I mean, heck — what better way to catch a glow-in-the-dark mouse?

It's 'Go Time' for my governorship of California, if my extension cord reaches

Now that the Ninth Circuit Court of Appeals has cleared up the confusion in California, and the recall of the gubernatorial recall election has officially been recalled, my bid for governorship has entered a critical stage known to campaign strategists (and many toddlers) as "Go Time." That's right. By Oct. 7, I must convince millions of California voters (and a handful of confused Floridians) that I am THE candidate who can return the Golden State to its former greatness. I will do this by rolling up my sleeves and calling for bi-partisanship, even if it means Republicans and Democrats working together; I will do this by tightening the belt around California's bloated (yet perfectly tanned and oiled) budgetary midsection; I will do this without the use of liposuction or breast enhancements; and, perhaps most importantly, I will do all of this while remaining a safe distance away here in Oregon.

However, before we get to the details of my plan (which includes a very popular referendum limiting the number of times a candidate can say *Kal-ee-fon-ee-ah* without an interpreter present), I'd like to answer the question regarding my absence at the televised debate held on Sept. 24. The truth is, I was kept from attending the debate due to security reasons following a series of anonymous letters threatening to, and I quote:

Terminate you like a T-1000 should you show your puny face anywhere in Kal-ee-fon-ee-ah.

Though we haven't been able to trace the source of these letters ourselves, I've been told that Arianna Huffington has agreed to step forward and, in a tremendous show of character, blame it on Cruz Bustamante. It's because of these threatening letters that my editor, in a touching show of support, refused to allow my participation in the debate out of his genuine concern for my safety so close to a deadline. Regrettably, after watching the debate on television, I realized I'd missed a tremendous opportunity to distance myself from the other candidates by being the only person on the panel who didn't need subtitles.

This included Peter Camejo, who needed subtitles so people could know what he was thinking about.

Clearly, this was yet another missed opportunity to boost my campaign. As some of you may recall, I was blatantly passed over as grand marshall for the Mexican Independence Day parade simply because, as one organizer put it:

He's not Mexican.

This has left me with one final opportunity to convince California voters that I'm the right person for the job. I will now do this by revealing what I call my "California Plan for Recovery."

Or CPR.

Step one is to solve the state's spiraling budget crisis. As Governor of California, my first act will be to tackle this issue by introducing an across-the-board silicone tax. According to my estimations, this tax could generate an actual budget surplus within a year.

Step two: Address the state's electricity problem at the source by mandating construction of the world's longest extension cord. This cord would be a safe, three-pronged design stretching as far as Ashland, Ore., where residents would have their choice of either (a) offering the last spot on their surge protector for a nominal fee, or (b) changing their outlets back to two prongs.

And finally, step three: Repair California's tarnished image.

This will require Californians to willingly serve as a reminder that our election system here in the U.S. — no matter how flawed it may be — is still better than whatever system they'll be using in Florida next year.

Okay, since you asked, here's an update on my California goobernatorial campaign

Since announcing my candidacy for governorship of California last month, I've received letters from actual Californians wanting to know how things are going. I'm assuming of course that they are referring to my candidacy, and not to the race in general. The biggest development of course is that the recall election may be postponed until March. This is due to concerns about the inaccuracies of the punch ballot system, which experts say could lead to as many as 40,000 votes being tabulated incorrectly.

"And that's a conservative estimate," judges from the 9th Circuit Court of Appeals said. "We really have no idea how many Floridians will turn out for this election."

What this does is give me even more time to chip away at the competition.

If you listen to the media, the field of legitimate candidates has pretty much dwindled down to Arnold Schwarzenegger, Cruz Bustamante and...

Hold on...

I know I'm forgetting someone...

Oh yeah — Gray Davis!

I'm here to tell you that my campaign is not only alive and well, but has me poised to become the true front-runner once people realize that Schwarzenegger has no chance of winning this election. That's because, in addition to the Democratic votes he'll be missing as a Republican, Schwarzenegger would also have to get elected without ANY votes from California journalists who — let's be honest — don't want to type his name any more than they already have to.

And, if a recent *Associated Press* article is correct (and, being a newspaper service, it has to be), Bustamante has now come under fire due to his shocking association with, quote: "A Chicano student group while attending Fresno State College in the 1970s — or thereabouts."

According to the article sent in by Jeannette Coomler of Salinas, Calif., one of the goals of this radical organization is to establish a separate "Chicano homeland" here in the U.S.! This has sparked a growing fear that, should Bustamante get elected, he could then carry out his diabolical plan by creating a Chicano homeland RIGHT IN CALIFORNIA!

Given the chance, I'd like to ask Mr. Bustamante how he plans to deal with the obvious legal issues California would face in trying to establish a "Chicanos-only" state, which would require relocating as many as 50 Caucasians. I think it's safe to say that Bustamante and Schwarzenegger will soon be out of the way, leaving Davis, porn star Mary Carey and myself as California's top choices for governor. However, if what my campaign manager says is true, a recent poll shows that Davis has lost his grip and is now behind Carey and slipping — an image that should easily make me the front-runner.

The next step in solidifying my governorship was supposed to be by serving as grand marshal for the recent Mexican Independence Day parade. This opportunity came after Schwarzenegger's invitation to be grand marshal was rescinded once officials realized the name "Schwarzenegger" wouldn't fit around the rim of his sombrero. That left me as the next logical choice because, as any Mexican-American will tell you, my name is exactly half the size of his. Knowing this was a big opportunity, I was ready to go out and win the Latino vote!

That was until Bustamante stepped in and agreed to wear a sombrero that simply reads: "Busta."

In spite of this setback, I am continuing on thanks to the support of California voters like Michael Setty, who emailed me to say I definitely had his vote, as long as I promised to stay out of California. Like most politicians, I'll make that promise if it means winning his vote. Unlike most politicians, it's a promise I'll actually keep.

Thankfully, most men will never have to butcher a cow while wearing high heels

My wife talked me into going with her to a fancy shoe store and, as expected, it wasn't long before women were falling all over me. That's because they were all trying on high heeled shoes, some of which were so towering that a special negotiator had to be called in to talk them down. These women apparently loved high heels so much that, once they discovered they couldn't afford them, they chose to end it all by unstrapping their Stilettos and leaping headfirst into the bargain table. I observed all of this knowing full well that if the shoe were on the other foot, men, given a choice, would rather have themselves hobbled.

The reason is simple: Men are physically incapable of walking in high heels without looking like a poodle balancing on its hind legs for a piece of cheese. We just don't possess that special gene that women have, which allows them to stride down the street in high heels with leggy confidence. And let's face it. Even if we did have it, chances are we'd still walk — with leggy confidence — directly into a post.

I am going to reveal something about myself that could mean the end of my career. Or, at the very least, the end of my wife's willingness to share a closet with me. You see, in order to prepare for writing this...

I dressed a poodle in high heels.

No. I tried wearing a pair of my wife's high heels. And let me just clarify that it did not include any type of accessorizing, unless you count the scarf, which was used to stop my nose from bleeding after I tripped headfirst into the coffee table. For obvious reasons, no one was home when I attempted this, which is to say that I risked my life for this column. One minute, I was making my way along the wall toward an arm of the couch (and feeling pretty good about the way my calves looked). The next minute, WHAM! My ankles were touching the floor and I was trying to remember the number for 9-1-1.

Don't judge me. I was a journalist in high heels putting himself in harm's way in order to bring you the truth. God only knows what would've happened if the dog hadn't broken my fall.

The irony in all this is that men were actually the first to wear high heeled shoes. That's right. An Egyptian inventor devised them as a way for butchers to elevate themselves off the messy stall floors. This practice of wearing heels lasted approximately 11 minutes, after which the chief butcher to the Pharaoh awarded the inventor his very own pyramid chamber, which he was immediately sealed into.

Eventually, high heeled shoes resurfaced again in the 1600s, when the French used them as a way to elevate themselves above anyone who wasn't French. Ha! Just kidding! They didn't need special shoes for that. However, fashion-minded women in France did hobble around on 40-inch heels, often using long sticks to balance themselves. This helped established Paris as THE fashion Mecca, and more importantly to travelers, as a place where crowded streets could be cleared easily using a single bowling ball.

Just like a pair of Stiletto heels, there is a point to all this, which is that men should be extremely thankful for all the sacrifices women make in order to look and feel more attractive.

Especially since they can do it without breaking the coffee table.

Tired of looking at the same old killer asteroid? Give it a new paint job

Scientists tell us it's only a matter of time before a giant asteroid threatens to crash into the Earth. This of course would lead to a cataclysmic event unleashing tidal waves, earthquakes, 6,000 years of winter, and, theoretically, mankind's final offering as an evolved species:

Survivor: Oh great—now what?

Scientists warn that the only way to avoid total extinction would be to somehow divert the offending asteroid into a different orbit, therefore altering its path into a collision course with something less vital, like, say... New Jersey. Until recently, experts believed that the only way to accomplish this would be through the use of nuclear missiles. These missiles could be launched from space and lodged into the asteroid, where they would remain undetonated until reaching the precise location astrophysicists determine would be far enough away to safely deflect the asteroid while, at the same time, still being close enough to scare the pants off of everyone on Earth.

However, a recent study suggests that there might be a more practical way of handling the situation by simply having someone go up and paint the asteroid white...

Wanted: *Commercial painter, must enjoy air travel, experience with spray gun preferred; will consider brush and roller if time allows.*

According to an article in *Science* magazine, changing the surface temperature of an asteroid can lead to a dramatic shift in orbit by creating an uneven release of heated gas known as the Yarkovsky Effect. As an illustration, this very same phenomenon has been observed in my own home, where it is known as the franks and beans effect; and Yes, in both cases there was a notable shift in orbiting bodies.

If it comes down to it, there are essentially three ways of changing temperatures of an asteroid.

The first, as I mentioned, would be to actually paint a large section of the asteroid white.

Or maybe even a nice mauve or fuchsia. This would not only induce the Yarkovsky Effect, it could potentially save the entire planet. More importantly, it could also be the first step toward adding some much needed color to what many agree is a really drab solar system. However, we need to remember that painting an asteroid isn't without its drawbacks.

For example: What if we get the thing painted, then decide we don't like the color? Unless we can talk someone into going back, we'll be stuck looking at a giant, orbiting eyesore.

Of course, this is assuming we can get paint to work in zero gravity in the first place. Even with gravity, it's hard enough not to lose half the paint down your arm while trying to paint the ceiling. Now try doing it while flying through the air at 800 mph and trying to keep your Dutch Boy from floating away in the shape of an orb.

Even if we were able to develop a special paint with its own super-gravitational pull strong enough to overcome the vacuum of space, who's going to lift it?

As you can see from this live ABC remote, Arnold Schwarzenegger and Hulk Hogan have just put on their painters caps and are entering the space capsule...

Our second option, according to Joseph Spitale of the UA Lunar and Planetary Laboratory, would be to "put a lot of dirt on the asteroid." Apparently, this would change the temperature and aerodynamics of the asteroid enough to potentially cause an orbital shift.

Probably.

Now, I'm no scientist, but wouldn't adding tons of dirt also make the asteroid BIGGER?

Ladies and gentlemen, the good news is that we successfully added an extra 60 tons of dirt to the asteroid. The bad news is that we've doubled its size and, consequently, doomed all of mankind. Still, we'd like to thank our premier sponsor, Bill's Gravel and Dirt...

This leaves us with our third and final option, which is to send a specially trained team of astronauts into space in order to intercept the asteroid and shift its orbit by heating it with a giant hair dryer.

Okay, that's just a subtle way of saying there IS no third option. Unless you include nuclear missiles.

Which is about the only way of guaranteeing that we can, once and for all, kiss our asteroids good bye.

Larger-brained humans will only lead to big heads

As if we didn't have enough problems already, according to a report in the journal *Science* the human brain is getting bigger. In fact, from what I understand (based on my in-depth analysis of a five-word headline in the *New York Post*), there's a good chance yours may be outgrowing your skull right now. Signs this may be occurring include: vomiting, nausea, dizziness, frequent headaches and bleeding from the ears. If you suffer from any or all of these symptoms, DO NOT PANIC! They may only be the side effects of your current FDA-approved medication for acid reflux.

Then again, your brain might have actually gotten bigger since you started reading this column. And not just because of the sheer quality of writing — which is always a possibility (keeping in mind the same symptoms may apply).

Before we go on, I should, as a responsible journalist, take a moment and actually read the article. In the meantime, I'd suggest applying equal amounts of pressure to both sides of your head, just to be safe.

OK. Sorry — false alarm.

After reading the article it has become clear the threat of spontaneous brain enlargement is actually very slim. In fact, the only documented case appeared in the *National Inquirer*, which reported that a young boy's head spontaneously grew three times its normal size during the Arkansas State Spelling Bee. Amazingly, nine-year-old Reggie Sims survived the incident and now lives in Southern California, where his oversized head goes virtually unnoticed. But for those of us living outside the Los Angeles basin, spontaneous head swelling remains extremely rare. However, researchers say the human brain is getting larger, albeit very slowly, through a process of evolution. At first, larger brains sounded like a good idea since bigger brains means a smarter gene pool, hence leading us toward a Utopian society free of want and suffering.

Or at least free from telemarketers.

The down side is that our great-great-great grandchildren could end up looking like one of those bigheaded aliens from a 50s science fiction movie. True, this could happen anyway — possibly even in my own lifetime — if I don't meticulously screen each one of my children's potential spouses. However, assuming neither my son nor daughter marries anyone whose head fits snugly into a standard tractor inner tube, there's still the matter of future generations to worry about. The journal *Science* article I read doesn't mention anything about other parts of the human anatomy growing in proportion along with our enormous brains which, as I'm sure many woman would attest, may in itself double the male IQ.

Biologists tell us that any "improvement" in the human anatomy is the direct result of evolution's attempt to meet the changing needs of mankind. For example: Our opposable thumbs. This uniquely human trait distinguishes us from other primates, most notably through our ability to use all three holes in a bowling ball.

Following that line of thought, larger brains is likely the result of our need as a species to absorb and process more information at a younger age. This was evident last night, when my five-year-old nephew whipped my behind in PlayStation 2 football.

He cannot read.

He cannot understand the tactical decision making required for offensive line formations.

He doesn't even know how many yards are in a first down.

Yet he can complete a hail Mary pass and run a bootleg while I — with my larger and ultimately superior opposable thumbs — push buttons and move toggles as my defensive line is left picking grass from its teeth. I can't say for sure if this has any connection to the evolutionary process. But if his head gets any bigger, I swear:

He's moving to California.

Surgeon General's warning: Eat healthy, lose weight or fight a lion

Like many of you, I'll never forget where I was when I heard the shocking news that obesity had officially become the No. 1 preventable health crisis in the nation. In fact, I can even tell you which super-sized meal I was eating. The truth is, it's time for us Americans to make some drastic changes in our eating habits before the unthinkable happens, and we're forced to apologize to the French for throwing the earth off its axis.

With that in mind, we scheduled a Q&A session with the Surgeon General to explain how we got so fat, and what we can do to reverse this trend so that Americans can get back to living a normal, healthy lifestyle cut short by smoking and drinking.

Q: *How did we get so fat?*

SG: We'll start around 200,000 B.C., when early man was scavenging for food and living in dirty enclosures littered with bones and debris — a way of life that can still be observed in many college dorms. The difference is that, in prehistoric times, "fast food" was something hairy traveling on all fours. While there are plenty of campus refrigerators filled with hairy food items, in most cases it has stopped moving by the time it's eaten. Because of this, early man had the distinct health advantage of burning fat in order to obtain food, compared to what many college students burn, which is generally a large Papa Murphy's pizza.

Q: *Then why do so many college students look so trim?*

SG: Because their metabolism is still very high. This allows them to continue their bad eating habits without consequence until around age 30, when their metabolism suddenly kicks into reverse and, without warning, starts sucking up fat like a industrial shop-vac.

Q: *What can we do to break this unhealthy cycle?*

SG: The problem is that food has become too convenient. It wasn't long ago that Americans were a trim people undaunted by the idea of actually walking into a fast food restaurant and standing in line before being fed. Now, drive-up windows hand us food bags roughly the size of a potato sack, which we plant between the seats in our tank-sized SUVs. To break the cycle we must return to our hunter-gatherer roots. How?

Q: *Hey, that's my line.*

SG: Sorry.

Q: *How do we return to our hunter-gatherer roots?*

SG: By making it more difficult to get fast food. This can be achieved any number of ways, starting with the implementation of smaller, highly mobile restaurants that are constantly on the move. You know where Taco Bell is today, but what about tomorrow? And if you do find it again, what if it runs off? True, there's always a chance of finding a herd of Arby's, but chances are you won't be able to bring one down by yourself.

Q: *I'm not sure about that idea.*

SG: Please keep your comments in the form of a question.

Q: *Fine: Are you nuts?!*

SG: Okay, instead of mobile restaurants, how about taking a page from our prehistoric past by making any fast food purchase a life-or-death situation by forcing consumers to fight a mountain lion.

Q: *A mountain lion?!*

SG: Just a small one.

Q: *Are you dieting right now?*

SG: I was hoping it wouldn't be that obvious.

Ratings decline requires the Oscars to get jiggy before things go wack

As you've probably discovered, we have entered the annual awards show season, which officially began with the Golden Globe Awards, and is due to wrap up some time in April, when David Hasselhoff hosts the coveted Intoxicated Karaoke Performance Awards live from Tijuana, Mexico.

Every year, I watch at least some of these awards shows because, as a columnist, it's important for me to keep up with cultural trends. I also watch because seeing Nicki Minaj always makes me feel better about the way I dress. However, according to a recent poll, ratings for awards shows have actually dropped. So much so that programming executives are calling it "an alarming trend."

Personally, I think the word "alarming" is a little strong.

Coolant levels steadily leaking from a nuclear reactor — THAT'S alarming; a decline in the number of people tuning in to see how long it takes for a fight to break out at the Rap Awards is actually pretty encouraging. The obvious reason ratings are down is because the number of awards shows is up. The entertainment industry must ask itself if it really needs The Golden Globes, The Oscars and The Peoples' Choice Awards in order to single out Hollywood's finest when they could just as easily save time and money by combining all three into, say...

The Peoples' Globes Awards.

Okay, bad example (although, it does sound like something that's probably available on cable). The monumental length of these shows is another problem. When a person can receive "Best New Talent" and the "Lifetime Achievement" award during the same broadcast, I say it's too long. I'll go even further and say that we could actually learn a few things from the Rap Awards when it comes to cutting the length of these programs — especially when you consider last year's Rap Awards lasted only 11 minutes (five of which showed nothing but an overturned buffet table moving toward the exit under gunfire).

After approaching several top programming executives about my idea, I was, of course, immediately wrestled to the ground. This led me to organize a brainstorming session with Rapp producers Bigg-E-Mac, Mac Daddy, and Dubl-Bigg-Mac-Combo — with the main goal being to come up with a comprehensive list of ideas aimed at shortening the Oscars.

And the secondary goal being for me to acquire a really cool "aka," which I was given almost immediately:

2-Wite-2-Rapp

What follows is a three-step process that could potentially save the Oscars by making them shorter, more exciting, and, quite possibly, a little more "jiggy."

Step one: Get rid of the red carpet arrival and limit each celebrity to one drive-by. Non-celebrities would also be allowed a drive-by, but only in groups of eight or more, and only from the back of a Lincoln Continental assigned before the show.

Step two: Upon arrival, each celebrity will be issued a posse which, in turn, will spend most of the evening glaring at another posse. This will no doubt speed things up as celebrities, sensing a rising tension between rival posses, cut their acceptance speeches in order to leave before things get "wack." And finally,

Step three: Move the Oscars from the Kodak Theater in Hollywood to an abandoned warehouse in Culver City. There are a couple of reasons for this. First, there's the obvious cost savings. Why rent a theater when, with a little planning and a phone tree, everyone could just arrive and take over an empty warehouse just long enough to hand out the awards? This would also add a dramatic element to the show as it tries to finish up before the police arrive.

And there you have it, a simple, three-step solution to save the Oscars, compliments of me and my homies.

Now if I could just find my posse...

Outlook for the future of education? Just Pee-Chee

Like many of you, we spent last weekend shopping for school supplies. We did this with the help of a convenient checklist which, judging by its size, was provided by the Mead Corporation. When I was a kid, our back-to-school "supply list" consisted of a Star Wars notebook and a Pee-Chee folder. The notebook helped us organize our assignments; the Pee-Chee folder was used for entertaining ourselves during class by drawing thought balloons for the athletes on the cover.

Football Guy: (Getting tackled) "Oh sure — run the old L-42 play, THAT always works..."

Relay Guy: "If my team likes me so much, how come MY baton has a fuse in it..?!"

Tennis Girl: "If my skirt gets any shorter, I'll be playing Olympic volleyball..."

You get the idea.

Just about everyone remembers this folder because, like Al Sharpton's hair gel, it has remained virtually unchanged since 1964. What has changed, however, is the growing list of items parents must provide at the start of each school year — in addition to rudimentary things, such as clothing, snacks and a recent urine sample. The reason is simple: The government is tired of wasteful spending, particularly in the educational system, where a special task force has discovered that schools routinely get bilked into spending thousands of dollars on paper alone.

"And, shockingly, most of this paper has turned out to be blank," said White House spokesman Fred Netterman.

The study, code-named "Operation: Waste Storm," was described by Netterman as "the first step in a three-pronged approach to end overspending in four areas of education."

Netterman later apologized, saying his initial figures were incorrect, and that it was actually a four-pronged approach.

"The point is, I've been promised as many prongs as it takes to get the job done — that's how serious we are," said Netterman, who revealed that scissors, glue and construction paper were other "pork barrel" items targeted by the study. "Obviously, we're approaching construction paper with a great deal of sensitivity since, in addition to money, it involves issues of color."

When asked if making additional cuts to education contradicted the President's "No Child Left Behind" law, Netterman said it did not, arguing that it was the President himself, back in 2000, who stated: "Rarely is the question asked: Is our children learning?"

Netterman went on to explain that withholding $60 billion from education will encourage schools to do more with less, which will go further in preparing children for the real world than making paper hats and collages — items which, as he pointed out, could be outsourced to children in Taiwan and imported for half the price.

"In addition to the cost savings, think of how it would bolster our relationship with the Taiwanian people," said Netterman, who underscored his statement by pointing to a map of Japan.

So, how will all this affect our children's education? To be honest, I'm not sure.

But I'm sure, eventually, everything will be just Pee-Chee.

Nowadays, the womb is no place for slackers

Parents used to be satisfied with sonogram images of their child developing in the womb, even though, for all we knew, we were actually watching video footage of a school of mackerel on a depth finder.

"And if you look closely, you can see your baby ... right ...

about ... whoops! It's gone. Something must've scared it."

The doctor would then print copies of these images, which we carried in our wallets to share with family, friends, and anyone unfortunate enough to make brief eye contact. At the end of nine months, the only real expectation any of us had for our child was that they come out headfirst. Laughably, we actually felt it was enough for them to grow from a microscopic egg into a full-fledged human child within nine months.

Those babies, of course, were total slackers.

Thankfully, today's fetuses are on the fast track to success with the help of new Prenatal Education systems. These products are specifically designed to "maximize" a child's time in the womb — time which, until now, was frittered away on eating, growing, and using Mom's bladder for step aerobics. The philosophy behind this new trend is best summed up by the makers of the BabyPlus prenatal educational system, whose official marketing slogan is:

You're never too young to learn.
In fact, you don't even have to be born.

As a parent who learned of this opportunity much too late, I say why even TAKE THE RISK of stunting your child's intellectual capacity by wasting valuable time and waiting until you're actually pregnant? I suggest you start reading a thesaurus to your ovaries right now. Think of the pride you'll feel when your child emerges from the womb and, with full command of the English language, announces to everyone:

Slap my behind and I'll sue you.

The above scenario may be an exaggeration. But it illustrates an important point, which is that our entire judicial system could eventually collapse under the weight of frivolous lawsuits brought on by talking babies. It's not that there aren't obvious benefits to exposing your child to sounds while it's still in the womb. Like many parents, I too placed headphones on my sleeping wife's abdomen to see if our baby reacted to Pink Floyd. I feel the exposure broadened his musical appreciation, though it did cause him to cover his ears and inadvertently prolong pregnancy for an extra week.

However, accidentally frightening your unborn child with rock music is one thing. Enrolling them in a 16-week Prenatal University program is another. This program, which was developed by a California-based obstetrician, promises to intellectually enrich fetuses using a special microphone and strict conversational regimen aimed at stimulating the developing brain.

I don't know how long this program has been available, but, from what I can see, so far it hasn't had much of an effect on California.

The truth is, at the rate my 11-year-old daughter is learning, she's still going to be smarter than I am by the time she's 12. Why would a parent want to hasten this intellectual gap and risk being outsmarted by someone who does their best thinking while chewing on a binky? The bottom line is that I'm not sure how smart children really need to be before they come into the world.

Maybe there's a reason the umbilical cord doesn't come with an intercom system?

Your space adventure awaits! And mine will just have to keep waiting

So you want to be an astronaut?!

OK, neither do I. But suppose we did. And let's suppose I didn't routinely freak out anytime I'm launched higher than a pogo stick. Then we would all be very excited about all the recent advancements in the area of private spaceflight. Even now, it is possible for us to take a "slingshot ride" to the edge of the atmosphere and back, providing adventurers like ourselves with a breathtaking view of the earth, a few minutes of weightlessness, and, hopefully, at least one change of underwear.

You'll notice there are quotation marks around the phrase "slingshot ride," which is the actual term one expert used in describing the flight so that people like me, with no aeronautic experience, could picture themselves being flung headfirst into the stratosphere by something resembling a giant jock strap.

This, of course, would never happen.

At least not in the U.S.

Thanks to the FAA, we can rest assured that any flight heading into the cosmos will first have to meet the same rigorous federal safety standards set by The Jetsons 50 years ago. Knowing this, spaceflight entrepreneurs have spared no expense in designing flight packages cool enough to justify the $98,000 per-person price tag, which includes a disposable flight suit and wacky souvenir vomit bag that reads: **Sack Launch**.

So far, the front runner in this fast-growing industry is Space Adventures of Arlington, Va., which claims 100 would-be astronauts have already made large deposits — which I'm assuming means currency. If that's the case, then we're one step closer to realizing the ultimate space adventure: An orbiting hotel.

I know what you're thinking.

You've seen the luxurious accommodations of the International Space Station, and for $50 you can have the same experience by locking yourself in the bathroom of a Greyhound bus traveling between Jackson, Miss., and Scottsdale, Ariz. However, in this case, we're talking about a $500 million "cruise ship" capable of carrying 100 passengers and 50 crew members into orbit around the moon! Imagine the excitement of being aboard the largest, most luxurious space ship ever built! Imagine being among the first passengers as it departs on its historic maiden voyage! Now imagine doing that WITHOUT thinking about the Titanic.

Fortunately, there is another way to experience a trip through the cosmos without actually leaving the ground. And, no, it doesn't require a six-pack and a copy of Disney's Fantasia. As you might've noticed, Russia's space program has been a little slow lately. So slow, in fact, that no one realized there was a cosmonaut still orbiting in the International Space Station until, by chance, his video transmission was picked-up by the WB channel as a mid-season replacement for failed reality TV show, *Singing Bachelor Apprentices Who Can Cook.*

Thanks to this discovery, Russia has now begun offering action-packed cosmonaut training packages, which include everything from MIR space station simulators, to learning how to navigate by the stars, to spacewalk training, to an actual real-life cosmonaut rescue mission!

To be honest, I'm a little suspicious about that last one. Especially after they showed me my pogo stick.

Angry fans diffused by Kobe Bryant sock puppet

Like many of you, I watched the Pacers-Pistons debacle in utter disbelief. How could any self-respecting sports fans allow themselves to be seen on national television, in front of millions of viewers, wasting a seven-dollar beer? Somewhere along the way we've forgotten that sporting events are supposed to inspire the best in us — an ideal that professional athletes remind us can only be achieved through hard work, sacrifice, and the purchase of sneakers so expensive they require short-term financing. It's hard to know why angry sports fans have gotten out of control, but in the words of Italian soccer star Fabio Perfecto, "I hope it never happens in my country."

What is most disturbing, say sociologists, is that this type of behavior is now spreading to sports no one even cares about. For example, the recent World Ping Pong Championships in Seattle, where the only spectator at the event suddenly leaped from stands and, without warning, began hurling ping pong balls at the visiting Chinese team. The situation intensified when the Chinese, brandishing their paddles, relentlessly backhanded enough balls into the assailant to render him unconscious. Though some felt the response was excessive, investigators declined to issue any formal charges against the Chinese since no player actually left his seat during the volley.

"It is our conclusion that the Chinese acted with proper restraint, given the fact that, had they wanted to, they could have killed their attacker in less than 10 seconds," said a chief investigator.

Aggressive fan behavior has already prompted threats of a strike if security measures aren't tightened before the start of next year's Pro Bowling Tour. "We don't intend to make the same mistake as other sports," said a PBA spokesman. "The time to act is NOW, before we have spectators we don't actually know."

Psychiatrists argue the only way to reverse this trend is by teaching fans constructive ways to voice their disapproval. In a recent experiment conducted by the American Psychiatrists Association, Lakers fans were issued sock puppets resembling Kobe Bryant and told to "Sock it to Kobe" by telling the puppet how they felt.

"We all agreed it was a success when, at one point, there were literally 20,000 spectators in the stands yelling and screaming at sock puppets," said one psychiatrist. "We also agreed never to do it again because, quite frankly, it was the creepiest thing we'd ever seen."

In spite of a promise from NBA commissioner David Stern to protect athletes from unruly fans, "even if it means restricting alcohol consumption by raising the price of beer," agents and union officials say it's going to take more than promises to quell the anxiety many athletes now feel when stepping onto the court.

"Getting sucker punched and shanked by a defender is just part of professional basketball," said union director Billy Hunter. "But no athlete should be expected to go out, night after night, knowing he might get hit with an empty beer cup — or worse, a paternity suit."

When asked to comment on talk of a potential strike if tighter security measures aren't in place by season play-offs, Hunter called the rumors "laughable" and denied any plans to strike because of security issues.

"If we strike, it'll be for more money," said Hunter. "Sadly, after paying for child support, defense attorneys and anger management classes, many athletes are dangerously close to making the league minimum of $1.3 million — which sounds like a lot, until you factor in the cost of tricking out a 16-seat Humvee."

On a personal note, I plan to continue viewing professional sports from the safety of my own living room; the beer is cheap. The seats are more comfortable. And if I get angry, I have my own set of sock puppets.

Before deciding it's art, wait for the janitor to remove his mop bucket

I do not pretend to know anything about art. At least, not unless I happen to be at an actual show. In which case, after an appropriate amount of study, I can offer an interpretation so vague that it could possibly be mistaken as insightful:

You see, what the artist is saying is that man's self-imposed repression, symbolized by the overturned Volkswagen hood piled with rusty toasters, is a crucial part of his own inner struggle, as a human being, to find the correct Pop-Tart setting.

It's because of this that I am regularly contacted by art galleries (and sometimes even by the artists themselves) and asked to please stay away from their shows. I should make it clear that I have great respect for any artist whose work can provoke me into seeing or understanding something in a different way. For example, I once saw a piece called "Eternal Hunger," which, cleverly, was an empty room with a single pea glued to the center of the floor. I remember standing there in the doorway and quietly thinking to myself:

I'll probably never like peas.

Though it's not really my place, I'd like to offer a few suggestions that could help make art shows a little less intimidating and a little more inviting to people like myself, who often have trouble understanding some of the basic principles needed to appreciate art — such as why there are never any meat-based hors d'oeuvres at these things?

Let's be honest: a person can only eat so much sour grass hummus and tofu brochette before being moved by something other than the art.

I'd like to point out that visitors to an art show last week in Albany, NY., were not only greeted by a 5-foot-tall foam replica of a bacon strip, but, while browsing through a provocative collection of paintings and sculptures, were treated to bowls of freshly-cooked bacon bits. True, this was the second-annual Bacon Art Show. But it still illustrates an important point I've been trying to make about art, which is that my love for bacon isn't just an obsession — it's a form of self expression that should be celebrated.

Especially when it goes on sale.

But I digress.

In the past, I've always just shown up at art exhibits and remained as quiet and introspective looking as possible. This was accomplished by standing in front of a piece of art and giving it careful consideration before concluding that it really WAS just an empty hors d'oeuvres plate someone had left near the drinking fountain. With that, I — along with 10 to 12 others — would move on to the next potential masterwork. The goal, of course, was to stumble onto an actual work of art before engaging in rule #1:

Take time to think about the art and what it means to you before expressing your thoughts to the artist.

This brings me to my next suggestion for art galleries, which is to have the artist tell US what his or her thoughts are BEFORE we open our big fat mouths and express how deeply we were moved by an overturned mop bucket — which, coincidentally, appears to have just been purchased by the janitor.

Lastly, there are those uncomfortable situations when someone, such as myself, accidentally finds himself sitting on, leaning against — or cleaning his teeth with — an actual piece of art. To avoid this, I'd like to offer a simple suggestion, which is to go right now and make reservations for next year's Bacon Art Show.

Food-poison your face into a youthful glow

We humans have always had a certain preoccupation with wanting to look younger. This dates back to cave people who, while watching a boulder roll down a cliff during the very first *New Year's Rockin' Eve* celebration, said to themselves: "How does Dick Clark stay looking so dang young?!"

We also know that Egyptians, out of concern for personal appearance, made use of cosmetics and beauty parlours some 6,000 years ago. In the tomb of King Tutankhamen, for example, archeologist found items such as moisturizing cream, tweezers, nose-hair trimmers, and a shaving kit. In addition, they also discovered a series of hieroglyphics that, roughly translated, reads:

How does Dick Clark stay looking so dang young?!?

Given our history, it only stands to reason that modern humans are still looking for new ways to look younger — the most recent of which is through the use of botulism. That's right. Sick of aging? Food poisoning could be the answer!

Botulism, you see, causes severe paralysis by blocking the neurotransmitters responsible for triggering muscle contractions...

Neurotransmitter: "Hey, it's time to contract."

Muscle: "I can't. I'm being blocked."

Neurotransmitter: "By what?"

Muscle: "I don't know. Must've been something I ate."

In the case of your heart, this can lead to major fatigue, loss of consciousness and, in some extreme cases, a compelling episode of *ER*. Ironically, it is the toxin's ability to relax muscles that scientists are now using as a way to reduce the signs of aging. In small doses, botulism toxins have been formulated into an anti-wrinkle drug called Botox, (Yes, it's pronounced pretty much the way Forrest Gump says "butt-ocks.) which many people are now using as a way to look younger.

BUT WAIT!

Before you go rifling through the cupboard for that jar of canned rhubarb you got in the fall of 1972, you should know that it took years of scientific research to discover the exact strain of botulism toxin that can remove wrinkles without any pesky side effects, such as an agonizing death. Furthermore, the toxin must be injected directly into the wrinkled area to prevent it from spreading and relaxing ALL the muscles in the face. (This was only learned after Botox was mistakenly used by Ted Koppel as a facial scrub.)

Even with the risks associated with using this product, according to the American Society for Aesthetic Plastic Surgery, more than a million injections of Botox were given last year. In 2002, that number is expected to double as Botox injections become available to someone other than Dick Clark.

What this means, of course, is that we'll soon have a chance to recapture our youth.

And if that doesn't work, we can always capture Dick Clark.

Cell phone usage, volleyball-playing super models linked to short term blindness in men

I do own a cell phone. And yes, I have used it, but only as a last resort. That's because, aside from my fear of accidentally contacting a foreign satellite and suddenly being airlifted — car and all — to Guantanamo Bay via the Department of Homeland Security's free shuttle service, I'm also NOT a technologically adept person. After two years, I am just now figuring out how to access the pre-programmed numbers my wife entered into the phone 15 minutes after we got it. And though she went over the process with me at least a dozen times, most of my attempts to utilize this time-saving feature resulted in me calling myself, getting a busy signal and then hanging up. For the first six months, I thought everyone I knew was constantly yapping on the phone.

It doesn't help that all cell phones are apparently required by law to be smaller than a standard Saltine cracker. This leaves buttons the size of Braille, which I must somehow read while driving, just so I can place a simple call, get a busy signal and then hang up on myself. I know there are hands-free phones available. But if I'm going to be driving down the road having an animated conversation with no one else in the car, I want the phone to be highly visible; preferably hunter orange and the size of a microwave oven.

A friend of mine recently bought a new cell phone that (surprise) is so small that it actually fits inside your ear. Because it picks up vibrations as you speak (and hopefully those are the only vibrations it picks up), you don't need to talk into something in order to have a conversation. Like most people, he uses his new cell phone while driving, shopping and eating out. The difference here is that, without an actual piece of plastic that says *Hey, I'm on a cell phone,* he looks like a 35-year-old who wears a hearing aid and is talking to himself in Safeway.

To top it all off, according to a study just released by the National Safety Council, it appears that your driving is impaired no matter WHAT kind of cell phone you use. This is due to a condition called "Inattention Blindness." This occurs when a driver's attention to the visual environment is distracted enough that he fails to recognize objects within his immediate field of vision. For example: Suppose a man is driving along the beach in

Miami with his wife. Then suddenly, BAM! Without warning they find themselves driving past a nude beach where Playboy is shooting a video involving volleyball-playing super models.

The result? That's right: Inattention Blindness. The husband will suddenly be unable to recognize objects within his immediate field of vision if he wants to save his marriage and, quite possibly, his very life. Because of this danger, I will keep using my cell phone as little as possible.

At least until I get out of Guantanamo Bay.

Search for 'nuggets' believed to cause stress in chickens

As you may have heard, the new Carl's Jr. commercial is raising quite a flap among chicken advocates. As you may not have heard, there really is a group of people who work full-time advocating for the rights of chickens (though, as far as I can tell, not a single member of this group is, indeed, an *actual* chicken.) The ad in question is the one that shows a group of scientists examining a live hen as they search for its "nuggets," which, for me at least, helped explain a few things about my last doctor's visit. But members of United Poultry Concerns, a chicken advocacy group based in Virginia, don't see it that way and want to have the commercial pulled because they say the mock examination "caused the chicken undue stress."

In a recent statement given to the *Los Angeles Times*, UPC president Karen Davis was quoted as saying, "There's no question that the bright lights of filming, in combination with the numerous takes, would make the experience stressful for the chicken."

Considering that the chicken in that commercial was at least alive and flapping, one can only imagine how stressed-out a chicken must get when told it's going to be in a commercial for

KFC. Needless to say, executives at Carl's Jr. were extremely careful in issuing a response to the UPC charge. In fact, several meetings with the company's public relations and legal departments took place before CEO Larry Brayman finally released this carefully worded public statement:

Hey, it's a chicken.

Okay, that's not really what he said. But he did say that there was "No quantifiable evidence that chickens do or do not have feelings." It is this very point that UPC is contesting, thanks to a new book by Dr. Lesley Rogers called: The Development of Brain and Behavior in the Chicken, (which I should clarify, is not even the tiniest bit like *Chicken Soup for the Soul*). In her book, Dr. Rogers concludes that chickens are not only self-aware, but capable of experiencing emotions similar to those exhibited by some primates and even a few British Petroleum executives. Rogers summarizes her findings by saying, and I quote:

"Even vastly improved intensive systems are unlikely to meet the cognitive demands of the hitherto underestimated chicken brain."

I'm not exactly sure what all that means, but it sounds like we had better go ahead and meet the demands of this mysterious chicken brain before it's too late. In addition to its campaign against Carl's Jr., UPC is also lobbying against Burger King, which is offering children something called a Silly Slammer #5 Chirpy — a plush, yellow bird that emits a "chirp" whenever it is thrown against something. UPC's argument is that, understandably, this can only lead to the mass creation of serial killers (or, at the very least, to the mass extinction of Silly Slammer #5 Chirpies). Following that logic, my son has a plush toy that resembles Drew Carrey's head (I believe this was done on purpose) which, when tossed against something such as a wall or chicken, says: "Boy, my head hurts."

In spite of this, I feel pretty safe that my son, given the chance, would not actually try to do this to the real Drew Carrey. Unless, of course, he turned out to be extremely plush and missing his entire body.

Assuming, of course, that the mysterious chicken brain doesn't get to him first.

The best part of waking up is civet droppings in your cup

Some of you are probably familiar with the civet cat, a tree-dwelling marsupial related to the mongoose family that looks like a cat and sprays its enemies with a stinky oil. Naturally, we humans harvest that oil and make it into perfume, which in turn is used by department store clerks in the women's section to spray enemies with during the holiday shopping season. What many of you may not know is that civets have recently entered the coffee bean producing business — something that is fast becoming the most frightening beverage concept since the introduction of New Coke.

(For those of you with a weak stomach — or who happen to be drinking coffee at this very moment — neatly fold this section of the paper, then prepare yourself an Ajax mochaccino to cleanse your pallet with before reading on.)

Let's start with a little history.

Bean growers on the Indonesian islands of Sumatra, Java and Sulawesi have long regarded civets as pests because of their propensity to climb coffee bean trees, eat only the choicest berries, and talk incessantly about their stock portfolios while emitting a shrill sound similar to that of an espresso machine. However, at some point, someone suffering from the biggest case of caffeine addiction in the history of man decided he was desperate enough to "harvest" the civet droppings as a way to get his coffee fix. Though the trail leading to the identity of this "pioneer" is not complete, coffee genealogists have determined that it was someone visiting from the Seattle area.

From those humble beginnings comes the coffee bean known as Kopi Luwak which, loosely translated, means "Butt Coffee."

Fine. I made that part up.

It actually means "coffee" (Kopi) "weasel" (Luwak), which isn't much better — and a name advertising agencies won't be rushing to trademark any time soon. This brings us to our next question: how to market such a product? Getting folks to buy something, which as its biggest selling point can boast of being pre-digested by a skunk-like animal, is going to be a tall order for any add agency to swallow (at least, not without liberal amounts of cream and sugar).

And with an average sticker price of $200 per lb., don't bother looking for it in the bulk coffee section of your local supermarket — unless, of course, U.S. manufacturers come up with a "generic" equivalent (the only thing more frightening than Kopi Luwak itself). Given that the U.S.D.A. allows a certain amount of "foreign matter" in processed meats and canned goods, what kind of standards would be kept on a product that begins as "foreign matter" in the first place?

Let's move on.

There are a number of Kopi Luwak suppliers in America, with M.P. Mountanos Inc. being the first company in the U.S. to import the beans after trying them out several years ago. According to the company, the decision to purchase 70 kilos of the beans was finally made after a seven-year search for a "reliable" and "stable" supplier.

Whether that's in reference to civets cats or growers, I'm not exactly sure.

What I am sure of is the potential market this opens up for us here in the Northwest, where pre-digested black berry jam can be found in abundance along most logging roads in the spring. For anyone interested in pursuing this venture, I wish you the best.

As for me, I'm content in just bringing you the straight poop.

Computer acting up? Back-hand it with an antistatic wrist strap

Today, we will be covering basic troubleshooting techniques for your computer. By the end of this column, you will know how to identify a problem within your system, and then determine whether you can:

a) Fix it yourself, or

b) Save yourself the trouble by taking your computer somewhere and shooting it.

To begin with, most of us have absolutely no idea how a computer works. This is illustrated by the fact that, when there's a problem, we get really mad and yell at the monitor. This is sort of like yelling at the refrigerator because the container we thought was "Cool Whip" actually turned out to be refried beans left over from last year's Cinco De Mayo party. The fact is, refrigerators and computer monitors are just boxes filled with stuff coming from somewhere else; over time, improper maintenance can result in something that really stinks.

One of the reasons we know so little about computers is because they keep making them easier and easier to use. This in turn makes them harder and harder to understand because, as technology makes things smaller and smaller, there's less and less actual STUFF inside. Right now, you can still look in and see a few wires and some solder melted onto a plastic motherboard, which makes it possible to at least PRETEND you understand what's going on:

You see! If I take a piece of aluminum foil and touch this part to that shiny blob over there I can AAAAAGH!

At the current rate of technology, that's all going to change as ever-increasing macro-technology scales down the internal components of personal computers to little more than a $5 coupon for Windows 13 — and air. This means we need to take better care of our current computers so that we can pretend to understand them for as long as possible. It does not require being able to tear apart and reassemble your entire PC system. In fact, a recent study conducted by Falcon Safety Products, Inc., showed that 70 percent of computer malfunctions are simply caused by...

You guessed it: People shooting their computers.

No. Actually, according to a nationwide survey of 1,300 computer technicians, most computer malfunctions were caused by things like food, dead rodents, cockroach nests, and, in the case of one Pittsburg, Calif., technician, "a stash of marijuana" that mostly effected the computer's memory.

This brings us to how to clean your computer. You will need an antistatic wrist strap, a can of compressed air, and, if at all possible, a drug-sniffing dog. Once you have these items, you can remove the housing from your computer and use your antistatic wrist strap to begin cleaning. Depending on what you find inside, you can utilize the alligator clip attached to the wrist strap as either 1) a conductor to keep static electricity from discharging into the sensitive internal circuitry of your computer, or 2) a way to keep from burning your fingers.

Once this phase of cleaning has been completed, use the can of compressed air to blow out particles in some of those hard-to-get-to places—such as the nostrils of a drug-sniffing dog. Repeat this process at least twice a year, or, depending on your situation, as often as you'd like for the next three to five years.

By then, of course, it will be time to get a new computer.

Cold medicine: the key to true introspection

I'd like to start by apologizing for this column.

Technically speaking, I'm still writing it. However, given the volume of cold medication I have consumed, and keeping in mind that I have finally given in and, as a time saving measure, moved my workstation to the commode, there's a good chance my current location is exactly where this column is headed. Making matters worse, the laptop I'm using is about 10 years old. Getting it open was like shucking a Pismo clam. After opening it, I realized it's the very same model that caused panic aboard a flight to Miami when it overheated and singed the thighs of an intoxicated businessman.

True, I am not on a plane. Yet there are still some frightening similarities:

I am under the influence of Codeine.

I am in a seated position.

And if this morning was any indication, I won't be leaving my seat for the next few hours.

The upside is that if my laptop should suddenly burst into flames, unlike that unfortunate business traveler, I'll have the option of quickly extinguishing myself by removing the lid to the toilet tank and jumping inside.

(Did I mention I'm on Codeine?)

The good thing about getting sick is that it has forced me to slow down for a day.

I have time to reflect on things.

Be introspective.

For example, while sitting here, I've discovered that static electricity from this laptop makes the hair on my legs stand up. Chances are, I never would have made this discovery at work. At least, not without receiving a warning slip. I've also come to realize that by pressing our toilet plunger to the floor, then carefully manipulating the exchange of air while simultaneously working the plunger up and down in a breathing pattern, I can make it sound like Darth Vader with a really bad head cold.

Again, had I been at work, it's likely this would have gone undiscovered (although I can't say for sure).

(Have I mentioned that I'm on Codeine?)

Yep, it's just me, my thoughts, and the frequent spray of air freshener in our small, unventilated bathroom. The fact is, the longer I sit here reflecting, spraying and medicating, the less I care about slowly growing numb from the waist down. Especially if it means having an opportunity to reflect on some fundamental questions, such as why I've never noticed there's a spot in our wallpaper pattern that resembles Tina Fey?

I like Tina Fey.

But to be honest, I'm getting a little tired of her staring.

I'm also noticing some other things for the first time. I'm not going to get into them here; it would probably sound a little crazy. Suffice it to say, once I'm feeling better, we will be changing the wallpaper, shower curtain, and quite possibly the floor tiles. What I will tell you is that I've noticed our bathroom has an underlying aroma. Something that smells like, I don't know...

Searing flesh?

Hold on a second ...

OK, I'm back. Just a little problem with my laptop.

The good news is, I was able to put the flames out before any serious damage was done to my thighs. The bad news is, I had to move to the upstairs bathroom because the downstairs commode is no longer functional. If we'd installed a low-flow toilet, things might have turned out differently. Just ask Tina Fey.

She saw the whole thing.

Cold snap puts deep-freeze on taking out the trash in your underwear

It's not often that it gets really cold here along the Oregon coast. And by REALLY COLD, I mean cold enough to warrant using an ice scraper. Now, to someone from Michigan or Illinois — where an ice scraper is a six-ton piece of diesel-driven steel with studded tires and a nine-foot scoop — scraping down my windshield with a four-inch piece of beveled plastic that has a smiley snowman on the handle wouldn't exactly be called a winter crisis. (On the East Coast, this is what is commonly known as "spring.")

However, for us coastal Oregonians, who are kept reasonably warm by jet streams that push cold air to the north and allow naturally abundant hot air to make its way up from California, pulling out the ice scraper means it's time to revisit some cold-weather-safety procedures. To do this, we will use a couple of real-life examples from an actual area resident. Because some of these examples could prove embarrassing to this individual, we will protect his identity by referring to him only as *Den Noskcih.*

(To further protect his identity, please do NOT hold this page up to a mirror.)

The first line of defense against cold weather is your clothing. This is especially true when taking out the trash at 6 a.m. in nothing but your underwear — which brings us to real life example number one:

Upon hearing the garbage truck, Den leaps out of bed and rushes his can to the curb during a hail storm.

As you might imagine, this breaks a number of cold-weather-safety rules, not to mention more than one city ordinance. Amazingly, the whole thing could have been avoided by taking a few preventive measures — beginning with champagne. You see, because Den drank too much of it on New Year's Eve, he opened his big fat mouth and made a resolution to take the trash out every week without any reminders from his wife. If Den had just stayed away from the champagne (or made his resolution in front of the cat instead of his wife), he could have avoided ending up face-down in the recycle bin during a hail storm, dressed in nothing but his tighty-whities. (As you might expect, Den is currently looking for a new trash service.)

This brings us to real life example number two, Cold-Weather Grooming. Here is our example:

Because he's running late, Den rushes out of the house with his hair still wet, the result of which is a hair-doo similar to that of "Mr. Freeze."

When temperatures drop below 32 degrees, water freezes — yes, even if it's in your hair — and the colder it is, the faster it freezes. Therefore, a good rule of thumb is to not leave your house unless: a) The temperature rises above 32 degrees; b) Your hair is completely dry; or c) You really hate your hair anyway and would like to start over again from scratch.

Our cold-weather-safety discussion wouldn't be complete unless we talked about firewood. In Oregon, most homes do not have natural gas. Therefore, we rely on firewood and re-runs of *Temptation Island* as our primary heat sources. To burn firewood in your home, you really should have a fireplace or wood stove (although this is optional, depending on your degree of fire coverage).

Preferably, it should be equipped with a device called a "catalytic converter." This device is absolutely essential because it converts all of your firewood into "catalites," which are small creatures that eat lots of fiber and emit a natural gas that burns even longer than firewood.

This helps to slow down your wood consumption, which is really important because it's not like firewood grows on...

Well — you know what I mean.

As much as I'd like to continue this discussion, I really have to leave now.

I think I hear the trash truck coming.

Every Monday should start with a comatose computer

Sometime between Sunday afternoon and Monday morning, my computer slipped from its normal "sleep mode" and into a deep coma. This became apparent after hitting the space bar and getting no reaction whatsoever, not counting a low-pitched whirring sound that — if I didn't know better — I could swear was snoring. Realizing there might be a serious problem, I gathered all of my computer troubleshooting experience and, over the course of the next 10 minutes, applied that experience by hitting the space bar no less than 400 times. When that didn't work, I unplugged the computer and plugged it back in. Tried a different outlet. Switched keyboards. Wiggled my mouse. Considered finding a different occupation, preferably one involving explosives. I eventually realized the only thing left to do was call the Help Line listed in the service manual and hope someone there could either a) talk me through this or b) talk me down should our conversation move to the rooftop.

As expected, I was greeted by an automated voice telling me, in that creepy robot word-splice tone, that my call was important to *them* and to please hold until the next representative became available, just as soon as his larynx had been removed and cyber-genetically fitted for a generation of artificially intelligent beings slowly taking over the earth.

Thank.
You for.
Your patience.

Next came the music, a collection of Michael Bolton, Celine Dion, and Whitney Houston standards re-mixed — I'm guessing — by either John Tesh or Yanni to keep people on-hold from growing impatient. This is a little like trying to talk a suicidal jumper off the ledge by giving him a pogo stick. Making matters worse, I was reminded every 30 seconds by that same creepy robot voice that my call was "very important to *them*" and to remain holding for the next available representative, keeping in mind that my weak, carbon-based body was slowly deteriorating with each passing minute.

Again thank.
You for.
Your patience.

When my service representative broke the line 20 minutes later asking for my computer's serial number, I was unprepared. Not just because it was the first unsynthesized human voice I'd heard in nearly an hour, but also because I didn't have the serial number ready. That's when I was told I could easily find the number by going to my computer and — very carefully — turning it upside down. Upon hearing these helpful instructions I cocked my head to one side and, while pinning the phone against my shoulder, fought off an aneurism. I was then instructed to call back when I had the serial number readily available, to which I replied I was "readily available" to catch a flight to Atlanta and strangle him with a USB cord unless he waited for me to flip my computer over and read him the number. After entering the serial number into his data bank, he informed me all the hardware was still under warranty. However, I needed to pay $45 in order for the service call to continue. I thanked him for his time and, before hanging up, told him how much I was looking forward to having a glass of sweet tea when I got to town.

My next move was to take my computer to an approved repair service located 60 miles away. The up side is that I could deal with real humans. The down side is that driving there would cost about as much as following up on my threat and actually flying to Atlanta. After careful consideration I decided to stay here. That's because, the way my luck was going, "Chaz" was probably a 260-lb Martial Arts champion whose passion for the sport began when his wife left him for a loudmouthed humor columnist. Even if I got my computer fixed, what good would it do if I had to type everything with my tongue?

So, as of today, my computer is still in the shop. According to the repair guy they're just waiting for a new "logic board" to arrive which, well...

Makes sense, I guess?

In the meantime, I'll continue working on a back-up computer that is too old to handle things like getting on the Internet, updating my blog, or performing any function in under 10 minutes. I hope to have my computer back in a few days. Until then:

Thank.
You for.
Your patience.

Thanks to modern science, green-glowing mice can help cats with night blindness

I can't tell you how many nights I've spent lying awake, staring up at the ceiling and thinking to myself:

Gee, if only they could make a super strong mouse.

Because only THEN would there be a chance of one actually chewing its way through the ceiling and falling to its death on our bedroom floor. As I've mentioned in the past, from time to time we have a problem with mice. Our neighbors assure me that it's a common problem in the area, and that it's no reflection on how we keep our home — which, based on its rodent activity, I believe was insulated entirely with cheese curds. I bring this up because of several readers who sent e-mails regarding science news, all of which have to do with mice, and all of which I have combined into an informative feature we'll call:

Scientific breakthroughs that could inspire a horror movie franchise

We'll begin with a story about the creation of the first "super" mouse, which was sent in by Bonnie Higgins of Bridgeton, NJ, whose good intentions, I must assume, included keeping me awake at night armed with pepper spray and a sledge hammer. According to the article, scientists in Boston have created a mouse with giant muscles, "capable of enduring rigorous exercise for extended periods of time."

This is great news for people like me, who often worry that the traps they put out might actually *kill* a mouse. Now mice will not only have neck muscles thick enough to withstand the trap, but they'll also be strong enough to re-set those traps and then throw them back at me. If we're going to experiment with making something super strong, why not start with something more sensible?

"Hey, honey — have you seen the cat?"

"Last time I saw her she was chasing a mouse."

"Where?"

"Through that hole in the wall. I think she's on her way to the second floor. You can probably still catch her. The studs are slowing her down."

So who cares if mice become strong enough to open the refrigerator and get their own cheese? We can always use our superior intellect, right? Of course, this is the same intellect that we're now using to make mice smarter. This was bought to my attention by Jim Bricker of Lewiston, Idaho, who sent me an article headlined:

Geneticists Develop Big-Brained Mouse

I should clarify that this was not from the National Inquirer, and did not include a photo of a mouse with an enormous cranium writing on a chalkboard and wearing a propeller cap. According to Reuters health and science correspondent Maggie Fox, researchers at Harvard Medical School (again in Boston) have found a way to make a mouse's brain so large that it has to fold up — much like a human's — in order to fit inside the skull.

After reading this, two things are clear:

1) I will not be visiting Boston anytime soon.

2) Anyone who does plan to visit Boston should do so NOW, before it succumbs to a new race of highly intelligent mice with giant muscles.

And let's just hope none of these mice ever reaches the University of Hawaii because, if they do, they might also glow in the dark. That's right. According to an article sent in by Brandy Sherman of Cottage Grove, Ore., professor Anthony Perry has created an entire litter of green, glowing mice. This is very important because these mice can be utilized for things like...well...

Cats with night blindness? The world's most irritating night light? How the heck should I know?

What I DO know is that I plan to buy whatever kind of cheese it tells me to.

The Tom Ridge spring fashion collection: Fruit-leather chaps and plenty of duct tape

We are well into the fourth week of Tom Ridge's new Ready Campaign, which is aimed at easing our fear of terrorism through education, preparedness, and a nationwide call for all Americans to seal themselves inside their homes with duct tape.

"We must not be afraid; we must be ready," he said, adding that, at the very least, we should be prepared to tape-up anyone who isn't.

As a result, Americans rushed to their local hardware stores and bought as much duct tape as possible, creating a national shortage and ending the financial woes of Martha Stewart who, coincidently, bought thousands of shares in duct tape stocks a day before the announcement. The purpose for the duct tape and plastic sheets is simple. In the event of a biological or chemical attack, we can protect ourselves by going into a designated "safe" room, then sealing it up so that it is completely air tight. To demonstrate the effectiveness of this plan, I will now pull a plastic bag over my head and wrap it with duct tape. In addition, I will surround myself with fellow journalists who have just returned from lunch at The Enfermo Taco.

Let us begin. (Note: In the interest of time, we'll skip ahead to when my red-faced, teary-eyed colleagues are looking for the nearest exit.)

See? While journalists are falling all around me, absolutely NO outside air is getting to me. I am completely safe. Thanks to my protective barrier, I can laugh in the face of any would-be terrorist attackkkkkkkkkkkkkgggggggggggggggggg]]]]]]]]]]]]]ffffffffff ffffffffffffffffffzzzzzzzzzzzzz............

Sorry, I must've blacked out.

But the point is, I would have easily survived the assault if not for a complete lack of oxygen. It's these kinds of helpful tips that we can expect to get from what Ridge describes as an "on-going, multi-year campaign" to fight the spread of fear in America, especially if it happens to come from terrorists. This week, the Ready Campaign is expected to unveil its next preparedness tip:

How to shield yourself from deadly radiation using a tin foil hat and 32 fruit roll-ups

Rumor has it that the President himself was instrumental in turning what would have been a really boring "hazard" suit into a sassy pair of fruit-leather chaps.

As part of the Ready Campaign, families are being encouraged to prepare an emergency supply kit and establish a clear communication plan. Given that my wife can be heard from anywhere in the house, she is now our chief communications officer. Our three-year-old son is second in command because, essentially, he never stops talking. He is also proficient at identifying colors. Therefore, we plan to buy him the new Tom Ridge Learning Primary Colors Through Terrorist Warning Levels Can Be Fun! chalkboard, which he will update each morning after our daughter visits the Homeland Security Website to determine the likelihood of attack for the day.

Meanwhile, I have been put in charge of organizing the emergency supply kit which, so far, contains Kool-Aid, a three-foot-long licorice whip, and 27 rolls of duct tape. Thanks to the countless ways we're reminded each day of being in imminent danger with warnings from Tom Ridge, the Department of Homeland Security, the Ready Campaign, and the Citizens Preparedness Initiative, I've completely forgotten about the fact that, no matter how much I prepare for a terrorist attack, I could still get run over by a delivery van.

And with my luck, it would probably be delivering a shipment of duct tape.

Today's election process requires conventional wisdom

Aside from watching something on "The Dust Channel," I can't think of anything less interesting than the upcoming political conventions.

Watch, I'll show you...

See?

Nothing.

And the worst part is, it'll be on every major network, with commentary offered by shell-shocked correspondents picking confetti from their hair and wincing between air horn blasts that are supposed to make us all wish we were part of that kind of fun. In actuality, Peter Jennings, Dan Rather and Tom Brokaw don't want to be there either, but they will; and by gosh, if they've got to be stuck in a skybox for a week, we're going to watch. Now, this isn't to say making the conventions even remotely interesting isn't possible. In fact, if the campaign gurus would study the ratings, there are plenty of examples of what could be done to make things more exciting by following a few, simple rules:

Rule No. 1: Voyeurism is in.

Greed, Big Brother, Survivor, even *Who wants to* [fill in the blank] *a Millionaire* are, at their core, really about watching some poor sap squirm on national television. So why not presidential nominees? If nothing else, it'll give Americans a chance to see how the future president will handle his affairs under pressure. Well, you know what I mean.

Rule No. 2: There needs to be something at stake.

In most cases, it's an enormous sum of money. For this scenario, we could use the whole "most-powerful-person-in-the-world" thing, and maybe throw in a tobacco lobbyist or Viagra endorsement spot.

And, Rule No. 3: You've got to have a sharply dressed, highly irritating host. Combine these three key elements, add a political context, and you have the ultimate in convention coverage: *Big Brother Wants A Greedy Survivor.*

Each episode will begin with host Ross Perot in a helicopter as he flies over the nominees, who have been dropped into the heart of East L.A. with nothing but a baggy T-shirt, "Dickey" pants and a pair of $200 basketball shoes. They will also get three life lines:

A blue bandanna,

A red bandanna,

And a 50/50. (Gang members will be instructed to close their eyes for one minute while contestants run, allowing them a 50/50 chance of getting away.)

During the five-day airing, each nominee will have to scrounge for food, at times resorting to ethnic cuisine and tap water as they battle to survive long enough to reach Friday night's finale — a question and answer session for cumulative electoral votes:

Complete this famous quote: *"We the* (blank) *of the United States..."*

Is it:

a) Pot-smoking hippies ruining this country,

b) Perot conspirators from outer space,
c) People, or
d) Present White House administration responsible for creating that "giant sucking sound."

Gore: "If I get this wrong, I'll still keep my 100 electoral votes, right?"
Bush: "I say give them the chair, heh-heh... Wait, are we on, cowboy?"

The bottom line is, by convention time, there's about as much anticipation to find out who the parties will nominate as there is in watching milk curdle; the result comes as no surprise, and neither is particularly pleasant to swallow.

Then again, at least you can take something for a sour stomach.

If your name is Larry, call me; we've got a bad connection

There are three things I know about "Larry." He is a contractor; he lives somewhere in Multnomah County; and he has the same cell phone number that I do. The calls started about a month ago, presumably about the time "Larry" got his contractor's license and began making bids. Since then, he has been a busy man, picking up jobs and making sure that his clients know they can call him any time. Day or night. For any reason at all.

Which they do, to *my* cell phone.

The Hansons, for example, call whenever they change their mind about what color tile to use around the bidet in their new bathroom. For the Gilmores, deciding between cedar shakes or aluminum siding requires at least one consultation a day. And the Reyboulds are still contemplating the ripple effect of kitchen cabinets without knobs. Mrs. Reybould thinks knobs would make their kitchen look more inviting; Mr. Reybould believes not having knobs would stymie their 2-year-old and keep him out of the cabinets for at least another year.

Over the course of the last month, I've gone from politely explaining that there is no "Larry" at this number, to a more direct approach, which is that "Larry" died — killed in a freak shop-vac accident that was a gruesome, yet impressive, testimonial to the workmanship of Black & Decker products. I was certain that this tragic revelation would solve my problems. That was until the calls started up again, no doubt after "Larry's" apparent resurrection from a 3-gallon-capacity shop-vac canister.

This left me only one choice.

When the Hansons called this afternoon asking for advice from "Larry" about their decision to use apricot-colored tile around the bidet in their new bathroom, I told them, as their contractor, they could save themselves a tidy sum of money by simply purchasing a better brand of toilet paper. [Click — dial tone]

One down.

For the Gilmores, who were still agonizing over the decision between cedar shakes or aluminum siding, I suggested ditching the house for a double-wide trailer covered in simulated wood paneling and accented with a fence made out of used shipping pallets. [Click — dial tone]

Two down.

The next time the phone rang, I snatched it up on the first ring. "Larry speaking." It was the Reyboulds, looking for help on reaching a final decision about those kitchen cabinet knobs.

"It seems to me that the perfect combination would be something inviting and deceptively hard to open," I said, and heard the Reyboulds agree. "Might I suggest installing some beautiful ceramic knobs on your cabinets, then nailing the doors completely shut."

Mrs. Reybould hesitated before asking, "And where are we supposed to store our dishes?"

"Hey, I'm offering a solution! If you want to bicker over functionality, find another contractor!" I snapped.

There was an awkward silence before Mr. Reybould grabbed the phone. "What kind of nails would you suggest?"

[Click — dial tone]

Though I hung up on them I do plan on calling them back at some point. In the meantime, if "Larry" happens to be reading this, please call me so we can straighten this whole mess out.

You know the number.

Cover your phone bill with mustard

With energy costs on the rise, around the Hickson household we've been scrutinizing our monthly utility bills a bit more carefully. Among them, our telephone bill. Now, in the past, we'd considered ourselves savvy consumers because we took the time to look for things like calls to Kohldazhell, Russia and any connections lasting for more than 24 hours.

Any 1-900 calls were categorically disputed — and then I'd call the phone company and do the same.

However, all those itemized surcharges in small print at the bottom of the bill were sort of like the little tag you get inside of your new clothes that says "inspected by No. 10" — I'm not sure who he or she is, or what that inspection process entails. I just assume it's important enough to include in my pants.

But in this case, as we began looking more closely at our phone statements, we started questioning the validity of some of the charges that, until now, had been averted like the list of ingredients on a package of hot dogs: you know they're there, you know they're ugly. But you also know you can cover them with mustard.

All together, there are 17 "extra" charges on our bill. For the most part, I understand five of them: bill statement fee, federal tax, public utilities commission fee, residence line fee, and the state 911 fee. While I understand these fees, I don't necessarily agree with them. The $1.50 I pay for receiving my billing statement each month could just as easily be dropped if they'd just stop sending me a bill in the first place.

And though I'm not sure why I pay a fee to the utilities commission, I figure it's worth one penny a month to keep them from holding a telethon.

That said, the remaining 12 charges seem, at the very least, questionable.

First of all, there are a number of "universal" fees I incur, beginning with a charge for "Universal Connectivity." For those of you who may be wondering; Yes, "connectivity" is really a word, which means one of two things according to Webster's Dictionary:

1) To connect something.
2) The connective muscle tissue that holds antlers in place.

Since I'm (nearly) certain that my monthly expense of 42 cents doesn't go to help deer suffering from DAS (Droopy Antler Syndrome), then I can only assume it's for being connected to the universe. The thing is, I get at least five calls a week — usually while I'm eating — asking about long distance service. I think if someone had called to offer phone service to places other than my own planet, I would've remembered.

In addition, there is the Federal Universal Service Fund, Oregon Universal Service Surcharge, and the Oregon Universal Service Surcharge for long distance. I believe the reason Oregonians are charged twice is because, as Oregonians, we're already in our own universe; calling outside of it costs extra.

Though there are other fees that seem questionable, such as a separate "User Charge," which sounds a lot like what I'm paying for in the first place, there is one charge that I find a bit unsettling:

"Resident Service Protection Fund."

When I called to dispute this fee, the phone company said they'd be happy to eliminate it—as long as I understood that my protection would no longer be guaranteed. I decided to go ahead and pay the extra dime, leaving me just enough pocket change for a hot dog.

Heavy on the mustard.

Laughing at cows can be dangerous, especially when playing bingo

As you probably know, it's national Be Kind to Animals Week, and just when Florida was beginning to re-gain a small measure of respectability by working hard to draw absolutely no attention to itself, the "Chad State" is once again in the national spotlight — this time because of some highly publicized bovine activity.

I'm talking, of course, about the controversy surrounding Cow-Patty Bingo. For those who might not be familiar with this activity for reasons of sanity, we'll just take a moment to cover the basics.

First, you need a cow.

Second, you need a REALLY BIG bingo card.

Okay, I was just kidding about the second part. But you really do need a cow, preferably one that has just eaten a lot of fiber — like, say... a 55-gallon drum of granola. Next, you need a large field or yard (such as a neighbor's) that can be divided into numbered grids. Once you have the cow and the grid, it's time to start selling squares. This requires finding people who think that poop is entertaining. If you know anyone who watched *Jersey Shore,* that would probably be a good place to start. The rules to Cow-Patty Bingo are simple. Each square is numbered and sold for $5 each, and you can buy as many squares as you like. Keep in mind, however, that the more money you spend on squares the less you can spend on beer, which is something you'll need a lot of in order to cloud any memory of yourself standing in the bleachers screaming "POOP IN MY SQUARE!"

It's also important to note that, in order for a "drop" to qualify, it must be deemed "clearly visible" by the judges. This is actually a lot harder than it sounds. That's because, in order to prepare for this level of scrutiny, judges, on average, consume twice as much beer as spectators at these events. Now that we've covered the basics, it's time to talk controversy. According to an article sent to to me by Jack Ortiz of Reedsport, Ore., a recent Cow-Patty Bingo fund raiser held at Florida Southern College became the target of protests from PETA (People for the Ethical Treatment of Animals) which said, and I quote: *Cows are adversely affected by laughter.*

(I should clarify that PETA was referring to human laughter, and not cows getting laughed at by other cows. I should further clarify that, as far as cows are concerned, the poop thing just isn't that funny anymore.)

Furthermore, Amy Rhodes, a caseworker for PETA, strongly denounced the college's participation in Cow-Patty Bingo, saying that it was "...a dangerous message to send to kids." I completely agree with this, and can see how prolonged exposure to this type of activity starting at an early age can only lead to one thing — and that is retirement and REAL bingo.

Probably somewhere in Florida.

While there are certainly no easy solutions to the growing controversy over Cow-Patty Bingo, I think finding some common ground would be a good place to start. From there, we can finally move forward.

Just as long as everyone watches where they step.

Excuse me; I'd like to expose my blog

I'm about to do something a little risky (possibly even controversial) by explaining how you could be the first person, aside from my wife, to see my blog. Exposing my blog is something I'm not entirely comfortable with. However, considering how hard I worked to get my blog up in the first place, I'd like as many people to see it as possible.

And though I'm sure this goes without saying, I'd like to clarify that what we're talking about is my new Internet weblog.

Anyone under the age of 25 knows exactly what a weblog is. Which is why, as a 46-year-old man, I recently found myself declining the advances of a young woman who was offering, rather enthusiastically, to launch my blog. I explained to her that I was extremely flattered, but also happily married to a woman whose Latin roots include, among other things, castrating bulls. After which, she responded with a lesson about blogs.

What they are.

How they work.

And why, on second thought, she would not be getting anywhere near mine.

Being a man, I instinctively responded by telling her I didn't need her help anyway because I was perfectly capable of launching my own blog. Probably in half the time. This, of course, was a mistake. Not only because it stopped most of the conversation in the room, but also because I realized the only way to save my dignity was to make an actual weblog available on the Internet. This meant utilizing a part of my brain that often shuts down after just 10 minutes of trying to re-program the TV remote; this meant tapping into a series of synapses so gapped and corroded from disuse that getting them to fire would require surgically implanting 10-gage wiring; this meant, above all else, running the risk of exceeding my brain's operating capacity to the extent I find myself writing paragraphs that are merely a string of sentences joined together by semi-colons.

I decided the first step in building my blog was to get on the Internet and look at other people's blogs. This, as you've probably heard, is extremely easy to do. In fact, I'd say there are more people on the Internet wanting to show you their blogs than just about anything else. From there, I came up with a list of ideas, some of which, until surfing the Internet, I honestly didn't know you could do with your blog.

Next, I staked my claim on the World Wide Web and chose what is known as "domain name" which, from what I understand, is mine forever. Or at least until I do something stupid that inadvertently causes the collapse of the Internet and, quite possibly, draws the attention of Homeland Security. For this reason I gave the name a lot of thought before finally — in a moment of epiphany — lightning struck: www.nedhickson.com.

Of course, there's a lot more that goes into creating and launching a weblog than this. For example: whining continuously until your web-savvy friend agrees to help you. This only came after waking up at 3 a.m., face down on the keyboard, with my spacebar short-circuiting in drool. That said, I hope you'll check out my blog.

But please, keep any comparisons to yourself.

Only real men can iron clothes at 3,000 feet

I have reached the conclusion that most of the world's ironing is now being done by men. I say this because it's the only explanation I have for a sport called extreme ironing, which is actually being lobbied as an Olympic event by "ironing enthusiasts" — a phrase referred to in the Bible as a sign of the coming apocalypse.

And four horsemen will come from the sky. And they will lay waste to the land, but not before having their robes pressed by ironing enthusiasts.

It's easy to understand how extreme ironing evolved if you keep in mind a simple truth about the male species: Given enough time, any man performing a mundane task will find a way to hurt himself. And if you can hurt yourself doing it, then it's practically a sport already. Sure, bowling and golf might appear to be exceptions to this rule. But ask anyone who has ever jammed their finger in the ball return, or inadvertently left a tee in their back pocket, and they'll tell you there is plenty of danger involved.

As a man who irons, I know, firsthand, the danger that comes with pressing my daughter's favorite clothes. Especially if I use the wrong setting and turn what was once a flowery cotton blouse into our newest hand towel. Until recently, men who ironed were looked upon as being wimpy. This was a stigma left over from an earlier time when men brought home the bacon and women cooked it... then cleaned the kitchen, vacuumed, washed the dishes, bathed the kids, and did all the laundry. Back then, men who refused to perform domestic chores were still called masculine things such as "The Breadwinner," "King of the Castle," and "Man of the House."

Generally by other men.

Today, men who want to bring home the bacon while avoiding any domestic chores are called other things, such as "single" or "recently divorced." As a result, we men have come up with a way to demonstrate our unquestionable maleness by 1) taking a simple task and 2) making it as difficult as humanly possible. This is the general idea behind extreme ironing which, according to its web site (www.extremeironing.com), "combines the excitement of an 'extreme' sport with the satisfaction of a well-pressed shirt."

Being a man, I can appreciate that kind of logic; any woman can iron a pair of slacks; it takes a MAN to do it while jumping out of a plane.

Because of this, I have decided to train for the 2013 Extreme Ironing World Championships, for which my family has pledged their support by providing me with as much ironing to do as possible. In fact, as a demonstration of their unselfish commitment to my goal, everyone recently purchased an entire new wardrobe, none of which is "wrinkle free." My hope is that the experience will draw us even closer together as a family.

At least, once I can find them on the other side of this pile of ironing.

Your investments are more secure, thanks to me and a select group of financial dunderheads

Given the state of today's economy, it's hard to know who to trust when it comes to investing your money. You could trust ME of course, but that would mean giving your money to someone whose greatest return on an investment came when I accidentally got a 75-cent candy bar out of a vending machine using only two quarters. The truth is, I know absolutely nothing about the financial marketplace. This is why I currently do not own any stocks, bonds, treasury bills, money market accounts or, for that matter, any actual *money*. However, it's because of this — and what the White House calls my "unique financial perspective" — that I was asked to join the Presidential Advisory Board on Corporate Fraud, where our motto is:

For every dirty business we wipe out, there's somebody taking a bath

It's our job to sift through literally thousands of highly complex financial reports sent in by America's corporations, and then analyze each one for signs of fraudulent activity. You may be wondering how someone like myself — with the financial IQ of a Rhesus monkey — could possibly hope to find ANY sign of shenanigans somewhere in the complicated maze of bookkeeping ledgers, profit statements, and Hooters receipts. It's actually very easy. That's because we've been painstakingly trained on how to study a document and quickly spot signs of fraudulent activity — such as finding a yellow sticky note with the words "fraudulent activity" written on it.

Using this technique (based on the Evalyn Wood speed-reading method), we've been able to scrutinize the financial dealings of more than 600 major corporations in just under 36 hours (including lunch breaks, naps and a tour of Washington D.C.). I'm proud to say I believe our efforts have had a major impact on ending corporate fraud because, so far, we haven't found a single incident. By itself, this may not be enough to restore your confidence in the financial marketplace. But remember this: Right now, the President's newest economic stimulus package will soon be making its way through Congress on the "fast track" (a special system designed to speed up the review process by avoiding any contact with the president whatsoever).

This new plan is the result of high-level meetings with economic advisors, corporate analysts and CEOs from around the country. In fact, the President is so sure of his plan that he said, in a direct statement to Congress, that he would personally be handling his package as often as possible, and that he wouldn't stop handling it until the bill was passed.

"For obvious reasons, we hope the bill passes quickly," said a White House spokesman.

So what does all of this mean to the average American? Investment opportunity, of course. A big part of the President's stimulus plan will include more tax cuts — particularly for larger businesses. This makes perfect sense because, as we all know, the first thought any CEO has when his company gets a million-dollar tax break is: *Let's use this extra money to create more jobs!*

Known as the “trickle-down effect,” this will lead directly to a sharp drop in unemployment as the demand for yachts and private jets increases. At this point, many of you are probably asking yourselves: *So, what should I invest my money in?*

Being that I am now a member of an important government board that investigates corporate fraud, providing you with that type of information could get me in really big trouble. However, I CAN tell you about an investment opportunity that will guarantee a one-quarter yield.

The only catch is, you really have to like candy bars.

Open contempt for those in better shape is the first step to a healthier you

Like millions of Americans, I recently stripped down, prepared myself for the worst, and stepped onto the scale. Soon after, I retrieved the scale from the front yard and accepted the fact that, yes — it probably was defective. At my wife’s suggestion, I tried our neighbor’s scale. This led to the discovery that, of the 23 scales I tested within a five-mile radius of our home, every single one was off by exactly 11 pounds. Being a journalist, I had to wonder: Was this a widespread problem? Were we being duped into needless exercise by faulty scales?!

I immediately brought this to the attention of my editor, who, realizing the implications, told me to stay out of her candy drawer.

The truth is, I have no one but myself to blame for putting on these extra pounds. This is why, every year around this time, people just like me make a commitment to start going to the gym. I know this because I recognize most of these people from last year. We all have the same expression: grim determination mixed with a sense of purpose in knowing that, afterward, there’s a KFC right across the street. We come dressed with headbands and towels over our shoulders even though we spend most of our time wandering around the gym looking for water bottles.

After making this realization, I was motivated to do things differently this time. Never again would I splash water on my face, then stand close enough to someone to appear as though we are workout partners. It was time to get serious about fitness by accepting the fact that the closest I'll ever get to having buns of steel is if I happen to leave the bread box open overnight. I'm nearly 40, married, and have two children; what do I need washboard abs for when I know perfectly well that my wife gets more turned on by me doing the laundry?

With these things in mind, I put together a list of goals that will motivate me because they're actually achievable.

First, buns of steel are out. Instead, I will settle for buns of aluminum foil; as long as they can hold their shape and don't leak, I'm happy.

Second, I understand that my metabolism is slowing down and that, as a result, my body's fuel-burning efficiency is similar to that of a Humvee. Unless I'm careful, I will also weigh as much as a Humvee and require a government subsidy just so I can fill up with gas.

Third, I will no longer waste my time comparing my body with anyone else's, especially if theirs is better. This should make my workouts twice as productive since I will be avoiding eye contact with everyone else at the gym.

And finally, I will stop using the scale as my measure of success. What's the point, really?

They're all wrong anyway.

Through hypnosis, you can become a better golfer — unless you think you're a chicken

Our universe is full of mysteries.

Easter Island. The Bermuda Triangle. California.

And perhaps the biggest mystery: Why I was chosen to captain a team at the Florence Chamber of Commerce Golf Scramble for a *second* time. Being asked the first time could be attributed to Chamber members not realizing how bad a golfer I really am. Though none of the injuries sustained during last year's tournament were life threatening, having six golfers (two of whom were playing the hole behind me) knocked unconscious by balls with my initials on them — I thought — would become my golfing swan song.

(Speaking of which, I'd like to take this opportunity to apologize once again for the tragic death of that swan near the putting green. Had I known the difference between a putter and a pitching wedge, things might've turned out differently for that majestic creature.)

Because of this, I fully expected a letter from the American Golf Association (and PETA) denying me access to any course that doesn't include a windmill and tokens for a free hot dog. Needless to say, when I was asked back for this year's golf scramble, I naturally assumed that, at some point, hard liquor had become available in the clubhouse.

As it turns out, being the worst golfer in Ocean Dunes Golf Links history actually makes me a hot commodity! That's right! With my handicap, the only way a team I'm on can lose is if, over the course of 18 holes, I accidentally knock each of my teammates unconscious with my backswing.

Which is why I'm determined to make this year different. How? By hypnotizing myself into believing I'm a good golfer.

That's right. Thanks to golf hypnotherapist Dr. Kenneth Grossman, I will utilize the power of my subconscious to golf in a manner that is, quote: "Relaxed, self-confident and, unless you purchase both CDs, amazingly like that of a chicken."

The program, called Hypnosis for Golf (available at www.hypnosis4golf.com) comes with a no-risk guarantee that if I'm not completely satisfied, my money will be refunded "...within a period of time considered reasonable by many third-world countries."

Like many of you, I was a little skeptical about the idea of hypnotizing myself because I figured it meant standing in front of a mirror with a shiny object and repeating:

You're getting very sleepy.
Very sleeeee-peee
Very s-l-e-e-e-e-p—
THUD.

That was silly, of course. Dr. Grossman is a man of science, and his method is scientifically proven to induce the trance-like state necessary for self-hypnosis. This is achieved by having the subject go to a quiet room and, for 15 to 20 minutes, watch golf on television. If you happen to be among those who are more resistant to hypnosis, then switch to bowling. However, Dr. Grossman warns that prolonged exposure can send subjects into a catatonic state similar to a coma. If that happens, change to something more stimulating, such as the blue screen on your auxiliary channel.

With two weeks left before the Florence Chamber Golf Scramble, I feel there's plenty of time for me to become a better golfer. Or at least a less dangerous one. I plan to practice Dr. Grossman's technique each day until I can approach the fairway with complete (entirely unfounded) confidence.

I'd also like to say to my team members that, if for some reason I don't show up, I'd appreciate it if someone would come over and change the channel.

Graduates taking that first big step should remember their roller blades

To this year's graduates:

As you cross the stage to receive your diploma, remember that you're crossing a brand new threshold in your young life. That's because, in most cases, your parents have already arranged for the contents of your room to be hauled onto the front lawn and sold, probably during the graduation ceremony itself.

Or maybe even at the graduation ceremony itself:

Before we call our next graduate, I'd like to turn your attention to the roller blades I'm wearing. They, along with other items belonging to Billy Schlependorf, will be available for purchase after the ceremony in the courtyard.

That's right; by the time you get home, you'll be lucky if you're room still has the same light switch. I know this may sound harsh, but it is something that parents do out of LOVE. It's about your parents helping you make that important transition into independence, even if it means turning your bedroom into patio space between the new hot tub and gazebo. I know it's hard to believe, but that's how much your parents are willing to sacrifice in order to help you find your place in the world — which, by the way, doesn't include living in the attic, basement or any of the utility closets. This means finding a job. Something that will allow you to apply the cumulative knowledge you've acquired through years of higher education. It means competing in today's tough job market against like-minded graduates.

It means, in many cases, a career in the food service industry.

For those who might be contemplating this opportunity (or who might be wearing a hair net at this very moment), keep in mind that some of the world's most successful business people got their start in the food service industry. And keep in mind that just because I can't think of any right now doesn't mean it's not true, because I'm pretty sure I read it somewhere. Really.

Okay. Fine.

I'm a big fat liar.

It doesn't mean that working in fast food can't be rewarding. In fact, ask any journalist, and they will tell you that there's nothing more rewarding than being a fry cook. To prove it, I'm going to stop writing at this very moment and pose this question to each of my fellow journalists here in the newsroom...

...You see?

Just as I expected: every reporter I talked to agreed that there is nothing more rewarding than being a fry cook.

[Editor: Please note that you are surrounded by big fat liars.]

So, what does all of this mean exactly? For you graduates, it means taking your first steps into the world on your own. As you do, I'd suggest you stop by that table in the court yard.

You never know when a cheap pair of roller blades might come in handy.

Being safe means avoiding Jessica Simpson during a lightning storm

Here on the Oregon coast, lightning is a rare phenomenon. So rare, in fact, that most of us have absolutely no idea what to do in the event of an electrical storm. I know this because, as an Oregonian, I can attest to the fact that most of us run to the nearest plate glass window to watch lightning, often while wrapping wild game in tin foil and exclaiming, "Wow, did you see how close that was?! We better take the TV antenna down!"

It was because of this that Hands Across America did not include holding hands with anyone in Oregon. As a columnist with the awesome power of the print media at my disposal, I have an opportunity — an obligation, really — to help educate my readership and perhaps save the lives of as many as a dozen people. However, before we talk about safety, we must first understand lightning and its relation to space.

Space is what I must fill each week in order to keep my job; therefore, we will start with the atom.

If you were to break the universe down to its most basic element, you would get in really big trouble. You would also get one of the smallest forms of matter known to man: the atom.

To give you a sense of scale, it takes nine atoms to make one Jessica Simpson bikini. Following that line of thought, it takes approximately nine Jessica Simpsons to make one Oprah Winfrey. And while one Oprah Winfrey makes more money than nine Jessica Simpsons, you will eventually discover a fundamental law of physics, which is that one bikini will not fit around nine Oprah Winfreys.

Especially if that bikini belongs to Jessica Simpson.

My point, of course, is that if I ever want to see my wife in a bikini again, I really need to move on. This brings us to static electricity, which is caused by the interaction between protons and electrons within an atom. Protons contain "positive" charges. Electrons contain "negative" charges. As atoms come into contact, they exchange protons and electrons, creating charges that eventually show up on your Visa bill in the form of static.

For example: If my wife were to find the purchase of a Jessica Simpson poster on our credit card, the result would be...?

You guessed it: Static!

That static is then carried directly into the atmosphere on sound waves created by...?

You guessed it: My wife!

Once it reaches the atmosphere, static is then transformed into super-charged electricity as it comes in contact with other bits of static from other wives whose husbands weren't smart enough to use cash when purchasing their own Jessica Simpson poster. It is this super-charged static electricity that eventually forms lightning bolts, which return to the earth and strike unsuspecting husbands — usually while they're watching the American Music Awards.

Okay, now that we understand where lightning comes from, it's time to discuss safety. First, it is a common misconception that the safest place to be during a lightning storm is inside a car. While a car certainly offers a protective barrier between you and a rogue lightning bolt, it's still not as safe as the protective barrier created by...?

You guessed it: Nine Oprah Winfreys!

Still, the safest place to be during a lightning storm is indoors. This is because metal plumbing and electrical wiring create a protective web that will carry a lightning strike to the ground. Because of this, it's important to stay away from windows, plumbing fixtures, electric appliances and, if at all possible, Jessica Simpson.

I hope this has been helpful.

Now, if you'll excuse me, I promised my wife I'd put more tin foil on the TV antenna.

A jury of your peers could include Strom Thurmond and a dead cockapoo

It's time once again for us to open our law books and try to answer a nagging question first raised in 1998 by a woman who sued McDonald's after tragically burning her chin on a hot pickle slice:

How do we balance the Scales of Justice when one side has more nuts?

I say this because of a lawsuit filed against Burger King, Wendy's, KFC and (of course) McDonald's, on behalf of Mr. Caesar Barber, whose lawyer claims that they unjustly "sold his client food that made him obese." This is a little like Hannibal Lecter giving up meat, then suing the North American Vegetarian Society after choking on a Tofu Burger. It's these kinds of cases that illustrate exactly what our judicial system desperately needs: Man-eating judges.

And also a system for determining a lawsuit's validity before it actually makes it to court. This process could take place during a quick, pre-trial hearing, held in private chambers, without any lawyers present to muck things up...

Judge: I see here that you would like to sue the Dairy Farmers of America for the mental anguish and emotional distress you suffered after accidentally spitting a mouthful of sour milk into a pan of hot bacon grease.

Plaintiff: Yes, your honor. It was very frightening.

Judge: Was anyone hurt?

Plaintiff: No. But I can't even look at buttermilk gravy anymore.

Judge: I see. And it says here that you're filing a separate lawsuit against the American Pork Farmers Association.

Plaintiff: That's right.

Judge: You do understand that, between these two cases, you could tie up the courts indefinitely.

Plaintiff: But my lawyer says I could get $1 million.

Judge: Let's bring him in; we can discuss the rest over some fava beans and a nice bottle of chi-a-a-a-anti...

All I'm saying is that if there was some type of consequence for people who initiate stupid lawsuits — such as being eaten alive by a maniacal, cannibalistic judge — then we might see a drop in the population of those cases. Or at least in the population of lawyers, which couldn't hurt.

The reason I bring this up is because I believe stupid lawsuits are the reason a lot of people are becoming less and less willing to serve as jurists. For example, a study conducted in California found that only nine percent of the 4.4 million people summoned for jury duty in Los Angeles County last year actually elected to become part of the judicial process. This, of course, doesn't include those who became part of the process after fingerprinting.

In all fairness, I should mention that not every potential juror would've qualified for duty anyway. That's because there are very strict guidelines when it comes to the initial phase of the jury selection process — the first of which is that you actually have to be alive in order to render a verdict.

It may sound a little nit-picky, but this is a requirement in every state, except South Carolina, where being alive isn't even required of its senators. In spite of these stringent guidelines, a report commissioned by the American Tort Reform Association discovered that, in its desperation, Los Angeles County not only summoned dead people for jury duty, but also people's pets. As shocking as this sounds, there is some good news in that none of these pets were dead.

While the study was able to determine that absolutely NO PETS had played a part in the final outcome of any cases, it did point out that, in at least once instance, "It was only because that little cockapoo couldn't read the darned verdict," said the bailiff.

The truth is, the only way to increase participation in the jury process is to restore the respectability of the judicial system by eliminating stupid lawsuits that waste everybody's time.

The fastest way to do that, of course, would be to require the people who file them to serve as jurors.

Stranger danger also includes Komodo dragons

As you've probably heard, the executive editor at the *San Francisco Chronicle* was attacked by a 7-foot-long Komodo dragon last week. Oddly enough, it wasn't a letter to the editor gone horribly wrong, or even a marketing stunt for the summer release of *Crouching Editor, Hidden Dragon* that spurred the attack. It actually happened during a special behind-the-scenes tour at the Los Angeles Zoo. As a result, officials are now going to "re-evaluate" the special visiting privileges reserved for major donors.

(Without question, feeding yourself to a seven-foot lizard definitely falls into the "major donor" category.)

Nevertheless, because of this incident, any hope I had of covering myself in A1 Steak Sauce and visiting the lions' den at the Portland Zoo is now over. What does remain is the question of how zoo officials, who utilize these types of fund raising devices as a way to purchase dental floss for their Komodo dragons, will find ways to attract major donors in the future. While there are certainly lots of other, safer animal exhibits that could be toured by big spenders, the danger factor — and story-telling value — drops off considerably once you leave the man-eater realm.

Being at a dinner party and telling how you stared down a Siberian tiger, then narrowly escaped its claws, is definitely more impressive than recalling the time you held off a hungry Toucan with nothing but a tranquilizer gun and a box of Fruit Loops. The same goes for tales of survival that have anything to do with ovulating ostriches or outrunning giant, spitting tortoises (even if what you were wearing was labeled dry clean only).

The fact is, these stories are a lot like microwavable pork rinds; lots of sizzle, very little pop.

It's a situation that has fund raising officials scrambling for new ways to reward their major contributors; the trick being to find an acceptable balance between offering donors danger without also offering them as dinner. As you can imagine, brainstorming sessions have produced a number of ideas, all of which are top secret. However, through an inside source, I was able to obtain a list of titles for some possible "special visit" activities.

Among them:

One potato, two potato, three potato, Roar!
Share your Big Mac with a Razorback.
Can You Find the Piranha in the Sauna?
Crouching Tiger, Hidden Exit.

Jack is nimble, Jack is quick...but Jack is still asking for a much bigger stick.

The truth is, there's no need to waste time coming up with new ways to thrill big contributors. All officials need to do is take a closer look at the dangers an average attendee confronts during a routine excursion to the zoo. Just consider how frightening it is to walk past the guy who bends and contorts balloons into animal shapes. It's like maneuvering past someone twisting multi-colored explosives together; one false move, and the chain reaction could blow the fur off a mountain yak.

Ever run out of food pellets while you're in the middle of the petting zoo? The only way out is to be air lifted — and then, only after your hair and shoes have been eaten by goats. I'd just as soon skip the details about the monkey house, but let me just say to any honeymooners out there that, if you walk by it at the wrong time, they won't be throwing rice.

Which gives me a thought: If zoos were to stop providing special privileges to major donors, they could skip this monkey business in the first place.

Full-contact bowling could get more men to yell at their TVs

Like millions of other red-blooded, unathletic men across America, I will be spending a good portion of Super Bowl Sunday sitting on the couch, eating handfuls of assorted snack foods, and whining every time a player from my team makes even the teeniest mistake. It doesn't matter that these men are performing feats of athletic skill I can only achieve in my dreams (after which I usually wake up with a pulled groin muscle). And it doesn't matter that each of these men possesses more muscle mass than my entire body weight plus a mid-sized SUV.

The reason these things don't matter to us men is because we know THOSE men can't actually hear us. If they could, then Super Bowl parties as we know them would cease to exist:

"Did you see number forty-two?! That idiot completely missed the tackle!"

"Hey, Bill — I think he's looking at you."

"What...?"

"Try moving over by the cheese dip — oh yeah, he's definitely looking right at you."

"What's he holding up?"

"I think it's some kind of fancy GPS device."

"Why's he smiling like that?"

"Quick, Bill! Change the channel!"

This obvious exaggeration was done to make a point, which is that, aside from leaving for work one morning and being tackled through the screen door by a 310-pound linebacker, nothing can keep a man from shouting at the TV during a sporting event. In fact, my father-in-law, who owns one of those giant TVs with picture-in-picture viewing, has taken this to a new level by learning to yell at four different games at once. While this is certainly an impressive display of multi-tasking, watching a game with him is like watching a game with a sports fanatic suffering from Multiple Personality Disorder.

I should clarify that not all sporting events fuel a man's primal need to yell at the TV. One example is bowling. The reason is simple: There's no element of physical danger involved. True, there's always the underlying risk of someone's fingers getting pinched between two bowling balls, but it just doesn't evoke the same level of danger as it would if bowlers had to actually compete for the ball in a tip-off before each frame:

"...The ball goes UP-and-now-down, off the head of Czechoslovakia's Sirius Kunkussion, and onto the foot of Floppy Sesamoid, who is now gasping for air from the hand blower..."

It's pretty much the same thing for golf and tennis; no real danger involved. And even though golf does use exciting terms like Water Hazard! Sand Trap! and Sudden Death!, we all know the only real danger is Arnold Palmer forgetting to pack a sweater for the senior tour. However, in both sports, a few well-placed scorpions could make all the difference:

"What a beautiful shot by Tiger, eh Tom?"

"Yes it was, Frank, but he seems a little hesitant to get his ball."

"Well, Tom, Tiger's a smart young man. He knows there's a good chance that one of the three remaining scorpion hazards is probably in that cup."

"That's a good point. But remember: He does still have one last caddy-option left. The question, of course, is whether to use him here, or save him for the sand trap."

Or tennis:

"In case you're just tuning in, it's advantage Agassi, which means Chang mus t win this next point if he wants to stay alive — no easy feat, I must say."

"That's right, Tom. As you can see, they have just released the scorpions on Chang's side of the court. One wrong step, and he could — WHOA! I think we've just lost another ball boy..."

Now, before I get a bunch of angry letters from bowlers, tennis players, golfers and scorpions, I just want to say that I have nothing but the utmost respect for those sports (and for scorpions in general). The last thing I want to do is offend anyone with a racket, golf club, or good enough aim with a bowling ball to drop a 7-10 split.

Especially since we just had the screen door fixed.

My greatest childhood fear? Being bitten by a radioactive moth

For most of us, there comes a time in our lives when we must face the truth, and accept the fact we will never actually possess any type of super-human powers. This includes the ability to fly, shoot laser beams out of our eyes, look good in a skin-tight costume, or spontaneously emit a cloud of paralyzing gas. (Let's be clear on that last one; if it requires eating a Taco Bell value meal and a 30-minute waiting period, technically your paralyzing gas is NOT a super power.)

As a child, I spent countless hours thumbing through comic books and dreaming of the day I would be bitten by a radioactive insect — and knowing full well that, with my luck, it would probably be something stupid like a moth:

"Curses! It's Moth Man, here to foil my evil plans! How can I stop him? Hey — maybe I'll try this porch light..."

In fact, I was so sure that I would end up as a lame super hero that, with the help of my friends, we came up with a plan to MAKE me into Spiderman before there was any chance of me being bitten by a radioactive moth, ear wig, silverfish or stink bug.

Our plan was simple.

Step one: Find a spider — preferably a small one — and expose it to high levels of radiation.

Step two: Make it bite me.

Now, finding just the right spider proved tricky. That's because there were certain genetic traits that I did not want incorporated into my DNA. For example, really hairy spiders were out. So were those spiders with the big squishy bulb in the back. Maintaining a secret identity was going to be crucial, and trying to do that as a seven-year-old with a giant rear end and thick body hair would be nearly impossible. After eventually capturing the perfect spider specimen, it was time to expose it to high levels of radiation. This, of course, meant gaining unfettered access to the most potent source of radiation at our disposal: The microwave oven.

Since there's a good chance that many of you are actually reading this at breakfast, I'll spare you the details and just tell you that I never ate out of that microwave again. I also never gained any super powers. I did, however, gain an appreciation for the super powerful absorbency of *Brawny* paper towels.

The reason I'm bringing this up is because of an incident last week that proves that there ARE those among us who aren't willing to give up the dream of having super powers. According to a CNN report, a man entered a bank in Utah, walked across a lobby full of customers, and began taking handfuls of money from the vault without filling out a withdrawal slip — which he didn't figure he needed to since he was completely *invisible*. In fact, it wasn't until being tackled from all sides by bank security and a mob of angry customers that he suspected his invisibility scroll, which he'd purchased from a "sorcerer" for $625, might not be working.

Though it's true the incident ended badly for him, it's a real positive for the rest of us if this is the direction that super villains are headed. Heck, maybe it's time I pulled out my old Moth Man costume.

Assuming it doesn't have holes in it.

Spring officially starts once you've mowed over your hibachi

The official start of spring is almost here. I know this because I received a Sears catalogue depicting what appears to be an all-American family taking time off from its busy modeling schedule to cook hamburgers on a brand new stainless steel grill large enough to accommodate an entire side of bull elk. As you would expect, children were in the yard squirting each other with water toys and running barefoot over a perfectly manicured lawn which, judging from the size of the family dog, must be self-cleaning.

Mom was nearby, well oiled and lying on a lawn chair in her bathing suit, still recovering from her recent *Victoria's Secret* lingerie shoot in the Bahamas.

Around the Hickson household, summer starts out a little differently. I was reminded of this yesterday as I stood in our back yard, waist-deep in weeds, swatting at a mosquito with a rusty spatula and trying to remember the last time I saw our hibachi. Each year, I promise myself I won't begin the spring by embarrassing our entire family.

And each year, a search and rescue team finds me whimpering somewhere in our back yard, surrounded by weeds, lying in a fetal position next to our lawn mower.

My family has a hard time understanding this, especially since, in most cases, I'm found less than six feet from the house. I tell them not EVERYONE is born with a keen sense of direction, and that all of this could be avoided if I just had a riding mower with *Onstar*. I generally lose this argument because, as my family points out, I could find my way out of the yard by following my own clipping path IF I didn't insist on starting out with a crop circle every time. That's when I'm sent back out to mow the lawn with an orange rope tied to my belt. The mowing process can last up to several hours or, like yesterday, less than 15 minutes, depending on how long it takes me to run over the hibachi. While I can laugh about it now, I wasn't laughing when I was blinded by a spark so intense it flash-burned the hair off my legs.

The good news is that neighbors unfortunate enough to be facing a window — any window — at that particular instant are expected to regain their sight within a few days.

However, this still leaves me with a partially mowed yard and what is now a two-piece hibachi set. On one hand, having separate grilling surfaces is nice, but only if the total net volume of what you're cooking is equal to, or less than, one chicken drummette. For example, I tried preparing hamburgers for our family. This process took just under four hours, the last 15 minutes of which was spent waiting in line for our order at Burgerville. That experience has led me to consider buying a new grill. Something I can cook multiple items on, which would therefore make it large enough to avoid running over with the lawn mower. This is particularly important to me if we go with the propane model.

Then again, if I run over THAT, it could really speed up the lawn mowing process.

It's not a VW bus unless you can square dance in the front seat

When I first heard about Volkswagen's plans to bring back the Microbus, I immediately decided it would become our new family vehicle. That's because no mode of transportation offers the same level of excitement as riding in a VW bus.

Except maybe riding in a runaway mine car.

But that was always part of its charm, just like the seat belts that had to be double-knotted to the door handle; the innovative heating system that blended engine heat and exhaust fumes with just enough outside air to keep occupants from blacking out; and a horn that never EVER worked — and when I say never-ever, I don't just mean on mine. To this day, I have yet to meet anyone who has actually had (or witnessed the existence of) a working horn on a VW bus. Remember, this was way before side-impact bars, breakaway bumpers and so many air bags popping out of places that, last year alone, false sightings of Pamela Anderson rose by as much as 64 percent.

It used to be that comfort didn't have to come at the expense of safety. In fact, the total cost of safety features on an average VW was about $6, which was the price of a bracket for mounting a spare tire on the front. Once it was put in place, that circle of inflated rubber became your vehicle's most important safety feature.

Because, technically, it was the ONLY safety feature.

Admittedly, this doesn't take into account the bus's aerodynamic body design, which was modeled after a standard ACME brick, and therefore created enough wind resistance to keep the vehicle from climbing any grade steeper than, say...

A speed bump.

Add passengers to this equation, and your chances of getting into a serious accident were virtually eliminated unless you somehow managed to get into a head-on collision while parked in your driveway.

Because of all this, I was shocked to hear that Volkswagen described their new Microbus as "a vast improvement over the 1950s design."

This is like saying you have somehow improved on the design of your favorite pair of old underwear; sure, maybe they're not much to look at, and maybe the muffler's worn out, but at least you know you'll get a comfortable ride. At no time since parting with my own VW bus 14 years ago have I ever driven a more comfortable vehicle. And at no time since then have I managed to get in or out of a vehicle without resembling someone failing a yoga exam. That's because the VW designers of old didn't see a need to fill every available space with some kind of special feature. Aside from the essentials needed to steer, accelerate, shift gears, and slow the vehicle down enough to allow the drag of your foot to bring it to a complete stop, there was nothing else getting in the way of your driving experience.

There was literally enough room in the front for a driver, a passenger, and a pair of square dancers to all lock elbows and do-si-do, just as long as they avoided the gear shift.

Not anymore.

You see, the new and improved Microbus has things like an on-board multiplex theater, a DVD/video game console, and seven-inch TV screens built into the seats — which, by the way, are covered in white leather.

How can THAT be an improvement over the old seats? At least when THOSE cracked they could be fixed with a strip of electrical tape that not only blended perfectly with the seat, but also matched many accents in the black plastic interior.

And if you think you can still save money by working on the engine yourself, you can forget about it. The new and improved version is a computerized, 5-speed, 230 horsepower V6 engine with "Tiptronic" clutchless shifting. Now, I don't know what all that MEANS exactly, but I'm pretty sure that my standard VW repair kit, which consisted of gum, duct tape, a beer tab, three rolls of kite string, and a copy of VW Repair for the Complete Idiot, won't do me much good.

So, to set the record straight, we do NOT plan to buy a new Microbus. At least not until they introduce a new, UNimproved version of the 1950s design. I'd like to stir up a grass roots movement for this idea, so I'm asking anyone who'd like to see the return of the old-style of bus to please honk when they see me.

Of course, if you happen to be DRIVING an old VW at the time, then you'll just have to wave.

But don't forget to swing your partner first.

Looking for excitement? Try feeding your arm to a catfish

After living in the Deep South for 10 years, I occasionally feel a strong urge to return. When that happens, I just remind myself that as beautiful and historic and hospitable as the South is, it contains people who use themselves as bait for catfish that are roughly the size of an Airstream travel trailer. Generally speaking, these people are not intoxicated or medicated. Nor is there any evidence to support that they are the victims of mind-controlling aliens who have simply grown bored waiting for the invasion.

No. These folks WANT to hunt catfish by sticking their bare hands into underwater burrows, knowing full well it could be the hiding place of a cottonmouth, snapping turtle, or Dick Cheney.

Admittedly, the closest I've come to hand-grabbing a catfish occurred at a public golf course near Atlanta, when I waded into a water hazard to retrieve my ball and accidentally stepped on a gar. For those west of the Mason-Dixon, a gar is sort of like a barracuda, but with more attitude. To this day, none of us can agree on how big this gar was. My guess is about 12 feet long. And I'm pretty sure it had the hindquarters of a bull elk clenched between its jaws. Others in our group disagree, and say what I actually stepped on was a swollen bratwurst.

Which is totally ridiculous.

I think I'd know the difference between stepping on a dangerous man-eating fish, or a relatively harmless meat by-product. Although, to be fair, I can't say for sure because my eyes were closed and I was screaming.

In that moment it became clear to everyone in our group, — and anyone living within a two-mile radius — that I wasn't going to be bare-handing a giant catfish (or bratwurst) anytime soon. To fully appreciate this aggressive style of catting known as "noodling," you must keep a couple of things in mind. First, some catfish can weigh as much as 100 pounds. Fish biologists have documented enormous mouth radiuses, which is done by carefully extending the mouth to its largest capacity, measuring it on all sides, then comparing it to a scale reference provided by Mick Jagger.

The other thing you have to remember is that the South's most successful "noodlers" — those who have achieved celebrity by the sheer volume of catfish they've landed with their bare hands — generally have names like "Uncle Stubby," "Button-Nosed Jim" and "Three-Finger Jack." These men not only offer themselves for the sake of the sport, but vow to keep doing so, even if it becomes necessary for someone to physically insert them into a catfish lair once they've lost all their appendages. It's this kind of dedication that inspires people like myself to at least consider taking a risk and, despite the danger, order fried catfish that might contain a missing digit from "Three-Finger Jack."

To better understand this sport, I tried contacting several "noodlers" by phone to discuss what it takes to be successful. One thing I learned right away was to make sure the person you are calling is indeed a "noodler" before addressing them as such. This is especially true if you accidentally transpose the number and call someone who is, at that very moment, running late for an anger management class. As it stands, I have yet to talk with an actual noodler, many of whom were in Pauls Valley, Okla., this past weekend for the first-annual National Noodling Tournament, where the motto was: "No Hooks. No Bait. No Fear."

This is actually very close to my own personal noodling motto: "No Hooks. No Bait. No Cajones."

I will continue to follow this story. In fact, my editor has agreed to fly me back to the Deep South for first-hand research, and I definitely plan to go.

Just as soon as he includes a return ticket.

Online banking: Bringing Zimbabwe and Snakegut, Alabama closer together

It's not every day that I receive an e-mail from a Zimbabwean prince who needs help relocating $20 million into an American bank account as soon as possible. In fact, in the last five years, I've only received this letter maybe eight times. In each case, the letter explains that I've been chosen because I'm reputed to be a "dependable and trustworthy" person. Given that this letter is always addressed to *Dear Sir* or *Madam,* I can only assume that my reputation is in fact so great that I no longer need an actual name.

Either that, or I'm not the only person to receive this letter.

Each time I've gotten this email, I've deleted it because, let's be honest: Who wants to spend time figuring out how to access their online bank account? I'm doing good to make a deposit after my wife forges my name and fills everything out for me. I have no intention of adding to that headache (or potential jail time) by making a cross-continental transfer of millions of dollars from Zimbabwe.

Besides, having our checking account suddenly jump to over $20 million — I think — would look a little suspicious...

I'm sorry Mr. Hickson, but you don't have money in your account to cover...Oh, wait a minute. Scratch that. Will this bagel be everything?

At the same time, what if it were true? What if there really WAS a South African prince desperately trying to move millions of dollars into the online account of a complete stranger? And what if my wife found out that I'd deleted his letter nine times? And what if, after discovering this, she was sitting next me when 20/20 began telling the story of how Booger Jones of Snakegut, Alabama became a multi-millionaire after figuring out how to access HIS online bank account to help a Zimbabwean prince?

(And furthermore, why is it that, even after using Spell Check, the word "Zimbabwean" still looks wrong?)

Because of these nagging questions, I decided to do a little investigative work and make absolutely sure there was no "Booger Jones" living anywhere in Alabama.

To my surprise, I found 14 of them.

Which is why I decided to answer Prince Mbagi's plea for help. Now, in order for you to fully understand the scope of his situation, I will summarize:

Prince Mbagi, the son of a wealthy Zimbabwean farmer killed by members of the South African government, is trying to find someone in America who will "inherit" his family fortune in order to keep President Mugabe from stealing it. As a show of appreciation, this person will receive $5 million and a free cell phone.

The only thing Prince Mbagi needs is an online account to transfer his millions to.

I know what you're thinking, and NO — I had no intention of forking over my account number to a complete stranger until I could verify that the cell phone also came with free minutes. The first step was to contact Prince Mbagi at kmbagi @ phantomemail.com, which, I discovered, is an email service providing "completely anonymous internet accounts." Naturally, this made perfect sense for someone in his dire situation.

What didn't make sense was that I needed a password in order to leave a message. Because I didn't know it, I did the next logical thing, which was to try cracking the secret password by entering random combinations of the word "Booger."

Not really! Haha! That would be silly!

I contacted the webmaster, explaining that I was trying to help a Zimbabwean prince looking for someone who could be trusted with $20 million.

His reply was swift:

I have no idea what you're talking about.

Best of luck.
— Booger Jones.

Needless to say, I didn't make contact with Prince Mbagi. I did, however, learn how to spell "Zimbabwean."

Dating at an 'oxygen bar' could lead to heavy breathing

It all started with bottled water.

That's when we, the consumers, put our collective feet down and cried out in a united voice that there was a little thing called Te Law of Supply and Demand — and that we'd be willing to break that law for the chance to purchase an already free and abundant earthly element if it came in a squeeze bottle. The latest trend is oxygen, which can now be purchased at a growing number of hip

"Oxygen Bars" around the country. To prepare for your first venture, you must visualize the atmosphere of an oxygen bar.

[Pause here to catch clever irony of last sentence.]

[Thank you for waiting.]

Doing this is simple. Picture a singles bar with attractive people all sitting around conversing. Now, take the wine glasses and beer bottles from these people, and replace them with plastic oxygen tubes draped over their ears. Add to this sexually-charged atmosphere the constant hum of an oxygen pump, and there you have it!

The terminal-care ward on "General Hospital."

OK, that's the visual. Now let's work on etiquette. To begin with, flagellating into the end of someone's oxygen tube is not considered an acceptable "ice-breaker." Though there are many scent options to chose from, that is not one of them. Also, nothing exposes a first-timer faster than asking for the "smoking section" at an oxygen bar ...

Come to think of it, that's not entirely true.

The fastest way is actually not asking — and just lighting up. For you single men out there, remember that the whole purpose of breathing 97 percent pure oxygen is to clarify and revitalize thinking. So pick-up lines that may have sounded clever after four beers at a singles bar now sound something like, "I wish I were a Jedi Knight. Can I live under your couch?"

So instead, try one of these savvy lines to entice a prospective date at an oxygen bar:

1) "Excuse me, is this nose-piece taken?"

2) "Can I buy you another minute of air?"

Or,

3) "This reminds me; whatever happened to the group 'Air Supply'?"

As with any new and exciting trend, knowing the correct terminology and etiquette are crucial. Just as you wouldn't enter a biker bar and ask for a "Zima," you wouldn't want to ruin your first oxygen-bar experience by asking for a nose cannelloni instead of a cannula; while one will blow oxygen through your nostrils, the other will blow ricotta cheese.

So, let's get started by covering some basic terminology:

• Cannula — A stylish, plastic tube that delivers oxygen to your nose.

• Host — Someone carrying an illness that can be spread by sneezing on someone else's cannula (or cannelloni, for that matter).

• Ebola — A deadly, incurable virus made famous by the movie "Outbreak," in which Dustin Hoffman contracts the virus after trying to pick up on an infected monkey at a Peruvian oxygen bar.

• Life insurance — A policy that will pay your loved ones should you contract the Ebola virus from a cannula (or even a cannelloni).

• Swizzle shtick — The act of writing a humor column about oxygen bars.

If you're nervous about taking the first step into this new trend, remember that it's actually been around for a long time. Japan, for example, has had oxygen bars for almost 40 years. Mexico, California's down-wind neighbor, opened its first oxygen bar eight years ago — which, coincidentally, is right about the time Ross Perot started complaining about that "Giant sucking sound."

Lastly, if all else fails, just hold on to your cannula — and don't forget to breathe.

Working the late shift at Denny's? Compare SAT scores with 'Mr. Sizzles'

During the next few weeks, every high school senior who plans to attend a four-year college will sit in a room with dozens of other nervous seniors and be handed a 300-pound Scholastic Aptitude Test. Shortly thereafter, each student will open the exam to page one and choose between a) continuing on with the test, or b) sticking a No. 2 pencil in their eye. That's because they'll be answering questions they wouldn't otherwise face without at least one "lifeline" and a chance to win $1 million.

The reason it's important to do well on the SATs is because your score tells colleges how smart you are. The smarter you are, the better your chances of getting into a prestigious university because, let's face it: The last thing any university wants is a bunch of dumb students who need to be educated, even if they are paying $40,000 a year toward a degree which, in many cases, still won't provide them with their most valuable document: A food handler's card.

Being a writer, I've naturally spent many rewarding years in the food service industry. And I can tell you that SAT scores don't matter when you're working the late shift at Denny's next to a sweaty, one-eyed fry cook whose nickname is "Mr. Sizzles."

What matters is learning to stay away from his blind side whenever someone orders the fried platter.

But I digress.

Like it or not, you need to have a good SAT score if you want any chance of getting into college and experiencing that crowning moment when, surrounded by family and friends, you suddenly realize you're in a commercial for the new *Girls Gone Wild!* video.

Therefore, as a service to students, I'd like to provide some useful tips on how to prepare for the SATs. This information is based on my own experience when, as a high school senior, I was tested regularly for a period of 90 days following a trip to Tijuana, Mexico.

To begin with, page two of your SAT handbook clearly states that anyone caught cheating will automatically be expelled and the action duly noted on their student record. Naturally, this will be a huge disadvantage for anyone applying to anything other than Electoral College. My suggestion, as you might've guessed, would be to avoid this situation entirely by making sure you go into your exam fully prepared to rip page two right out of your handbook.

Ha! Just kidding! That would be irresponsible of me!

It's actually on page four.

Okay, seriously — cheating is bad. And, unless you have a very good press secretary, you're going to get caught. This means you'll have to study. Studying, as you know, requires organization and a willingness to sacrifice time you would otherwise spend doing something more exciting.

Such as lancing your own boil.

My point being that no one ever said it would be easy. However, I can promise you that the harder you work at it, the more gratifying it will be once people have stopped staring at the side of your neck. Especially during the SATs. That said, I wish you the best on your exam.

And so does "Mr. Sizzles."

Well soak my peas and call me Piggly-Wiggly: It's New Year's Day in the South

My ex-wife came from The Deep South. Because of this, we were required to eat a giant pot of black-eyed peas every New Year's Day. According to southerners, this ensures good luck the whole year through until, coincidently, they get stuck eating beans again the following New Year. This annual tradition was introduced to me during our first year of marriage while living in Texas. My assignment was to bring home a bag of black-eyed peas from the local Piggly-Wiggly, which is the actual name of a supermarket chain that exists only in The South. In fact, The South is full of supermarkets with really silly names like Jitney Jungle and Kroger's. Apparently, this was a final act of defiance at the end of the Civil War:

Those Yankee scoundrels may have claimed our beloved soil, but we will rise again! Until then, they will be forced to buy their groceries from stores with really stupid names! Ha!

Hey, wait a minute... so will we.

DAMN those Yankees!

—Jefferson Davis, 1865

Because I'd never actually seen a black-eyed pea before, I was provided with a description and told to look in the dried beans section.

"Not the dried peas section?" I asked.

"No, it's a bean."

"Then why do they call it a pea?"

She had no answer for this, so I can only assume it's another one of those southern things meant to frustrate northerners like myself, who have a hard enough time understanding how you can improve your luck by eating something that gives you gas. Finding black-eyed peas proved to be very easy. That's because, in the South, they are so popular around the new year that supermarkets actually replace the normal "impulse-buy" items (such as *Yosemite Sam* mud flaps) located near the check-out stands, with bags of black-eyed peas. These bags often include special seasonings and a coupon for hog jowls. For those of you who have never prepared black-eyed peas, pork is a crucial element because, without it, you might as well be eating boiled erasers. In fact, one of the more popular recipes includes peppered tomatoes, cajun seasonings and extra spicy Andoulle sausage. Appropriately enough, this recipe is known as "Hoppin' John," which, depending on how much you eat, pretty much describes what you'll be doing the morning of Jan. 2.

I should mention that the black-eyed pea thing isn't the only southern tradition that leaves northerners like myself scratching our heads and begging for biscuits until the baby cries (and Yes, that's a totally made-up colloquialism). There's also something called the "first footing," in which the first person to cross your threshold on Jan. 1, foretells the kind of luck you'll have in the new year. Traditionally, you hope for someone good looking, or someone with influence or, at the very least, someone you haven't seen in a while who owes you money.

Being Danish, I prefer a much more sensible tradition which is shared by the Dutch. And that is to celebrate by gathering those closest to you, then — in a symbolic gesture representing the "Full Circle" of life in the new year — eating a bunch of donuts.

This makes perfect sense to me.

However, my ex-wife still insisted on making her annual batch of black-eyed peas every year, including an extra-spicy "Hoppin' John" recipe, which was sort of a compromise. If I couldn't eat a donut on New Year's Day, I could at least be sitting on one.

Striking matadors could result in a lot of bull for Spain

Though the story hasn't received much coverage here in the U.S., Spain's impending matador strike is big news in Madrid.

Especially if you're a bull.

Spain's current crisis stems from concerns about the spread of "Mad Cow" disease. Even though no cases of "Mad Cow" have been documented in fighting bulls — which seems odd, since the whole idea is to get them mad in the first place — and the exact details of how a bull could contract the virus from a cow remain sketchy, the agricultural ministry insists that an eventual cross-over from cows to bulls to Spaniards is possible. It's a notion deemed ridiculous by many in the bullfighting industry, who insist that their health-conscious practice of cutting the animals up right after they die, then selling the meat to anyone passing by outside the ring alleviates any chance for the virus to spread to the general population.

What makes this such a volatile situation is the long standing traditions of bullfighting, which date back to a time when the first matador discovered that, for some reason, wearing a Mickey Mouse hat and red cape makes bulls really angry.

Since then, even the trappings of a matador, called *trajes de luces* (which roughly translated means "really tight pants"), have become, like bullfighting itself, an integral part of Spanish tradition. To help you better understand the sport, here's a general overview of what happens at a typical fight.

According to the *Beginner's Guide to Bullfighting*, six bulls are selected and allocated in pairs to three matadors at noon on the day of the event. This process is conducted by the event's impresario (promoter) and takes approximately four hours, which allows just enough time for the matador to eventually squeeze into his pants. When the president of the bullfight signals for the first bull to be released, a brass band begins playing *La Viva Loca* while a team of three assistants enrage the bull by flapping their capes at it and calling it "Geraldo."

The main reason for this is to see how the animal moves in the ring. The other reason is to allow the matador enough time to change his *trajes de luces* again after actually seeing the bull.

Once this has been accomplished, the matador enters the ring with a small crimson cape, a curved sword, and a can of Red Bull. It is at this point that he can dedicate the beast to an individual, the audience itself or his corporate sponsor. If he performs his task well, the audience waves white handkerchiefs as a sign of approval and affection for the matador; if the bull does well, it waves a small crimson cape.

Whichever side you take in this stand-off, given that July and August are the busiest months in Spain's bullfighting calendar, a strike by matadors could leave millions of fans in search of an alternative to their favorite summer past time — which just goes to show that, no matter how different a culture may appear on the surface, when it comes to the world of professional sports, all fans are used to a certain level of bull.

Anger issues? Don't beat yourself up over it

Hello and welcome to another edition of our special in-depth medical feature *Health Yak*, which has been recognized by the U.S. Surgeon General as "extremely topical," meaning that you should not attempt to ingest any portion of this column without first consulting your doctor. Today we will be discussing a study that suggests as many as 16 million Americans — or roughly the number of people who never receive their appetizers during an average season of Hell's Kitchen — suffer from periodic outbursts of anger.

I know what you're thinking:

What makes this different from a typical outburst of anger, like when I open the air vent in my car and release a cloud of spores the size of shiitake mushrooms?

The answer, of course, is that there IS no difference, at least not until someone funds a clinical study, at which point it becomes an official "disorder" treatable by a new drug with minor side effects, such having your liver grow to the size of Shaquille O'Neal's seat cushion. According to Dr. Emil Coccaro of the University of Chicago's medical school, which, as you may recall, conducted the definitive study on the yawning habits of the Tibetan mountain yak (Conclusion: After 3,000 yawns, researchers become suicidal), what used to be known as "road rage" has now escalated into a nationwide problem called Intermittent Explosive Disorder. By definition, IED involves "outbursts that are out of proportion to the situation."

For example: Let's say you're at a drive-thru trying to order a bacon cheeseburger and, for the seventh-straight time, the person taking your order insists there is no one named "Macon the Sheep Herder" working there, and to please place your order. And let's say, in frustration, you exit your vehicle and rip the image of a cheeseburger directly from the menu board and begin gnawing on it, causing those in line behind you to drive off through the patio area.

Chances are, you could be an IED sufferer.

According to Dr. Coccaro, his conclusion was based on the results of a nationwide, face-to-face survey of 9,282 adults who were scored based on their response to highly formulated and complex diagnostic observations, such as "I'm guessing most dogs would probably introduce themselves by sniffing your face."

Amazingly, all 9,282 participants in the study were identified as IED sufferers.

"Obviously, the disorder is more widespread than we thought," stated Coccaro, who then added, "You got a problem with that?!"

To determine if you might be an IED sufferer, answer "Yes" or "No" to each of the following scenarios:

1) When my computer crashes, I try to remain calm by thinking about the solitude and freedom of skydiving, descending through the clouds, and then letting my computer drop from 1,800 ft. into a lake.

2) On at least one occasion, I have attempted to affect change and contact someone in our nation's capitol by yelling at the top of my lungs.

3) I find it difficult to remain calm when, after paying $40 for gas, I have to pay another 25 cents for AIR.

4) Because I have been told it is an important social issue facing our nation, I am frustrated by my inability to really care where the heck Katie Couric goes.

And lastly,

5) Recently, I have been performing yoga as a way to limber up before handing out a good butt-whoopin'.

OK, tally your score by giving yourself one point for "No" and two points for "Yes."

Answer key: If you took the time to actually answer any of these questions you are an IED sufferer. According to the study, you should go ahead and join the millions of Americans already on some type of anti-depressant. And if you have a problem with that, you KNOW where you can find me!

I'll be waiting right here in the lotus position.

Somewhere in Atlanta is a landscaper without gas

After years of creating ad campaigns for high-profile companies like Coca-Cola, a good friend of mine in Atlanta has decided to do what many successful advertising people do when they reach that point in their careers where they can simply LOOK at a new product and, without any hesitation whatsoever, begin to vomit:

And that, of course, is to go into the lawn care business.

Like some of history's most successful entrepreneurs, Fred spent time studying his new market, its trends and the competition before assembling a detailed business plan, which he described as follows: "I bought a lawnmower."

On the surface, this may not sound like much of a business plan. But as Fred pointed out, what sets him apart from other lawn care enterprises around Atlanta — aside from his limited grasp of Spanish — is the TYPE of mower and equipment he's using. While other lawn care enterprises utilize gas-powered equipment and emit enough exhaust smoke to divert air traffic as far west as Alabama, "I use manual-reel mowers, electric gear and hand tools in order to reduce emissions and promote more responsible, planet-friendly yard work," Fred explained.

I considered this for a moment — this idea of promoting more responsible, environmentally-conscious yard work — before responding with, "Hahahahahahahahahahaha!"

"No, really," said Fred, who cited an EPA study that showed that a piece of gas-powered lawn gear actually creates more pollution than a car. "Unless it's a Gremlin," he added.

When I considered that it usually takes a full hour for the lawnmower smoke to leave our yard (a process I sometimes hurry along with a leaf blower), I realized he could be right. On any given weekend there are at least a dozen people around our neighborhood mowing lawns, edging grass, using gas-powered weed eaters, burning yard debris and branches (and, occasionally, portions of their fences and/or shrubbery), then tidying up with leaf blowers the size of a Lear Jet engine. After which they take a moment to enjoy their handiwork by — what else? — smoking a cigarette. Somehow, I have become desensitized to all of this, and the fact that our Labrador has passed out three times in the last month while relieving himself in the front yard on mowing days, possibly for periods long enough to cause permanent brain damage.

Sadly, we'll never know how much damage because, as I mentioned, he's a Lab.

I told Fred he was on to something big and asked how the business was going. He admitted he had miscalculated and started too late in the season. As a result, "MowGreen" hasn't really taken off yet despite an aggressive ad campaign.

"Plus, I think most of the fliers we put around the neighborhood ended up in a portable toilet at a construction site down the street," he said. "We used recycled paper, so at least we're still having an impact on the environment."

Fortunately, because of his years of experience in advertising, Fred saw the need to diversify his marketing campaign in order to keep it from...

Well, going down the toilet.

In addition to creating a website (www.mowgreen.net) and blog to explain his services and communicate with clients, he also came up with a high-profile promotional plan to spread his idea of "planet-friendlier" lawn care by offering a free mow to the first celebrity who asks.

"As long as it's within driving distance," said Fred. "If it's really far away, they'll have to split the gas with me. And possibly let me sleep over."

(Note: This offer excludes Joan Rivers.)

In the meantime, Atlantans, when you think of lawn care I hope you'll support the environment by thinking of Fred. Unless, of course, you're in a portable toilet.

Don't Panic. It's just your toilet paper getting smaller

I have a friend in Atlanta who I consider an astute observer. The kind of person who is aware of even the most subtle changes in routine or appearance. Which is why it came as no surprise when I received the following e-mail from him:

I think they shrunk my toilet paper.

According to "Derf" (Note: Out of respect for his privacy I have created a fictitious name that should not be held up to a mirror), his recent purchase of Scott toilet paper seemed "more narrow than normal." Because many of you are probably reading this over breakfast, I will not explain how he reached this conclusion, nor will I ever be caught without two-ply toilet paper should he come to visit. What I will tell you is that, after reading about his deductive process, I felt a need to go clean my hands, which I did, by dipping them in kerosene and lighting them on fire.

However, once the flames were out, my newspaper instincts took over and began pursuing the truth, in the tradition of other great investigative journalists (from the *New York Times*), by rolling up my sleeves and doggedly typing the words "smaller toilet paper" on Google. As I expected, "Derf" was right. According to a recent public announcement from Scott, the company has narrowed its sheets by nearly an inch. In my opinion, this decision seems to fly in the face of our nation's widening bottoms. (If that last sentence makes it in, you'll know my editor was asleep.)

Scott says the reason it can make its sheets smaller is because its new version has a "longer-lasting, softer and more absorbent texture" that was "extensively tested by consumers before being introduced to the market."

OK, first things first. I think we can all agree on one thing: Ewwwwwww.

Secondly, I admit I have no experience in the area of product testing, except for trying to avoid those freakishly enthusiastic people handing out free samples at Costco, some of whom — and I'm not proud of this — I've gotten past by performing a ninja roll. Following that train of thought, I have to wonder what qualifies as "extensively tested" when it comes to toilet paper, and whether there's a connection between the free food samples I'm constantly being offered while shopping, and the questionnaire I found hanging in the bathroom stall during my last visit.

I suppose I should be thankful there wasn't someone in THERE handing out free samples. Because, to be quite honest, performing a ninja roll at that particular time would've been out of the question.

Right now, you're probably asking yourself: What point is he trying to make?

I know I am.

Just kidding! Hahahahaha! Of course I have a point! I'm a journalist! It's my job to have a point; something thought provoking and informative that ties everything together with clarity and insight.

In this case, however, I think it might be too much to absorb.

Warning: Do not cover face with newspaper while driving

There was a time when manufacturers included warnings on their products as a way to provide useful information that could potentially save our lives.

Or, at the very least, our eyebrows and/or stomach lining.

However, at some point, that all changed. As far I can tell, it happened about the same time McDonald's had to cough-up a McMillion dollars to the lady who didn't realize that spilling hot coffee on yourself while behind the wheel of a car can lead to a condition commonly known as "The Open-Road Lap Dance."

Taking a deeper look, that condition is really just an extension of the more common rule known as "cause and effect," which states:

'Cause I'm dumb enough to place hot coffee next to the most vulnerable spot on my entire body, I am, in effect, going to do something even dumber by spilling it there.

Probably before I leave the drive-thru.

Though the woman claimed to be unfamiliar with either of these two concepts, she WAS familiar with the judicial system, and how her coffee mishap could lead to litigation and a new home in the Hamptons. That landmark decision opened the floodgates to a barrage of wrongful injury cases aimed at sending a clear message to American businesses:

We will buy your products.

We will use your products.

And, God willing, we will hurt ourselves with your products and retire early.

Because of this, manufacturers have been forced to hire consultants who do nothing but sit around trying to think up ways stupid people could hurt themselves. Recently, I was able to gain limited access to one of these brain-storming sessions (limited, of course, out of fear that I might hurt myself), and while I'm not at liberty to divulge the company's identity, I can tell you that there are at least five ways a stupid person could fatally injure themselves with a bar of Irish Spring. This topic stems from an actual warning label my friend discovered on the handle of his son's stroller:

Always remove child before folding.

First of all, I'd like to point out that this time-saving tip was NOT included anywhere in the instruction manual when my kids had strollers. Had I known how much easier this makes things, I probably would've used it a heck of a lot more. Instead, after spending nearly an hour trying to pry my son loose from the grip of his $200 stroller, I simply stopped using it.

I'm kidding of course. I never, at any time, actually folded any of my children up in their stroller! At least not without their written consent (which, by the way, my attorney keeps on file). This lead to the discovery of more examples of warning labels aimed at those who would otherwise be eliminated through the process of "natural selection."

This first one appeared on the bottom of a Band-Aids box:

For serious injuries please seek medical attention.

Good to know, at least until Band-Aid comes out with a super-absorbent "severed limb" selection, preferably in the less obvious "skin-colored" tone that I can wear to work.

This next one was on a box of nails:

Do not swallow nails: May cause irritation!

And that's just on the way down. Imagine how irritable you'll be during next morning's bowel movement.

This last warning was on a can of primer:

Do not spray contents into face.

That's right. If you seem to be going through a lot more paint than you expected, and your retina's are primer gray, try flipping the nozzle the opposite direction. I hope this has been helpful.

Don't say you haven't been warned.

Getting older: It's a slippery slope down a falling ladder

From time to time it's good to give yourself a refresher course on the basic laws of physics. This weekend I chose gravity. I did this by climbing to the top of an extension ladder and, for the sake of science and a clogged rain gutter, riding it to the ground while screaming. This impromptu experiment helped underscore several known principals of time and space, such as:

Given the space of 12 vertical feet there still isn't enough time to call 9-1-1 before hitting the ground.

My experiment proved this is true even if, as a safety precaution based on prior experience of yourself doing stupid things, you have entered the first two digits of 9-1-1 before climbing the ladder. In theory, there should have been plenty of time between points "A" and "B" to punch a single digit on my cell phone. Possibly even leaving enough time to speed-dial my favorite coffee shop and order a double latte for the ambulance ride. However, the experiment also proved that somewhere between "A" and "B" there was a previously undiscovered point, which is that I haven't gotten any smarter or more coordinated with age. This was demonstrated by the fact that, even with a full 2.5 seconds of "hang" time, I could not get my thumb, which was poised over the "1" button on my cell phone, to engage until after I was lying on my back looking up at our rain gutter — at which point my thumb locked onto the button and remained there for the next 30 minutes until the phone battery gave out.

In summary, we can conclude that Sir Isaac Newton was correct when, in 1667, he revealed his Third Law of Gravity: *What goes up must eventually come down, particularly if it involves a klutz on a ladder.*

Given that my ankle took the full impact of my ladder-ride-for-science, my wife urged me to have it checked out immediately. She said this was the logical thing to do and assured me it had nothing to do with my being nearly 40. I asked what she meant by that and she explained, being a man, I might see an immediate trip to the hospital as a sign of getting older.

I laughed, then assured her I was totally secure with my age. To prove it, I would go see the doctor.

"When?" she asked.

"As soon as there's reason to."

That reason came the next morning, when I woke up to find someone had surgically removed my ankle and, at some point during the night, replaced it with an eggplant. Two hours later, I was in the exam room, where I was told my X-rays looked good.

No broken bones; just a really bad sprain.

"However, I think I see the beginning stages of... Arthritis

...arthritis

...arthritis

It's in your lower ankle, right below that... Bone spur

...bone spur

...bone spur."

He pointed to a couple of spots on the X-ray as proof that I was, in fact, falling apart from the ankles up. Though he didn't come out and say it, I could tell by his expression I'd be lucky to make it back to my car before crumbling into a pile of dried carbon with an ankle brace. Suddenly, my life was flashing before me. I wanted to call my family to tell them I loved them. If only I hadn't burned out the "1" pad on my cell phone!

"Mr. Hickson?"

"..huh?"

"I see on your chart you'll be 40 this year."

"It's true."

"I've been there. Relax — you're just getting to the good part."

During the ride home I realized he was right. Sure, I might be hobbling around for a while but eventually my ankle will heal. Before long I'll be back to doing all the things I normally do.

Assuming, of course, none of those things involve a ladder.

Parenting Is As Easy As One, Two...Scream

(My fountain of knowledge is an open ~~bar~~ book)

Flaming Pop-Tarts, pets wearing boxer shorts means it's back-to-school time

Now that school is back in session, we have settled into our normal routine here at the Hickson household. This routine is based on a strict time schedule that my wife and I have developed over the years to ensure that, each morning at precisely 7 a.m., all hell breaks loose. This includes — but isn't limited to — at least one person (or family pet) running through the house in boxer shorts, and my wife locking the bathroom door for some "quiet time" while heating a Pop-Tart with her hair dryer.

Though we know this pandemonium could be avoided by just getting up a little earlier, the fact is, I am the only morning person in our family. As anyone in this situation already knows, this is sort of like being the only lamb at a coyote picnic. In order to stay alive, you must keep moving while, at the same time, drawing as little attention to yourself as possible. What makes this especially difficult is that, from time to time, I find it necessary to actually speak. Usually, I'm just trying to determine our progress by way of a simple question like: *Why is the dog wearing cowboy boots?*

That's when all eyes suddenly turn to me. And these are not happy eyes.

No....These are the eyes of pod people.

They are hungry. They are confused. And they know I am not one of them.

Fortunately, this is about the time the core temperature of my wife's strawberry Pop-Tart reaches its flash point, causing it to burst into flames and, consequently, be dropped into the commode. The dog, familiar with this routine, then races across the living room in his cowboy boots and runs head-first into the bathroom door, which my wife — also familiar with this routine — has locked again.

Given that I have nothing to compare it to, I have no idea whether our morning routine is considered "normal" by most standards. However, judging from the cereal commercials I've seen on television, I'd have to say no. That's because getting my son to eat a "well-balanced breakfast" isn't nearly as important to me as making sure he leaves the house without his pants on backwards. This often means deciding between making a nutritious breakfast of juice, toast, cereal and an egg, or tackling him when he least expects it so I can verify that his pants are in position and completely functional.

After looking through some self-help books and trying to pick up some tips, I came to the conclusion that, for the most part, these people are single. I know this because of suggestions like:

Set aside some quiet time each morning for you and your children to talk about your goals for the day. This will help your whole family begin each morning with a clear direction!

Better yet, why not provide each reader with clear directions to your home so they can set aside time to come over and whack you with this book? The only author who seemed to have a handle on things AND be an actual (living) parent was a retired lawyer who lived in a small town in West Virginia with her husband of 24 years, four children — and a full-time English nanny.

Of course, there was nothing in the book suggesting what to do in case you couldn't afford a nanny, nor was there any indication that one would be appointed for me. nWhat this means is that we'll stick with the routine we already have.

At least until the dog stops wearing cowboy boots.

You can't swim with one hand on your woggle

I wasn't born to swim. This became evident early in life after habitually swimming into the side of pools, then immediately sinking head-first to the bottom. A number of factors can be attributed to my being hydro-challenged, beginning with the fact that I can't actually breathe under water. This traumatic realization was made one morning after watching *Aqua-Man* on T.V. and then, as a test to ascertain my level of super powers, trying to inhale running tap water from the kitchen faucet. The experience was a wake-up call, and forced me to admit that the closest I'd ever get to being an underwater super hero is if "dog paddling" and "consuming large amounts of pool water" qualified as special powers. Needless to say, I wasn't exactly waiting for a call from *The Super Friends*.

Twenty-five years later, I'm still not much of a swimmer, which led me to enroll our son in swimming classes; just because I'm not a good swimmer doesn't mean that my son shouldn't be able to be used as a flotation device. For those of you thinking of signing your kids up for swimming lessons, there are a number of things you can do to prepare your child — and yourself — for getting the most out of class.

First, swimming trunks that enter a body of water too quickly will deploy like a driver's side air bag. Add cargo-style pockets, and your child will be lucky to touch the water at all.

Secondly, if your child uses a "woggle" or "noodle" to float on in the water, wean him off of it now. Aside from adding a false sense of security, it's nearly impossible to swim efficiently with one hand on your woggle.

And that's as far as I'm going with that joke.

One way to accomplish this transition is by trimming away small portions of the woggle in the weeks leading up to the first day of class. This worked well for our son, who showed up for his first lesson with a piece of green styrofoam roughly the size of a Lumberjack Biscuit. We will complete the final step in this elimination process next week, when we replace what's left of his woggle with an actual biscuit — which will then swell up and break apart in the pool.

Something a lot of people aren't aware of is that chlorine actually causes temporary deafness in adults. This affliction is an indirect result caused by the fact that your child — along with 20 to 30 others — will be SCREAMING EVERY SYLLABLE THAT LEAVES THEIR MOUTHS THE ENTIRE TIME THEY ARE IN THE POOL. Unless you leave the building all together (or are immune to high-decibel sounds because you regularly work on the deck of an aircraft carrier), ear plugs aren't a bad idea.

The most important thing, of course, is that your children learn to swim, especially if they live anywhere near a body of water.

Your children will thank you.

I will thank you.

And most importantly, *The Super Friends* will thank you.

Which reminds me; they still haven't called yet. I guess until Aqua Man hangs up his fins, there won't be a need for Dog-Paddling Woggle Man to flail into action.

And for all our sakes, let's hope there never will be.

For a father, it's never too early to begin sabotaging your daughter's dating prospects

I had a frightening dream last night. In it, I was wearing an alpine yodeler outfit. The kind with the brown shorts, the white knee-high socks, and the little cap with the feather in it.

Wait, it gets scarier.

I was on vacation with my family. Our kids were older, and my daughter had a boyfriend with her. A space ship landed, and an alien came out yodeling the theme from *Close Encounters*. My wife was calling to me, trying to be heard over the yodeling alien, when I finally heard her cry out in utter desperation:

The cat likes to play checkers.

As you might expect, I woke up in a cold sweat, unable to shake that vivid, terrifying image of...

That's right: My daughter with a boyfriend.

True, she's only 12 years old right now. But time passes quickly, and in another 15 years she'll begin dating. To me, this dream was a clear indication that I should begin preparing myself for the inevitable. When I explained this to my wife, she laughed.

Hard.

I've seen drunken pirates with more emotional restraint.

For some reason, mothers are better able to deal with the whole dating prospect. I think this is because, statistically speaking, they aren't men. They have no idea what it's like to be a 15-year-old male. Well, I DO, which is why I will personally be screening each one of my daughter's potential suitors before rendering my final decision to boot each one of them right off the front porch. This may sound harsh, but, in the long run, will save my daughter the embarrassment of having to explain why her father has latched himself to the underbelly of her date's car like Robert De Niro in *Cape Fear*.

Or why the only parties she can attend are costume parties, where the theme is Camelot, and all males are required to dress in full plate armor and a cod piece. If necessary, I will forge them myself. No cod piece? No date. I say this because I've seen what happens to fathers once their daughters begin dating. I have several friends who are just beginning this process. In most cases, this has included talk of buying a new home outside the city, and establishing a refuge for crazed Rottweilers along a moat surrounding the family compound. Even to me, this sounds a bit extreme. At some point, you have to establish a certain level of trust with your daughter. You have to allow her a sense of freedom.

And you have to do it without letting her know she's being followed.

You can try doing it yourself, but there are only so many times you can get away with "accidentally" crossing paths at the movies, Dairy Queen, and an abandoned gravel pit all on the same night.

Because of this, I've already begun interviewing private detectives. You see, to a father, money is no object when it comes to providing his daughter with the false sense of freedom that she deserves.

At least until a) his social security runs out, b) she becomes a national karate champion, c) he becomes a national karate champion, or d) preferably all of the above.

My wife, of course, thinks I'm being totally ridiculous.

"Over protective and irrational," she laughed.

But, as I poignantly reminded her, at least I'm not the one who yelled out "The cat likes to play checkers."

From the mouths of babes: Plenty of reasons for Dad to avoid eye contact with Mom

Few things can turn a pleasant, family drive along the coast into 50 miles of hell with an ocean view faster than when your son 1) says something inappropriate that 2) sounds like it came from his father.

Case in point: While taking a leisurely drive this week, my four-year-old son suddenly blurted out "When I get bigger, I'm gonna have a girlfriend."

Okay, no big deal. With one hand on the wheel, I exchanged a wink with my wife and smirked.

"I'll bet you are, son."

"Yeah! I'm gonna have TWO girlfriends!"

This, of course, brought a raised eye brow from my wife, who smiled and waved a finger at me. Chuckling, I raised my hands in mock defense, then explained to my little Casanova that, if he was a lucky man, he'd have a wife and family some day.

This was apparently the response my wife was looking for because she reached over and took my hand.

"But I'm not gonna have a wife," my son added. "Just a girl friend — then a mean witch will turn her into a wife."

Case in point number two:

There's no place to run in a car.

Being that I was the driver, I had to make sure the road was my primary concern even though my hand, which remained in my wife's possession, had suddenly lost all feeling.

"Where would our son ever get an idea like that, *Dear*?" my wife asked. At that moment, I would've given anything for someone — ANYONE — to get car sick or have a bowel movement.

Or both.

Especially if it was me.

Time stopped as my mind contemplated the proper response, which meant finding just the right combination of words and body language — such as "Marriage Rocks!" and then leaping from the car into the grill of a passing Winnebago. At this point, I turned to the collective wisdom of men gathered through millions of years of evolution. Utilizing this wisdom, I avoided all eye contact by driving as though I was guiding a nuclear sub through heavily mined waters (which, in essence, I was) and, clearing my throat, said in a distinct voice:

Absolutely nothing.

That's right. As I said, this is the collective wisdom of men.

I didn't say it would actually work.

"*Well..?*" my wife said, squeezing my hand even tighter. (I know this only because my daughter suddenly poked her head between the seats and said, "Eeewww, Dad's hand looks really weird.")

It was clear that I wasn't going to get out of this without some kind of distraction, such as a 50-car pile-up. That left only one option, which meant going against everything I'd been taught as a man and, regardless of the consequences, actually saying something in my defense. Taking a deep breath, I broke my gaze from the road just long enough to make brief eye contact with my wife's forehead before offering my confession:

"Please don't be mad, but I think he got it from Barney and Friends."

"Eeewww — Dad's hand!" my daughter screamed.

"I'm serious!" I pleaded. "The Story Lady — she has weird books! She's from Jamaica!"

My wife wasn't buying it (even though I really do have concerns about someone with a magic door and — as far as I can tell — no permanent address).

The truth is, we still have no idea where our son came up with such a ridiculous statement, which, I'd like to add, in no way reflects the opinion of any married man I know. I'd also like to say to any unmarried men who might be reading this, when you DO meet that special someone, use the collective wisdom of men.

And find yourself a good hand surgeon.

Unless you are taking it with you, never sit in a kindergartner's chair

Though it had been five years since our daughter's first parent/teacher conference, my wife and I felt the same familiar anxiety as we entered our son's kindergarten classroom, sat across from his teacher, and realized:

Neither of us is getting out of our tiny chair without having it surgically removed.

This is what is going through the mind of every parent at every conference for the first two years of their child's education. Sure, we may be smiling and nodding and looking at samples of our child's work while listening to assessments regarding key areas in their curricular activity, but, in reality, we're just trying to keep our tiny chairs from becoming impacted. When a voice from the intercom interrupted our meeting and briefly called the teacher away (possibly to help with an emergency chair extraction), my wife immediately turned to me and asked if I'd heard anything that had been said during the past 10 minutes. I told her I'd basically missed everything after, "Hello Mr. and Mrs. Hickson. Please have a seat."

My wife, who was obviously upset by this, asked what we were going to do. I told her, from what I remember, at this stage kindergarten was about basic numbers and writing their names, and assured her that our son was probably doing just fine.

"I mean about these *chairs*!" she hissed.

I told her I didn't have a plan. However, if we were going to come up with one it needed to be now, before the teacher returned, or before our chairs were no longer visible — whichever came first. We decided the first part of our plan would be to, very carefully, try standing up. This was achieved after several attempts, the last of which involved a maneuver similar to something I saw in a Jackie Chan movie. I can't really be more specific than that because 1) this may go to trial, and 2) my wife would kill me.

Not necessarily in that order.

The second part of our plan was to replace our chairs with something less invasive. We agreed it would have to be a subtle change. Something that would allow our conference to continue without drawing attention to the fact that we were no longer sitting six inches off the floor with our knees up around our ears, like a pair of grasshoppers ready to leap over the table.

Knowing our time was running out, we made a quick scan of the room and improvised as best we could. When our son's teacher returned, it was apparent that our plan had failed. Partly because the switch wasn't one hundred percent complete.

But mostly it was because, in our haste, we hadn't taken into account that the SpongeBob Squarepants bean bag chair — while tough enough to survive several years of hyperactive kindergartners — was never intended to withstand the impact of two full grown adults leaping onto it simultaneously. The result was a loud pop, followed by a burst of high velocity bean bag buckshot peppering the chalkboard and a good portion of the reading area. If not for being shielded by an oversized world atlas, there's a good chance Biffy the mouse would not be alive today.

Once the bean dust settled, the only thing left to do was untangle ourselves, climb to our feet, retrieve our tiny chairs, and sit on them with as much dignity as possible. Given that we had none left, the rest of our conference went very quickly. On behalf of my wife and myself, I'd like to apologize for what happened. In the future, we will be happy to sit on whatever chairs are made available to us.

Assuming we're allowed to sit at all.

Parents: Lung capacity key when choosing inflatable toy

We live less than 15 minutes from our favorite lake. The problem is, it also happens to be everyone else's favorite lake, which means in order to get a spot within the vicinity of actual water, you have to be there when the gates open at noon and participate in something similar to the Oklahoma Land Rush. It's not uncommon to see small children strapped to inflatable toys and tossed ahead of the crowd in order to claim prime territory. As a parent, it's not a gamble I'm willing to take with my child. Especially since, as a general rule, it only counts if your child is in an upright position once they skid to a stop.

The good news is that once the initial pandemonium is over, things generally settle into a state of peaceful co-existence as, one by one, parents begin passing out while blowing up inflatable toys. Sadly, the evolutionary process has not been able to keep up with the growing demand for larger and larger inflatable animals. Unless you are a pearl diver by trade, chances are your lung capacity is nowhere near what it needs to be in order to fully inflate your child's favorite water toy. This has created a generation of children who are routinely disappointed by their parents during the formative "summer vacation" years, when parents are trying to build a foundation of trust and respect — something that's hard to do when your child sees you pass out facedown between the tail fins of a plastic humpback whale.

I speak from experience. My son's favorite water toy is an inflatable "Shamu" that, when fully inflated, can be seen from space. Though I consider myself relatively fit (and by that I mean relative to other people standing in line with me at Burger King), I have not yet, in a single sitting, been able to inflate my son's whale beyond the point it stops resembling a decomposing whale carcass. That's about the time dizziness and suspected cerebral hemorrhage force me to breathe pure oxygen — which, fortunately, is now available to parents in single-use canisters at the snack bar.

Sure, we've tried inflating the whale before driving to the lake.

Once.

We quickly discovered there wasn't enough room in our mini van to fit a fully inflated whale and both children. This left us with three options:

1) Bring the whale and leave the kids.

2) Stay home and let the kids drive the whale to the lake themselves.

3) Strap the kids to the top of the van and hope for the best.

We went with our third option, but strapped the whale on top instead of the children when my wife raised an important point:

Aerodynamically speaking, the whale would give us better gas mileage.

I'm no Boy Scout, but I know how to tie a knot. I stand by that to this day. Just as I did in court, when I argued that it was a single, unexpected 120 mph wind gust — and not defective knot tying — that caused a nine-foot inflatable whale to go tumbling into oncoming traffic. Thankfully, no one was injured, although a family of six on its way back from the local aquarium is still in counseling. Because of that experience, and a court order, we save the "Shamu" inflation process for the lake.

Naturally, the same goes for the deflation process which, in many ways, is even more demoralizing. That's because in order to get all the air out, I — a grown, 38-year-old man — must roll around on top of a plastic sea mammal while holding onto a tiny air nodule located in a region SOMEONE should have realized was going to look highly inappropriate. In addition to depleting any respectability I had in the eyes of my children, it has also created an image my wife admits "Is hard to get past sometimes."

However, in the end, ask any father who wants his kids to have fun and he'll tell you the same thing: It's just part of the rising cost of inflation.

If a man is attacked by his tent in the forest, should he make a sound?

Our family loves to go camping. In fact, we make sure to get out and pitch our tent — without fail — once a year. Traditionally, this takes place during the busy Labor Day Weekend so that as many people as possible can witness a grown man being attacked by his own tent.

In my defense, I have to say our tent is very large; especially when it is lying flat on the ground.

If I hadn't lost the step-by-step instructions that came with it, I'm sure the assembly process would be a lot easier because, as a man, I could use them to, step-by-step, blame everything on having lousy instructions.

What this means is that over the Labor Day Weekend my handiwork will again be mistaken for a hot air balloon that has crash-landed into our family's camp site. I bought this tent 20 years ago while living in Texas. As you know, everything is bigger there — including tents — which is why I tried to find the smallest model available. This turned out to be a tent called Quick Camp, which was a handy, two-compartment structure roughly the size of a jet hanger. Despite its size, the salesman assured me that the assembly process was very simple. He said that the entire thing could be erected in less than 20 minutes with a little planning. And he was right.

As long as our plan included staying out of the tent.

For some reason, it collapses on me every time I go inside. I'm not talking about an inconvenient buckling of the walls; this is more like an instantaneous implosion of water-resistant nylon that required the assistance of a search and rescue team:

"Listen up! Team 'A' will start at the west quadrant near the mosquito netting. Team 'B' will take the dogs and follow the perimeter until we can —"

[Woof! Woof!]

"Quick — over HERE! I think someone's moving under this giant door flap!"

In spite of these experiences, I still feel it's important for our family to go camping together. That's because, as a parent, I know our kids really hate it. I mean, sure — it's pretty exciting while Dad is flopping around under 200 yards of nylon. But once that's over, and I've decided that we're all going to sleep out under the stars LIKE REAL PIONEERS! they begin to realize that everything they know about civilization has been left behind.

And by "everything," I mean cell phones and television. In the primitive world of camping there is no Jersey Shore. No American Idol.

There is only dirt.

And time.

And if they're lucky, enough fire to cook a marshmallow.

Eventually, as the shock of not having their devices wears off, children enter what I feel is the most important phase of their camping experience: Realizing that we, the parents, are the key to their survival.

This epiphany starts the moment I pull out the old camp stove, give it a few pumps, then light the picnic table on fire. In that instant, the only thing that matters is reaching out together as a family and finding the nearest fire extinguisher.

So, during Labor Day Weekend, if you happen to be in the neighborhood, feel free to stop by our tent.

I'm sure the rescue team could probably use your help.

It takes more than the help of G.I. Joe to break the power of Barbie's mojo

The act of "playing" is a crucial part of how a child establishes self image and a basic understanding of the world. I know this because, as a progressive father of today, I have read extensively about this very topic — which is why I progressively freaked out when I found my son playing in the shower with a Barbie doll.

It wasn't the fact that he was playing with it that bothered me, it was the fact that it was still completely intact. This is something I don't expect from a child who routinely disassembles my office chair and a good portion of my desk in less than four minutes using nothing but a three-piece *Bob the Builder* tool kit.

I decided something needed to be done. It was time to enlist the help of an old friend; it was time for G.I. Joe to break Barbie's mojo.

Looking back on my childhood, I spent countless hours playing with G.I. Joe, The Six Million Dollar Man and Big Jim. And let me just clarify right now that they were all Action Figures.

Not dolls.

That's right. dolls do NOT have muscles, dragon tattoos, and/or weapons. Dolls have "accessories" like hair brushes, a change of clothes, and red pumps. *Action figures* have bionic powers, or

"Karate Chop Action," or one chrome arm that detaches to become a rocket-fueled pogo stick. I've never seen a commercial with Barbie hanging from a helicopter fighting for mankind against Dr. Steel and his deadly eye rays. Although, to her credit, Barbie does have a Winnebago that folds out into a tanning salon, which she uses to avoid harmful UV rays.

I should also clarify that, as a kid, playing with action figures wasn't always about fighting; It was also about tolerance and acceptance. When G.I. Joe lost part of his head in a tragic Fourth of July sky-rocket explosion in 1972, Big Jim and Six Million Dollar Man just pretended not to notice when he came back wearing Spiderman's head. I sincerely doubt that Barbie's friends would be as accepting under the same circumstances.

Along with my decision to purchase a G.I. Joe for my son, I thought it might be helpful to familiarize myself with Barbie so that I might better understand how to exploit her weaknesses. Finding information on Barbie is very easy. That's because she has at least 40 bazillion people with websites devoted to her. (Note: Only six of these people are actually young enough to justify being THAT enthusiastic about a plastic doll; the other 994 bazillion should really consider moving their Barbie collection to a well-ventilated area.)

I started my search by looking back on Barbie's history. That's when I discovered some unsettling "coincidences" between her and G.I. Joe which, if nothing else, might help Ken in the event of a divorce. For example:

In 1974, Barbie's figure became bustier AND completely bendable for the first time. That same year, G.I. Joe coincidently developed Kung Fu grip. And when Barbie was going through her mini-skirt and halter-top phase?

That's right: Say hello to Eagle-Eye G.I. Joe.

In light of this discovery, it seemed to me that G.I. Joe's moral standing has been tarnished. I can not, in good conscience, encourage my son to develop his self image with the help of G.I. Gigolo. And since Six Million Dollar Man and Big Jim have long since retired, I've been left with only one choice when it comes to filling that void. It's going to take a little work, but I'm hoping to have Big Six Dollar Ken ready for my son's next birthday.

Don't push the (belly) button

As with most explanations I find myself giving as a parent, things started with a simple "No."

In this case, it was: "No, you can't save chewing gum in your belly button." My son then countered with the inevitable "Why?"

"Because it's gross," I explained, then added for good measure: "What if it gets stuck?"

"It won't, Dad."

"It might — so take it out."

A roll of the eyes, droop of the shoulders. "But why-y-y-y-y?"

"Because I said so."

Eventually, it always comes down to that answer, which isn't an answer at all. But for some reason it seems to do the trick.

At least it used to.

Apparently, my son had awakened a little wiser — and with a better understanding of the difference between battles and wars.

Oh joy.

It wasn't long after my victory at the Battle of Bubble Gum Ridge that I noticed my son fidgeting with something.

"What are you doing, son?"

"Trying to get this marble to stay in my belly button."

His troops had been assembled and were now flanking my border. War had been declared, and I was still looking for a musket.

"You shouldn't do that. Your belly button isn't made for holding marbles," I said.

He looked up at me, launching the first of his newly acquired smart bombs. "What's it made for?"

I was still tamping "because I said so" down my rifle barrel when the first missile struck, taking out a large chunk of my artillery and forcing a new battle plan.

"Actually, that's how you used to eat while you were in your mom's tummy," I countered, and managed a momentary lull in the attack as his forces regrouped.

"How did I DO that?"

"You guys shared a tube between your stomach and hers."

Taking advantage of the disruption, I moved my troops forward and positioned them for a final assault. "Onions, cabbage, spinach, it didn't matter — whatever she ate, YOU ate. "

The marble dropped from his belly button to the porch step with a thud. "Eew-w-w!"

In the distance, I could see his battalion backing away from the ridge.

"If you keep doing that," I said, "we'll have to hook it back up."

"Gross!"

With that, I heard the call of retreat as his troops ran from the porch, passed the dog and into the back yard.

Later that afternoon, sitting at his plastic, multi-colored picnic table, we entered into negotiations over soda and chopped olive sandwiches. We agreed that if he left his belly button alone, I wouldn't reattach his umbilical cord.

With our truce in place, I walked away from the meeting secure in the balance of power we had established — and keenly aware of the advancements he could make by morning.

Dignity is easier to swallow with hot sauce

Within our lives there are certain moments that inspire a deeper understanding of ourselves. I experienced such an epiphany yesterday morning during a quiet moment of introspection, crouched in the backyard, sprinkling dog poop with hot sauce.

To clarify, I was not attempting to create the world's most disgusting Cajun appetizer. According to a book on canine behavior, this would train our dog to avoid eating his "leftovers." It was in that moment, while clutching a bottle of Tabasco and trying not to be seen by my neighbors, I came to realize that somewhere along the way providing our dog with decent manners had become more important than maintaining my personal dignity.

How did this happen?

I'm a 46-year-old man who survived the diaper phases of two children — both of whom were heavy eaters. I've had my share of high profile, low-dignity diaper changes, one of which required quick thinking, commando-like precision, and a paper plate.

I've sat across from my four-year-old son at a busy restaurant in downtown San Francisco, handed him a cheese stick appetizer, and watched him yak up what appeared to be everything he'd consumed since graduating to solid foods. I tried to salvage the situation by waiting for a lull in gastro activity and then racing him into the men's room. And let me just say that had the rest rooms been clearly marked, we probably would've made it.

What got me through those times, of course, was knowing, as a parent, I could look forward to eventually becoming an embarrassment to my children once they entered middle school.

However, as I crouched over our Labrador's latest pile with my Tabasco bottle at the ready, one thought kept running through my mind:

You can't embarrass a dog. Particularly one with questionable intelligence.

This meant I had either (a) matured to the point of not caring what others thought of me based on their own one-dimensional perception, or (b) succumbed to the realization that the last of my dignity had been wrung out into a mop bucket in San Francisco. In either case, it meant I had moved on to a new phase in my life. A time that will eventually prepare me for my later years, when I'm secure enough in myself that the opinions of others — or even the basic rules of traffic — no longer matter. However, reaching that level of self-assuredness is still years away, which is why, after noticing I'd been crouched over the same pile for several minutes, I quickly sprinkled it and moved on.

As far as I can tell, Stanley is no longer interested in his “leftovers.” I know this because he has stopped coming in from outside and standing with his tongue in the water bowl. At the same time, it's proven to be a trade-off since I can’t put Tabasco on my eggs without getting queasy.

The important thing is that the experience has allowed me to achieve some personal growth, thanks to a few moments of introspection about fodderhood.

I repeat: Aliens have NOT invaded your children – It’s just Fathers’ Day

Soon it will be Fathers’ Day, and as any father will tell you, it’s a very special day. That’s because it allows you to see what it would be like if your children came from another planet. On Father’s Day, children are required (and I’m pretty sure this is an actual law) to do things they would otherwise only do if there was some serious chocolate involved.

It is essentially a day similar to how you envisioned each day would be, back before you actually had children; back before reality set in, and you came to realize that, although insanity didn’t previously run in your family, there was a good chance it would be starting with you. For example, on Fathers’ Day, there’s always enough hot water for my shower. That means plenty of time to wash-up, shave, and even get the mirror foggy so that, by squinting, I sort of look like Brad Pitt in the shower. Squinting.

That's on Fathers' Day.

On normal days, the hot water lasts just long enough for me to realize that, in the time it takes for me to squint, I'm already OUT OF HOT WATER.

This is because I usually take a shower after my daughter, who, at age nine, defies the natural laws of physics by requiring close to 700 gallons of hot water to wash a surface area equal to three fruit roll-ups. Though I've tried to explain to her that most sea mammals get by on less water in their entire lifetime than she consumes in a single shower, she only listens to me one day a year.

Which brings us to Fathers' Day rule number two: Children actually listen to Dad the first time he says something.

Again, this goes back to those early dreams of fatherhood, when a raised brow was all that you'd need to bring order out of chaos. In reality, of course, that raised brow has now become part of a nervous tick that is a direct result of repeating yourself so many times that you've begun to sound like Dustin Hoffman in *Rainman.*

But this isn't the case on Fathers' Day.

That's right; when we go out to breakfast, my children will listen the very first time I tell them to stop eating sugar packets — at which point they will, instead, politely begin consuming crayons, place mats and/or whatever happens to be stuck under the table. I think it's important to note that what makes Fathers' Day different from Mothers' Day in our house is that, for my wife, the transition into parenthood was easier for her than it was for me. That's because, like many women, she had time to prepare for dealing with children because, well ...

She was married to a man.

I, on the other hand, was NOT.

(Which makes absolutely no sense, but really illustrates my point about that "insanity" thing I mentioned earlier.)

In a way, tomorrow is about children expressing their love and appreciation for their fathers by trying to be on their best behavior. It's a day filled with attentive faces, quiet voices, good manners and no squabbling.

To be honest, I'm glad it only happens once a year. Otherwise I'd go insane.

I love you, kids.

And that's definitely worth repeating.

The Great (hamster) Escape

When you find yourself force-feeding Pepto Bismal into your child's constipated hamster, you figure you've faced one of your greatest challenges as a parent.

But you would be wrong.

"Dad, I can't find Squiggles."

Those words, uttered just three nights later, transformed a quiet, Wednesday evening into a full-scale hamster hunt. Within minutes, our team was assembled around the kitchen table for a briefing.

"There's no telling how long he's been on the outside," I said. "There's a good chance he's already assumed a new identity — perhaps as a mouse or gerbil. Keep you eyes open."

A collective nod from the team.

"We're going to concentrate our efforts in the area between the guest room, hamster cage and attic — It's called cross-triangulation."

"I see... like the Bermuda Triangle," my wife said.

Ignoring her, I gave everyone their assignments, then dispersed the posse. "Let's go do some good!"

Excitedly, our one-year-old broke from the group and rushed through the kitchen with his flashlight, then promptly sat in our dog's water bowl.

Things pretty much went downhill from there.

What makes hamsters so hard to catch is that... well, they're *small.* And they can make themselves even smaller just by thinking about it. They also have no bones and can run in excess of 70 mph. None of this is covered in the handbook, which portrays hamsters as funny, quizzical characters that have special little pouches for storing food on either side of their jaws.

What the book *doesn't* tell you is that those "little pouches" can actually stretch to accommodate food items much larger than the hamster itself — similar to an anaconda's ability to swallow the entire Budweiser draft horse team. It was this thought that surfaced as I scooted belly-first through the crawlspace in our attic with a flashlight wedged between my teeth. I've never been keen on tight spaces, so when I caught the reflection of black eyes peering back at me from the insulation, I wasn't thrilled to discover that my rear end — which had slipped forward through the crawl space with minimal effort — was now meeting resistance similar to an elephant backing into a shower stall.

In front of me, Squiggles was preparing his pouches for something really big.

"He's over here!" I called out in a tone my wife mistakenly thought was a scream.

"Where are you?"

"Purgatory — or the crawl space in our attic, I forget which."

"Can you see him?"

"Yes, and he looks hungry."

"Can you grab him?"

"Not exactly; I can't move."

"Why does this feel familiar?"

"Remember when I got stuck under the Honda..?"

"I was being rhetorical."

"Oh — are you done?"

"Yes."

"Good. Now, how about being helpful and getting me out of here?"

I learned a couple of things during our recovery mission. First, given a choice, hamsters prefer fruit rolls to fat rolls. And second, cooking spray is as effective as WD-40 when it comes to loosening 39-year-olds out of tight spaces. Because of these things, I'm still alive and Squiggles is back in his home.

Now if we could just find the cat...

Family travel is easier, with the help of a licensed forklift operator

This morning, we left on a family vacation with our two children, four train tickets to Seattle, and approximately 700 pounds of luggage. This is a conservative estimate based on my wife's meticulous packing strategy, which means bringing anything that doesn't require the help of a licensed forklift operator. My wife says that we have a responsibility to our children to be prepared for all situations. Apparently, this includes any sudden shift in the Earth's core temperature that would render our entire summer wardrobe useless. For example: Our daughter's clothing options include both a full length fleece-parka AND two-piece bikini, with a choice of sandals, tennis shoes or mud boots.

Being a man, I naturally argue against hauling around this much luggage.

And, being a man, I naturally lose this argument.

This is because my wife is a woman, and therefore prone to supporting her argument with actual facts, such as: If for some reason there really WAS a sudden shift in the Earth's core temperature, I'd never hear the end of it.

As a result, I've learned to keep my mouth shut and just worry about my own packing. This is something I put a lot of thought into. First, because I'm a savvy traveler who refuses to bring anything that isn't absolutely necessary. And second, because my wife leaves me just enough room in our suitcase for a small shaving kit and whatever I can vacuum-pack into a one-quart freezer bag.

However, according to new travel restrictions listed in our Amtrak guide, my wife was forced to drastically cut back on luggage for our trip. This meant making some hard choices between what to take and what to leave behind.

After careful consideration, she decided I didn't need to shave, and pulled my razor kit from the luggage. Amazingly, it was just enough to put us within Amtrak's maximum weight limit.

For a circus train.

According to the restrictions, we still needed to get rid of another 180 pounds of unnecessary baggage.

Fact: I weigh 180 pounds.

But I'm also her husband. That makes me an important part of the family experience because, aside from being the man she loves, I'm also the man who carries my wife's baggage. And as I mentioned, she has a lot of it.

(Fact: We'll be gone by the time this column runs.)

In desperation, we turned to the internet in search of traveling tips. Though we didn't find anything that could help us with our packing, I did discover something just as important — which is that Hooters has its own airlines.

My wife didn't see that as particularly relevant.

I, on the other hand, thought it was very relevant, and supported that argument with my own fact: To assure great service, each flight includes two real-live Hooters girls.

As you can see, this is precisely why I lose these arguments.

I'm happy to say that we were eventually able to meet Amtrak's luggage restrictions and are, at this very moment, on our way to Seattle.

By bus.

We hope to arrive within a few hours of our luggage, which, according to my wife, should be waiting for us at the train station. Of course, it'll be my job to get all of it to the hotel. I'm estimating that this will require a minimum of two taxis — making two trips each — and, quite possibly, the help of two Hooters girls.

Fact: If I should come up missing, start by looking for a 180-pound suitcase.

Bond with your children this Halloween; dress them as portobello mushrooms

It was a conversation that we had been putting off for as long as possible, even though we knew it was our responsibility as parents to sit down and have *The Talk* with our daughter.

"It's better that it come from us rather than her getting crazy ideas from someone at school," my wife reasoned.

And she was right.

So we sat our daughter down and, presenting a united front, held our breath and asked: "What do you want to be for Halloween?"

For some of you, this is an exciting time that allows you to bond with your child by making their Halloween-costume dream come true. For the rest of us, it's a time when we cross our fingers and pray that our child's "Halloween costume dream" is hanging on a rack somewhere at Wal-Mart. Because if it isn't, we'll have to make something, and therefore put our child's emotional health at risk by creating a costume that could potentially scar him or her for life.

After 28 years, I still remember my mother carefully wrapping me in layer after layer of tissue in order to turn me into a frightening replica of The Mummy — and how it took less than five minutes for a light drizzle to turn me into the considerably LESS frightening Soggy Toilet Paper Man. Things weren't much better the following year, when I dressed-up as a pirate and missed out on all of the good candy after spending 45 minutes with my plastic hook stuck in the car door. By the time I hit the streets, all that was left were Sweet Tarts and half-opened rolls of breath mints.

However, as Count Dracula, I knew it was going to be MY year. Aside from maybe swallowing my own fangs, there wasn't much that could go wrong. I remember leaping from the porch and sprinting into the night with my long cape flapping behind me. I remember the sound of my polished shoes clattering across the pavement, and the eerie, greenish tinge of my glow-in-the-dark teeth — particularly as they flew out of my mouth after my cape caught on the neighbors' fence.

Granted, these situations weren't entirely about design flaw. In fact, I'm willing to accept the small role my own flawed coordination skills might've played in all this. However, that only adds to the pressure of coming up with a costume that can be safe, functional and, if necessary, used as a stretcher. Our son is still young enough that he has no real plans when it comes to what he wants to be for Halloween, which is fortunate. Not only because it makes our job easier as parents, but also because there's a good chance he won't remember freaking out last year after the cardboard robot costume I made him cut off the circulation to his arms, rendering them unresponsive for a full two minutes. This was discovered on our third stop of the night, when he tried to lift up his plastic jack-o-lantern for candy and, instead, fell head-first through the screen door.

This year, we're taking no chances; he will be going as a mummified football player, which means he'll be wearing a helmet, lots of pads, AND be confined to a sarcophagus that we can move from door to door. This brings us to our daughter, who likes to put her own spin on things. As of right now, she remains undecided. I will tell you that last Halloween, she was a ghost dog; the year before that, a cowgirl-fairy type of thing. So, being that her big fascinations right now are dinosaurs and mushrooms, I am already envisioning a fossilized portobello mushroom.

Not exactly something we'll find on the rack at Wal-Mart.

I checked.

Life without training wheels

We stood in the parking lot and eyed the expanse of empty, black asphalt.

"If I fall, it's gonna hurt," my daughter said, and absently rubbed at the notion of skinned knees.

I patted her shoulder, advising her to fall slowly — and immediately drew a disapproving stare.

"That's not funny, Dad."

Straddling her bike, which was now absent of training wheels, she surveyed the stretch of pavement from over the handle bars. What lay before her was more than a riding surface free of obstructions; it was her first step toward independence. As with most "firsts" in life, the moment was an uneasy mixture of opportunity and risk, willingness and fate. We both understood that after only a few cranks of the peddle, if she fell, I wouldn't be there to catch her.

As a parent, this would be my first step toward accepting that reality — and the notion of watching her peddle beyond the boundaries of my protection. Whatever mistakes she made, I would be too far away to prevent them; but close enough to see the hurt.

"Got your helmet cinched up good," I asked, making conversation.

"Yep."

"Remember what I told you — "

"I know, I know," she said.

I strummed my knuckles over her helmet. "Then let's do this."

She nodded, took a deep breath, tightened her grip on the handlebars — and rolled forward. While struggling for balance, she swung her feet onto the peddles and began turning the crank. Gradually, her speed increased. Her wobbling diminished. The pavement was passing smoothly beneath her wheels. Her smile broadened.

And I found myself alone on the asphalt, watching her ride away.

In that brief instant between momentum and balance, the world had changed for both of us. For my daughter, it had broadened; for me, it had just gotten a little smaller — or, at least, my influence over it had.

After making a loop through the parking lot, she returned and skidded to a stop in front of me.

"Did you see *that*?" she exclaimed, hands still locked onto the handle bars.

I gave her a squeeze. "Every second. I'm really proud of you."

We looked at each other for a moment, then out over the distance she had just crossed alone. After a moment, she glanced up at me. "I did just what you told me to, Dad, and it worked."

She then repeated the advice I'd given her.

Peddle hard.
Keep your balance.
Don't forget to steer.
And if you fall down, it's OK.

As she said this, I realized that maybe — just maybe — my influence still had a place in her broadening world after all.

Coaching kids? Start with jelly donuts

As I've mentioned before, I'm not very athletic. I made this realization in the third grade, when I was knocked unconscious 32 times playing dodge ball. After that first game, I remember waking up in the nurse's office and being told of a special program for "gifted" athletes who were so special they got to wear a football helmet during recess. Of course, I eventually figured out there was no "special program," and openly expressed my feelings of betrayal when I slammed my helmet on the desk of my high school counselor.

After which I was taken to the hospital with a broken finger.

I live with the memory of being an unathletic child on a daily basis. Particularly when I look in the mirror and see a man whose head still fits into a third-grade football helmet. For this reason, when my daughter asked me to coach her fourth-grade basketball team, I smiled, took her hand, and began faking a seizure. I panicked at the thought of providing guidance to a team of fourth-grade girls, any one of whom could take me to the hole. This includes my daughter, who has inherited a recessive "athletic" gene I call the "monkey factor" because, apparently, it leaps entire family trees. Of course, none of this mattered to my daughter; she just wanted Dad to coach her team. Knowing this attitude would eventually change (possibly by the end of our first practice), I made the decision to put aside my own petty fears and be her team's coach. In addition, I also put aside some petty cash for psychological treatment later.

To prepare myself as coach, I read books about fundamental basketball skills. I talked with other coaches. I installed a tiny basketball hoop over the trash can in my office. Before long, I had gained confidence knowing that with hard work and determination, someone would be able to undo the damage I was doing.

For our first practice, we worked on free throws and lay-ups. I chose these areas because, as everyone knows, they are the most common — and easiest ways — of scoring a basket.

Unless you are me.

As it turns out, repeatedly sending a wad of paper through a six-inch hoop over your trash can doesn't mean you'll be able to sink a regulation basketball from the free throw line. Particularly if your entire team and most of their parents are watching, in some cases using phone cameras to send live images to friends while laughing hysterically. Confident that I had taught my team an important lesson in determination, humility, and the value of having a "shared minutes" plan, we moved on to lay-ups. It was at this point I asked parents to please put their phone cameras away. In addition to the distraction it was causing, there were also safety issues to consider since many parents had now moved under the backboard to get a better angle.

When practice ended a week later (okay, but it felt like a week) we joined hands and reached an important understanding as a team:

The coach has no "game."

Apparently, my players don't see this as a problem. What matters to them most is if I can be trusted, as their coach, to coordinate the snack rotation. I assured them I could, and things have gone well ever since. They bring "game," I bring jelly donuts. My daughter and I are both happy with this arrangement, which has nothing to do with sugary baked goods.

The fact is, we don't even like jelly donuts.

Want to be a better father? Get a bigger grill

Tomorrow morning I will awaken to the sizzle of bacon and eggs, the aroma of freshly brewed coffee, and the shuffle of approaching feet as I lie in bed quietly thinking to myself, *My God, my wife is leaving me.*

Then I'll remember, *Wait — It's Father's Day!* A day when we fathers are revered for our wisdom, patience and, in a few rare instances, our neckwear. For one whole day I'll be the perfect father since my wife will be handling everything for me. She does this to help me relax and enjoy my special day. The problem is, it's hard to relax when, by handling everything herself, my wife makes it clear I could be replaced by a dishwasher and a few extra power cords.

Okay, that's not entirely true.

But it won't be long before my son can take out the trash. This will leave me with "The Grilling of Food" as my main contribution to the daily operation of our family. I have managed to keep this duty the way most men do, by making the task of grilling appear as complicated and miserable as possible, even if it means faking a heat stroke while grilling pre-cooked hot dogs. I realize there are many new fathers who have made themselves indispensable during the diaper-changing phase.

Just remember: Your indispensability in this area — much like this morning's tightly-wrapped dooty — will eventually disappear into the Diaper Genie. That's when grilling even the simplest things, such as a bratwurst, should be made to look as difficult as possible. To do this, you'll need a large grill. The bigger the better. In fact, if a hibachi is your main grilling source, go now, hop into your vehicle, and accidentally back over your hibachi several times and replace it with something more practical.

And, practically speaking, we're talking a grill roughly the size of a Miata.

Why?

You need a large cooking surface so that you can convincingly spray down flames and battle for control over a raging inferno that, if not for your grilling skill, would quickly consume everyone's bratwurst — and quite possibly the world. Unless you are highly experienced in pyrotechnics, or live near an open gas line, trying to produce this same effect on a hibachi is very difficult. Once you have your giant grill, you'll need to keep a spray bottle handy. Your wife will assume it's to prevent charring. This is partially true. But mostly you'll be using it to spray on your face and body to appear as though you are perspiring when, in fact, you are frequently supplementing any loss of body fluid with liberal amounts of ice cold beer hidden behind the grill.

Lastly, you should purchase a special, custom-made spatula that is so enormous and so heavy it can only be wielded with two hands. This will make the grilling process appear even more difficult by requiring a "spotter" every time you flip someone's burger.

Put all of this together — spray bottle, giant grill, two-handed spatula — and you'll have the dramatic image you want, which is that of a sweat-stained father staggering in and out of the flames of his grill, both hands gripped tightly around the handle of his 50-pound spatula as he devoutly retrieves the evening meal. Sure, this may sound like a lot of effort; you could fold clothes instead. But the effort is worth it when it comes to family.

Besides, it's really hard to keep beer cold when it's hidden in the laundry.

Frozen lima beans: The gift that keeps on gagging

It was 75 years ago this month that Clarence Birdseye, inspired by ancient food preservation methods used by Arctic Eskimos, made history by introducing the very first frozen food option: Savory Caribou on a Stick.

Though his first selection was met with little enthusiasm, Birdseye persisted, and eventually created a line of frozen vegetables that many of us are still gagging on today. I, for one, am still unable to walk past lima beans in the frozen food section without getting the dry heaves. This reaction stems from my childhood, and a spoonful of lima beans I've been trying to swallow since 1973. Unless you've been hermetically sealed and stuck in a freezer, you already know this is National Frozen Food Month. Coincidentally, I should mention this happens to fall in the same month as National Ear Muff Day, Extraterrestrial Abduction Day and National Pig Day, meaning that, for anyone whose pig happened to be wearing ear muffs at the time it was flash frozen by alien abductors, this is a big month for you.

For the rest of us, March is when frozen food manufacturers remind us to consider foods we wouldn't dish up without some type of extra incentive, such as giving it to a cell mate named "Big Red" in exchange for protection.

Which isn't to say all frozen food experiences have to be terrible. When I was a kid, I couldn't wait for Mom to pull my Libbyland "Sundown Supper" from the oven. That's because the makers of Libbyland provided enough games, toys and other distractions that, for all I knew, I was eating breaded eel.

In fact, I'm pretty sure I remember seeing an actual eel on the cover of the Libbyland box. This should have sent my childhood gag reflex into high alert. And it probably would have if not for the fact that this particular eel was wearing a cowboy hat and spurs. It didn't matter that a sea creature leading a wagon train through the high plains made no sense whatsoever. Or that the cowboy cook was a prairie dog who appeared to be stirring a pot of buzzard beaks. What mattered was that each dinner came with a packet of "Milk Magic" that turned my milk the color of gangrene and, even more importantly, grossed my mother out.

With those fond memories in mind, I went looking for the same kind of frozen dinner excitement for my own children. This led me to a collection of entrees that are either (a) the ultimate example of truth in advertising, or (b) menu items submitted by Hannibal Lecter.

The first thing I found was something called Jurassic Fried Chicken, which, for all I knew, meant really, really old fried chicken. I also grabbed Cheese Blaster Mac & Cheese, a Carnival Corn Dog meal, and, against my better judgement, Bug Hunt Fun Nuggets. The idea was to cook all four meals and let the kids have a frozen dinner buffet. This plan began to fade once I actually started reading through the meal descriptions, beginning with the Carnival Corn Dog: "A batter-dipped Frank made with chicken, pork and beef on a stick."

In this case, it wasn't the combination of meats that concerned me; it was the fact that "Frank" was capitalized.

This made the whole Bug Hunt Fun Nuggets concept of "finding" processed nuggets in the shape of insects a little hard to swallow. And to be honest, I had my concerns about how my five-year-old son's intestinal tract would react to a meal that included the term "Cheese Blaster." Of course, none of these concerns mattered to my kids; all that mattered to them was that Dad was grossed out.

Things probably would've ended there. But I felt obligated, as a concerned father, to show them my lima beans.

Geographically speaking, I have no idea what I'm talking about

When my daughter entered middle school this year, I knew it was only a matter of time before my worst fears were realized and, as a parent, I would have to help her with geography. As many of you know, I suffer from acute directional dysfunction — a disorder many famous historical figures also suffered from, including Christopher Columbus, who discovered America completely by accident while looking for...if memory of sixth-grade history serves me...a faster trade route to Wal-Mart.

I'm the kind of person who must enter and leave somewhere the same exact way in order to keep from getting lost, even if it means walking backwards out of a public facility, such as the men's room at Safeco Field. I've actually had nightmares about being a contestant on *The Amazing Race*. In it, I am partnered with my friend, David, who spent six years in the Marines and therefore still refers to distances in terms of "clicks," which is a unit of measure based on kilometers and the use of a special navigation device. Were I trying to find my way out of enemy territory, this device would be about as useful to me as a Super Ball. Because of this, my *Amazing Race* nightmare always starts and ends the same way, with everyone getting the first clue and then excitedly running off in the same direction, except for me, who excitedly runs in the opposite direction — and off a cliff with my "clicker."

It's a short dream but always traumatic, especially when I wake up lodged between the bed and the wall "clicking" my TV remote.

So when my daughter opened up her geography book and started talking about longitude and latitude, and the prime meridian, and flat map distortion, I knew it was time for me to buckle down and, as her father, at least try to get out of it by faking a seizure. Seeing her expression, I quickly realized I had already used this technique when asked about "where babies come from," "algebra," "geometry," and why her favorite shirt was now tie-died.

The truth is, I used to be good at helping her with geography, back when we could pour all the major continents and countries onto the floor and put them back together, usually with some parts of Hawaii missing because, as I explained, some of the islands were vacationing around Florida.

Clearly, this explanation would only lead to another pained expression from my daughter, and quite possibly the kind of parent-teacher conference I'd been hoping to avoid until she began chemistry.

"C'mon, Dad. I need your help. I can't figure the answer to this," she said, pointing to the last question on her sheet:

Using this flat map, determine the distortion ratio between these two continents.

"OK, looks like Russia and Africa," I said helpfully.

"Russia?" she asked.

"Yeah," I said, tapping what I knew to be the world's largest land mass, not counting Shaquille O'Neal.

"That's the Soviet Union, Dad."

Things weren't off to a good start but I pressed on. According to the formula, all we had to do was determine the coordinates of the farthest points on each continent, add them up, factor in the distortion ratio, then decide how much a "D" on this assignment was going to affect her overall grade. As it turned out, we actually DID figure out the correct answer. Don't ask me how because I honestly don't know.

However, in case you're wondering, it was still smaller than Shaquille O'Neal.

Now that you've graduated, YOU can find a place for that 70-pound ceramic pterodactyl

To graduating high school seniors: This is a bitter-sweet time for your parents, who are filled with angst and second-guesses, particularly if it appears that you won't be out of the house before the contractor is scheduled to demolish your room in order to finish the new Jacuzzi by July 4th. Don't get me wrong. Your parents will always have a place for you at home. It's just that, after the remodel, that place will have to be in one of the utility closets.

To help with this important transition, a lot of parents put together a "survival" package containing things like pots and pans, utensils, toiletries, dishes, tools — things from home that 1) you'll find familiar and comforting in your new life, and 2) they've been waiting to unload on you for years so they can buy all new stuff. To protect yourself, take careful inventory of this "survival" package before you accept it. Any small appliance — such as a toaster, blender or hot plate — that was made before standard outlets were introduced should be refused. The same goes for any "family heirlooms" that you've never seen before, but that your parents insist you loved as a child. In many cases, these items were never in your home to begin with, and are actually the result of an exchange program established by other parents of graduating seniors who are also trying to get rid of stuff they don't want.

The reason for this is simple: All parents know that whatever you leave behind after graduation will likely remain in the attic or garage until the reading of their wills. Because of this, they will stop at nothing to make sure you are accompanied on your journey by that 70-pound ceramic pterodactyl you made in fifth grade, as well as any other belongings that won't readily ignite should the garage be consumed in a "freak" inferno.

But, let's assume you manage to escape from home in anything smaller than a 27-foot moving van. Your next step as a graduate will be to settle into your new surroundings. For guys, this is a relatively simple process involving:

A nap.

And that's pretty much it.

Girls, on the other hand, tend to unpack as though each box contains a timed explosive device. If not stopped, each will detonate into a mushroom cloud of underpants revealing their true waist size to everyone within a three-block radius.

To complicate matters, many of you will also have a roommate your first year in college. It will probably be someone you've never met before, but whom you can rest assured has been carefully screened and, based on compatibility, specifically chosen as the perfect roommate. You will never actually meet this person of course, and will instead share a room with someone you once saw in a David Lynch movie. But that's all part of the college experience, which is aimed at preparing you for life.

(Or a life sentence, depending on how the whole roommate thing goes.)

Once you're settled, it's time to focus in on what you came to college for: An education.

Okay. Fine. Let's just be honest and admit that you chose a college based on which website had the best looking students playing volleyball in the fall leaves. Every college website has one of these photos, along with pictures of young, chiseled teachers lecturing before 300-seat-capacity halls filled with super models.

Warning: This is not real life! You will not find a lecture hall filled with 300 super models. In fact, your first semester, you'll be lucky if you find the lecture hall at all. And even when you do find it, chances are you'll be sitting next to your roommate.

That said, I wish all of this year's graduates the best of luck as they embark into the world with stars in their eyes and dreams in their hearts. And, if they weren't quick enough, a 70-pound ceramic pterodactyl.

Teaching a child to bowl is second leading cause of sterility

Teaching a child to bowl is truly a bonding experience. And by that I mean you should really consider taking out a bond before entering the bowling alley. As someone who escaped the experience of teaching his five-year-old nephew to bowl with only a minor skull fracture and minimal orthodontic surgery, I feel I've acquired a level of expertise that could be helpful. Let's begin with shoes. Changing into your bowling shoes while in the carpeted area will give you a false sense of security, making you less prepared for the realization that walking in traction-less

shoes on a highly-waxed surface is a lot like strapping soap bars to your feet and trying to cross a wet mirror. Ironically, a child has the natural ability to perform double axels over the same surface. Which isn't to say that you won't; it's just that theirs will be on purpose.

When it comes to selecting a bowling ball with a child, remember: At some point it will be hurled backwards and into your stomach, chin, and/or groin. So go light, and make sure the child's fingers fit the holes snuggly. A ball that's moving out of control but still attached to a small child can provide you with an extra two seconds of reaction time.

As most bowlers know, delivery style is a crucial element to success. A curve or spin placed at just the right arc can mean the difference between a strike or split. Fortunately, you won't have to worry about either since a child's delivery is closer to something like this:

Walk up to line.

Lift ball over head.

Throw ball straight down.

Get soda while ball is moved by earth's gravity toward pins.

It's at this point that the bowling alley's manager will offer your child free, personal instruction that begins immediately. Also, don't forget to ask for bumpers, which are metal gates about six inches high that extend to block the gutters and keep the ball in play. In addition to that, consider bringing along some extra fencing (chain-link is best) that can be attached to the bumpers. Though the metal gates keep the ball in play, the fencing will ensure that play remains in your lane.

Lastly, it's inevitable that children become infatuated with the ball-return mechanism, which, as I explained it, is sort of like a giant throat that hacks up bowling balls from somewhere beneath the lanes. At some point, a child will begin hovering around it in spite of your warnings that ball-return machines have been known to suddenly switch into reverse and suck small children into them, where they are forced to live as pin-setters until released by an 800-series bowler.

This makes no difference to a 5-or 6-year-old drawn to the mystery of the ball-return machine, which brings me to my final suggestion:

If you have children that bowl, always keep a spare.

Why is the Dog Wearing Cowboy Boots?

(They say pets help us live longer. “They” haven't met our dog.)

Learning to accept your pet's snoring problem could actually save your life

At three o'clock this morning, my wife sat bolt upright, yanked out her ear plugs and delivered the following ultimatum:

This has to STOP.

After propping myself up on my elbows and removing my ear plugs, I looked directly at her and said, quite frankly, she'd have to speak up if she wanted to be heard over the dog's snoring. Admittedly, it was my bright idea to have Stanley sleep in our room. That's because he's still a puppy, and therefore prone to chew up things we might leave out overnight.

Such as the living room or kitchen.

However, at three months old, his snoring sounds like a 250-pound man sleeping-off a three-day bender at the foot of our bed. Even with ear plugs, his snoring gets incorporated into my dreams, which has led to a recurring nightmare involving a race of giant wasps armed with chain saws. Part of Stanley's problem is genetics. Being half Shar-pei, he has a lot of loose skin and wrinkles. He essentially looks like a chocolate lab in need of ironing. In desperation, we took him to the vet, who told us that the loose skin around his face causes him to snore.

I'm not sure why he told us this, but I think there's a good chance Stanley has the same problem. Therefore, it made sense that some of the same methods used to treat snoring people might also work on dogs. At least it made sense at three this morning, when we started digging through the medicine cabinet in search of Breathe-Right strips. One thing we discovered right away is that these strips, while strong enough to flare even the largest set of human nasal passages, are no match for the elasticity of your standard pair of dog lips. The result was a series of fixed snarls which, if not for his wagging tail, would have been extremely frightening.

Next, we tried a throat spray specially formulated to stop snoring. According to the label, Snoreless provides "immediate results" by lubricating the throat and surrounding tissues, which often vibrate together and lead to chronic snoring. I don't know about all that, but I can tell you that our dog immediately yakked on the floor at supersonic speed thanks to his freshly lubricated uvula.

While cleaning up dog vomit at 4:30 a.m., we decided to call it quits. This decision came out of concern for Stanley's emotional well-being. These are the formative months, I reasoned, and there's a chance that having his lips taped back and being made to vomit in the middle of the night by the ones he loves could spell trouble later on. I know this because, as a pet owner, I have educated myself about my animals.

I am aware of their physical needs.

I am aware of their emotional needs.

I am also aware that in the past 12 months five people have been shot by their own dogs.

This was brought to my attention by Audrey Strausenberg of Grand Rapids, Mich., who sent in several articles detailing this disturbing trend. The most recent incident took place in New Zealand, where hunter Kelly Russell was shot in the foot by his dog "Stinky," who, authorities said, had no apparent motive other than being called "Stinky" for the last six years.

And for those of you who think this only happens with testy little dogs, think again. Last November, Joseph Tiffany of Grant, Neb., was shot in the ankle when his golden retriever (and I swear this is an actual quote), "Accidentally stepped on the shot gun, released the safety, and pressed the trigger."

Finally, there's the case of a 51-year-old man hunting near Stuttgart, Germany, who was shot to death while standing next to his car. Police ruled out suicide, and said that the shot gun must have gone off when the dog "accidentally" removed the safety, loaded it with shells, and then fired twice through an opening in the door frame.

In light of all this, should I somehow manage to get our dog to stop snoring, I doubt I'll be able to sleep anyway.

Today's pet care needs include cheddar cheese and a dog whisperer

Most of us expect to begin taking medication at some point in our lives, particularly those of us with small children. What many of us don't expect, however, is for the family dog to begin taking medication. I could be wrong, but I'm pretty sure this is the first generation to actually provide dogs with things like health insurance, plastic surgery, organ transplants and dentures.

When I was a kid, our dog seemed content eating table scraps, chewing on car tires and barking at the hot water heater. Those things were referred to as *character*.

Now, of course, these things are referred to as a *schizoid embolism* requiring psychological treatment, a diet plan and regular nightly flossing. Don't get me wrong: I'm not saying that we shouldn't provide our pets with the kind of health care they deserve. I'm just saying that I should have the option of being covered under my dog's health plan, which — with its dental coverage — is far superior to my own.

A few weeks ago, I took our Labrador to the vet after a series of "accidents" in the middle of the night. I believed this was the result of a) our dog having an incontinence problem, or b) the cat dipping our dog's paw in warm water.

Our vet said the only way to be sure was to obtain a urine sample from our dog for testing, at which point he sent me home with a plastic container roughly the size of a shot glass. As I feared, our vet explained that the sample had to go DIRECTLY INTO it in order to eliminate any chance of contamination.

There was never any question that I'd be the one stalking our dog with the shot glass, trying to catch a free pour until I either got the sample or was reported by a neighbor to the SPCA. I should add that our dog has always been a little jumpy, and a week of being stalked by someone trying to steal his urine hasn't helped.

After obtaining the required sample, I took it to the vet for testing and had my worst fears confirmed, which is that our dog does indeed have better health coverage than I do. We also learned that a dog's incontinence problem can be solved through a very simple, easy-to-follow combination of prescription medications, with one pill given once every other day, and a second pill given twice a day, every other day, but not on the SAME day as the first pill. After a month, the sequence is then reversed and continues until the incontinence stops completely, or both you and your dog are so confused that you don't care WHO pees on the floor.

Being that I am an organizer, I came up with a plan to keep track of everything by color-coding the pill bottles, then color-coding the calendar to match the correct sequence. As an extra precaution, I also created a spreadsheet that can be checked-off each night and, if necessary, used as a back-up in the event that we all go color blind.

Of course, none of this really mattered because our dog refused to swallow his medication.

When I tried sticking the pills in his favorite treat, it worked great. But it sort of defeats the purpose of having a prescription discount when you're spending $40 a month on cheddar cheese. That's when I, the dog-wrangler, decided I could force our dog to swallow his pills by placing them on the back of the tongue and poking them down with my finger.

In retrospect, this was clearly a bad idea.

On one hand, I can tell you our dog did swallow his pill; on the other hand, I can also tell you most of his stomach contents from that day. This brought me back to the cheese option, which I've stuck with for the last several weeks. While this has made giving prescriptions to our dog a lot easier and helped with his incontinence, the high rate of cheese consumption has created a different kind of problem — which has prompted a return to the vet.

And I'll tell you right now that if he wants a sample of THAT in a shot glass, he can do it himself.

Pack your bags, it's time to get the dog neutered

It was a foregone conclusion that we would have our dog Stanley neutered once he was old enough. Just like it was a foregone conclusion that, when it came time to deliver him into the hands of the vet, I would be playing the role of Judas. I thought about disguising myself and borrowing someone else's car so that Stanley would not associate me with his loss of malehood. My wife told me I was being silly. He's a dog, she reminded me, and capable of recognizing my scent no matter how I was dressed.

It didn't help the situation that my four-year-old son, after overhearing our conversation, had reached the conclusion that something serious was happening, and that it involved — but wasn't limited to — Stanley turning into a girl and biting daddy. Naturally, as responsible parents, we then sat down with our son and, together, convinced him that he had a hearing problem. We informed him the problem could be solved by allowing his ears to rest, which he should do by covering them as much as possible.

However, we realized our son would, from time to time, need to use his hands for something other than covering his ears. So, as rational adults, we also developed a secret code language in order to safely continue our discussion about Stanley. Using our new code, I explained that I was concerned how Stanley would react once he got home and discovered his luggage had been lost, and how he might hold me personally responsible since I was there when his bags were checked in.

My wife argued that dogs lose their luggage every day, and none of them go after the pilots.

I admitted she was right, but that most pilots aren't standing next to a passenger when they've just realized there's nothing waiting for them at the baggage claim.

That's when she explained to me that if Stanley missed his flight today, *my* luggage would be waiting for me on the front porch when I got home.

As I sat in the vet's office that afternoon, I avoided all eye contact with Stanley who, at 10 months old, still hadn't learned to fear people wearing latex gloves. When it came time, the vet explained that it was a simple procedure. That Stanley wouldn't be conscious during the operation, and that, as a male veterinarian, neither would he. But his assistants were perfectly capable of doing whatever is supposed to be done down there.

When they took Stanley away, he was happy.

When I picked him up a few hours later, he was still happy. Even though, with the cone over his head to keep him from licking his stitches, he looked like a dumb cousin to the RCA dog who had gotten a running start and gone headfirst through the small end of a Victrola speaker.

My wife called a short time later, and it was obvious that my son was with her because she asked how Stanley's flight went. I told her the plane landed safely, and that we would be home just as soon as I determined the physics necessary to fit a three-foot diameter cone through a two-foot-square car door opening.

Ironically, we'd probably still be there if Stanley hadn't fit in the luggage compartment.

Television for cats: Just one more reason not to have cable

Recently, the world's first-ever TV program specifically designed for cats began on network television. This groundbreaking show premiered — ironically — on the *Oxygen Network*, which demonstrates what can happen when creative minds are allowed to collaborate freely and openly in a room that is actually being *deprived* of oxygen. That's the only explanation I have for some of the things I saw on this show.

Things like cats doing yoga. Cat haiku. And a cat that eats with chopsticks.

Yes, I said a cat that eats with chopsticks.

As you might've guessed, the cat I saw doing this was Siamese, which is a breed known for its intelligence. I watched in amazement as Ying-Yow (which is Cantonese for "always hungry") demonstrated his supreme cognitive skills by using chopsticks fitted with special booties to eat a mixture of dry cat food and squid. As impressive as this was, he still isn't as smart as my two cats, who would have simply run away to find a new family.

But not before breaking the chopsticks and shoving them into the nearest booty.

This isn't to say that Meow TV is just a cat variety show. There are also long segments where the screen shows nothing but fish swimming in a bowl. Or sparrows eating in the park. This can last 10 to 15 minutes at a time without explanation or purpose, which is why I found myself checking to make sure I hadn't accidentally switched to watching Teletubbies.

For those of you who aren't familiar with Teletubbies, let me just say that after seven years I still have no idea what's going on. I know the names of the characters, and that they live underground in a spaceship somewhere in a magical forest. They all have some kind of antenna on top of their heads, each of which appears to have been damaged.

Probably when they crash-landed on Earth.

This would explain why they spend all of their time making baby sounds and dancing with a vacuum cleaner named "Noo-Noo" instead of accomplishing their supreme objective: To set up a base camp for the alien invasion. I say this because they have a highly advanced communication system complete with viewing screens mounted INSIDE their stomachs, and a giant transmitter disguised as a windmill that picks up images from anywhere on the planet — all of which they use for surveillance of things like....

Someone folding laundry.

As I said, I don't really understand what's going on in Teletubby land. All I know is that the Rev. Jerry Falwell doesn't either.

So, what's the connection between Teletubbies and Meow TV? First, our cats won't watch either one.

Second, when I took into account the many hours I've spent with my children trying to understand Teletubbies, I felt I owed our cats the same consideration when it came to Meow TV.

I'll now describe this experience in the form of cat haiku:

We tried cat yoga
Striving to reach inner peace
Before I bled out

That said, I hope those of you with cats have better luck than I did. My suggestion would be to avoid any form of yoga that places you within 20 feet of said cat.

Particularly if it has had to spend any time eating with chopsticks.

The horse yeller

By the time I hung up the phone, I was already picturing my strong, callused hand, toughened by years of rope burns and trail riding, reaching out to soothe a frightened horse that no one — including Robert Redford — could calm. It would be a communal experience, a sharing of untamed spirits and whispers, a life-bond between man and beast that would...

OK. Reality check.

It would be a week-long stint of horse-sitting that would basically shatter any fantasy I ever had of being a horse whisperer. In my mind, the whole thing would be as easy as dog-sitting, but with the fringe benefit of being a cowboy.

(Note: aside from the fact that both animals are quadrupeds, all similarities end there.)

Dogs do not weigh 800 lbs.

Dogs come when called.

Dogs can be manipulated.

And horses know this.

When it was time to bring them in, the horses had positioned themselves away from the corral, in the farthest corner of the pasture — somewhere near the Washington border. My instructions had been to carry a 10-penny nail and bang it on a bucket of oats. Once they heard the sound of the oat bucket, they'd come running because it was their favorite treat.

Except for today, apparently.

As I walked out in the field, both animals turned to face the sun, leaving me a view of "the moon."

Fine. No problem. Be gentle and patient.

Soothing.

I tapped the bucket, made horse sounds. Even whispered a little.

No response.

Tapped a little louder; called them by name. Gave the bucket a bang or two.

By now, I was less than five feet away, so I scooped up a handful of oats, extended it — and, after a frenzied moment of trotting hooves, found myself completely alone except for a cloud of dust, my oats, and a 10-penny nail.

The horses were now 800 feet away, on the other side of the pasture, back near the corral. For a moment, it was as if God had pressed "replay" on His universal DVD so He could watch this part again. Standing there with my nail and bucket of oats, I came to the conclusion that my whispering days were over. Instead, I grabbed a buggy whip from the barn, headed back out into the pasture, and began yelling — determined to chase the two delinquents into the corral.

The problem with whips is that, if you don't know how to use them, the self-mutliation factor becomes a serious consideration: For me, the goal was to get the beasts into the corral before I had whipped myself unrecognizable. The horses knew this, and were determined to change a few of my more distinguishing features.

After a good 30 minutes of running back and forth from one end of the field to another, I had successfully whipped myself into submission — and promptly returned to the corral. As I worked to stop the bleeding, I heard the sound of hooves approaching from the pasture. I looked up to see both creatures meandering up through the field and into the corral. Both stood there, eyeing me as I walked behind them and closed the gate.

"Gee, thanks a lot," I said under my breath, giving them each a handful of oats.

Don't mention it, I could swear I heard one of them whisper.

Insurance premium up? Thank my clumsy dog

Each year, we gather as a family to have our pets blessed on St. Francis Day. We do this because we want to give our pets every advantage, particularly if there's a chance — through divine intervention — that our chocolate Labrador's IQ could be raised above that of a standard carrot. I know this is supposed to be a general blessing situation, but I think God would agree there was a serious oversight during Stanley's creation process.

I know He is very busy.

I know He sees all.

But maybe He was also trying to catch the season finale of "Hell's Kitchen."

Whatever the reason, somewhere in the world there's a dog with two brains. Undoubtedly, its owners are very happy. They don't care that their dog's enormous cranium causes people and other dogs to stare. That's because their dog is smart. Their dog has an instinctive understanding of things like gravity. These owners give thanks to St. Francis each day because their dog, in spite of its bulbous cranium, would never high-center itself on a coffee table in front of company.

Stanley's problem is that he tries to move like a gazelle when, in fact, he has the dexterity of a bull moose. He may THINK he can leap over the back of the couch from a seated position, but repeated attempts have proven otherwise. I've given up trying to explain this to people; I simply tell them he must be choking on something and trying to give himself the Heimlich maneuver. It's less embarrassing than the truth, which, more often than not, prompts people to react as if their very life depended on not upsetting the lunatic dog before Animal Control arrives. However, Stanley does come in handy when trying to get rid of pushy sales people. All I have to do is open the door wide enough for them to glimpse a 60-pound dog repeatedly leaping chest-first onto the couch and then falling to the floor. On the rare occasion a sales person makes it through their entire spiel, I've yet to have one come inside even when invited.

I should mention that Stanley is more than a year old. The fact that he is still doing things like this concerns me. So much so that I began looking for a treatment. After hours of research and a lengthy discussion with my vet, we reached a disturbing prognosis for Stanley:

There is no treatment.

At least, not for him.

But I did find out that Stanley is not alone. According to a study conducted by Tesco Pet Insurance in England, Chocolate Labs are officially the clumsiest breed of dog on the planet. Tesco's study showed that Labs are twice as likely to hurt themselves while attempting something that researchers agreed, "Requires a crash helmet." In addition, 55 percent of Chocolate Lab owners filed a claim in the last year for damages to their home under the category "Act of Dog."

Unfortunately, this behavior is present in Labradors here in the U.S. as well. One example is a three-month-old Lab puppy in Oklahoma who recently blew the roof off his owner's house. As it turns out, "Jake" was fine and the family had left for the day. Firefighters speculate that the dog had chewed a hole in the gas line when a nearby water heater clicked on, causing a blast powerful enough to level the house.

This incident really put things into perspective for me. Come next year, when we gather our pets for St. Francis Day, I'll just pray for Stanley's continued good health and happiness.

That's assuming we still have a roof over our heads.

Women Are From Venus and Men Won't Ask for Directions

(Observations and insights that have gotten me into trouble.)

Balancing your checkbook is easy with the help of a Rhesus monkey

My wife is in charge of the checkbook and has been since we first got married almost 12 years ago. This was something we agreed on in advance of our wedding day, mostly because of the education my wife received as a business major in college. The fact that I was still keeping my money under an ice cube tray in the freezer also contributed to this decision. The truth is, even back when my wife's love for me blinded her to most of my shortcomings, she could still see that putting me in charge of the checkbook was like putting a Rhesus monkey in charge of...

Well, the checkbook.

This is because I am not a numbers person. While some people are able to solve complex mathematical equations dealing with numerical sequences and the square root of a hypotenuse triangle, others, like myself, still haven't figured out the correct way to read a tape measure:

Hmmm, looks like exactly seven feet, eight inches—plus about three little lines.

We recently looked into the cost of re-carpeting the living room. This, of course, meant determining square footage. For me, this was like calculating a trajectory for orbiting the planet Mars. After a series of failures that, had they gone unchecked, would've equaled enough material to carpet the entire house and most of the front lawn, I turned to the internet for help. It was there that I found an actual grade school math activity called Henry Carpets the Classroom, which teaches seventh graders how to calculate square footage. It was thanks to this website that I was able to determine the correct measurements by hiring a seventh grader to do it for me.

I am not ashamed of this.

I knew full well that my wife would find out when she balanced our account at the end of the month. But, as man of the house, I have nothing to hide.

"Who's Mr. Reggie Wilkins?"

"It's on the check."

"...Carpet consultant..?"

"Yeah, I wanted a second opinion."

"About what? Nap?"

It was at this point that my wife looked directly at me. I know this can only mean one of two things: Either she's forgotten to put in her contacts and wants to make sure the man she's talking to in the grocery store is indeed her husband, or she's expecting a reasonable answer in regard to something stupid that I've done.

Since we weren't in the grocery store, I deduced that she was looking for a reasonable answer, which, in this case, left me with only one viable response:

"FINE — then maybe I should balance the checkbook!"

The hope here was that the mere threat of ME handling our financial affairs would be so frightening that it would stun my wife to silence. This is known as a calculated risk, which is about as close to mathematical equations I get.

And, much like the few equations I've actually attempted, this one didn't work either.

"Okay — it's all yours," my wife said, and left.

Now, to give you an idea of the magnitude of fear that swept over me as I sat there alone in bed with a calculator and a pile of check receipts, insert the words "motion-activated nuclear lap grenade" after "alone in bed with" and you'll begin to understand the sheer terror of this moment. Of course, under no circumstances could I let my WIFE know this, which is why I briefly entertained the idea of just buckling down and hiring a seventh-grader to do it for me. Without question, this was absolutely wrong. (Just as it's absolutely wrong that a Henry Cooks the Books website doesn't exist.)

This meant either a) admitting to my wife that I was incapable of balancing our check book, or b) faking my own death and starting over in another country, preferably one that doesn't use the metric system. Because I love my family (and because there's no escaping the metric system anywhere outside of the U.S.), I swallowed my pride, admitted the truth, and offered a sincere apology.

In addition, I also offered to enroll in a personal finance course so that, at some point, I really could take over the check book and give her a much needed break.

My wife appreciated this.

She also appreciated my willingness to let her check out the cost of a Rhesus monkey, first.

Choosing colors with your pouse? Start with neutral corners

As I mentioned a few weeks ago, we are living in our home while it is being remodeled. This has meant making some adjustments in our daily routine. For example: learning to cook dinner while straddling a piano.

That's because the contents of our home are being shifted from room to room on a daily basis. It's a lot like having your home decorated by a feng shui expert with a serious drinking problem. Sure, you may expect to find a detached commode somewhere in the master bathroom. What you don't expect is for the master bathroom to be in your walk-in closet.

Since early June, each morning has essentially started the same way:

Get out of bed.

Stretch.

Walk toe-first into a piece of furniture.

Nighttime isn't much better. It has taken me years to learn to sleep walk from our bed to the commode. Now, even if I manage to navigate through our maze of furniture and back without getting a concussion, chances are I won't remember until morning that the commode was removed two days ago. In addition to the stress of living in a home that appears to have been the scene of a head-on collision between two cross-continental moving vans, my wife and I have entered into intense negotiations over room colors. This started with a trip to the paint store where we were introduced to even MORE colors my wife and I could disagree on. For example, there are at least 30 shades of puce in existence.

No one knows why.

Nonetheless, each shade has its own official name, such as “Gastro Sunset” or “Fermented Beet,” as well as a sample card, which professional painters collect and use in a game similar to “Pokemon.” The rest of us, meanwhile, take these cards home so we can get a clear idea of how frightening it would be to actually paint a room *that* color. Through this technique my wife and I selected a bold accent color: “Tainted Guava.”

After taking a sample home and painting a large section of wall with it, we realized there was a color we both agreed looked like vomit. We returned to the store and finally settled on a color I say is “plum,” my wife says is “burgundy,” but which is officially known as “Grape Ulcer.” This card is highly coveted in professional painting circles because the only thing that can stop it is the extremely rare “Satin Pepto” card.

Next came carpeting. I figured the worst was over because there were really only three considerations.

Is it a neutral color?

Is it soft?

Does it resist stains, i.e., contain enough Teflon to send our labrador across the house like a giant hockey puck?

Once again, things grew complicated. Did we want shag or short? Looped or cropped? Wall to wall carpet or area rug? All I wanted was for it to meet the above criteria and be guaranteed never, at any point, to spontaneously roll up like a burrito.

My wife wanted more. She wanted to scare me. She did this by using terms like “tackless skip,” “antimicrobial,” and “dimensional stability,” which made it sound as if we were planning to use our carpet to fly into space and fight microscopic aliens trying to destabilize the universe. Like most decisions within a marriage, it came down to an exchange of ideas and, eventually, a compromise. In this case, she gets to pick the carpet, and I get to walk on it.

Assuming I don't walk into something else first.

Navigating through heavy Traffic means being in the right hemisphere

It's a well-known fact that men and women think differently. This is because of the right and left hemispheres of the brain. While women tend to rely on the more creative, right hemisphere of the brain, which is responsible for verbal skills and abstract thoughts, men favor the more technical left side of the brain, which is mainly reserved for thoughts of sports and beer. This is why a man can deduce Anna Kournikova's exact measurements during a tennis match and, based on her perceived weight, determine exactly how many beers it would take before she would be intoxicated enough to make brief eye contact with him at a singles bar.

The difference between how men and women think has never been more evident than it was last week, during our family road trip to California. From the start, my wife insisted on being the navigator, even though, technically, navigation is a left-brain activity. I brought this to her attention, and, using her superior right-brain communication skills, my wife explained that, technically, I have the directional sense of a wind sock and would therefore remain behind the wheel and away from the Road Atlas at all times.

Admittedly, my wife was right about this point. When it comes to finding my way on the open road—or even on roads closed to thru traffic — nothing short of a full escort by compass-wielding Boy Scouts can keep me from getting lost. Several years ago while under hypnosis, I discovered that I was a Canada Goose in another life — a life that was tragically cut short after flying north my very first winter. Because of this revelation, I didn't argue about the driving arrangements.

At least not until we got to San Francisco.

You see, it was at that point that my left-brain processing skills discovered an interesting mathematical equation that goes as follows:

The time that is required for my wife to chart a course through heavy traffic is directly proportional to the number of lanes I have to cross in order to reach the appropriate exit.

Example: Positioned in the far left lane within eight lanes of heavy traffic, it takes my wife approximately six minutes to deduce that we should've taken the exit we passed five minutes ago.

That's because, in most cases, my wife is too busy shoving her feet through the floorboards and repeating the Rosary to worry about reading a stupid map that, in her words, "Was probably drawn-up by some left-brained, beer-swilling, sex-crazed, male with NO sense of direction anyway!"

Even though this announcement was made at the peak of rush hour traffic in the heart of San Francisco, it still illustrates the difference between how men and women think; In that same instant, MY thoughts were focused solely on traffic flow, and how, based on speed fluctuations and random lane changes, we could eventually catch up to the car whose driver I thought looked suspiciously like Anna Kournikova. In spite of these differences, we did find common ground once we left the interstate and went on foot into downtown. That's because, as man and wife, our bond of love and respect won't allow us to admit when both of us are completely lost.

But hey, if nothing else, at least we were in the right hemisphere.

Then again, maybe it was the left.

When it comes to a hot breakfast, nothing beats a flaming Pop-Tart

Cooking can be dangerous, especially when it includes all three components of what experts call the Triangle of Fire:

1) A heat source
2) Combustible material
3) My wife.

While I can vouch for her having absolutely nothing to do with any wildfires, she was in fact responsible for the 1992 Dallas, Tex., popcorn smoke-out at Keller Springs Apartments, which cost us a good stainless steel pot and most of our cleaning deposit. It only took that one experience for us to realize just how dangerous popcorn kernels can be once their internal temperature exceeds 6,000 degrees Fahrenheit — and only five more times before I banned the substance from our home completely, including microwavable popcorn. I'll spare you the details of what prompted that decision, but let me just say that if your microwavable popcorn bag is ever allowed to expand to the size of your favorite pillow, DO NOT open it.

Ever.

Our government has special underground dump sights specifically designed for this kind of toxic material; please use them. However, even with all of the precautions we've taken, it would seem that our family has been overlooking another potentially dangerous component in the Triangle of Fire:

The Flaming Pop-Tart.

According to a Philadelphia newspaper, that's exactly what happened to an unsuspecting New Jersey woman who said her kitchen caught fire after her cherry-flavored Pop-Tart "burst into flames like a blow torch!"

I'll be the first to admit that a fiery breakfast treat spewing artificial fruit filling would be a scary thing. In fact, aside from finding the real "Cap'n Crunch" floating around in my cereal bowl, I can't think of a more frightening breakfast experience. However, there are a couple of things worth noting about the flaming Pop-Tart incident — the first of which is that my wife had nothing to do with it.

She doesn't even know anyone in New Jersey.

Secondly, the Pop-Tart in question had been left unattended for 20 minutes while Brenda Hurff took her children to school. It was during this time that investigators believe the Pop-Tart "freakishly ignited" as a result of either a) the toaster malfunctioning, b) the pastry malfunctioning, or c) the surprisingly combustible nature of artificial fruit filling.

To ensure the safety of the general public, investigators called in agents from both the FBI and CIA to make sure that the burning Pop-Tart was, indeed, an isolated incident with absolutely no connection to any terrorist channels.

In addition, they also ruled out my wife, and any links to her watching *The Food Channel*. In case you were wondering, investigators have also decided against the possibility of spontaneous combustion as a cause for the blaze. This conclusion was reached after days of around-the-clock observation of assorted Pop-Tarts in a controlled environment, after which the following joint statement was released by the agents involved in the study: "We quit."

In any case, the fact that we don't have to worry about living in a world of spontaneously combusting Pop-Tarts is something that should help us all rest a little easier.

But I'd still suggest keeping them away from the popcorn, though. Just to be safe.

It's tax time, which means finding a way to claim that inflatable whale as a dependent

Just as we've done for the past 13 years, my wife and I arranged to have some quiet time so that we could go insane doing our taxes together. This process generally requires an entire day because my wife insists on keeping accurate financial records. These records are then piled on the kitchen table next to tax forms, booklets, a calculator, and last year's tax returns, all of which she organizes and obtains weeks in advance— and NONE of which, I remind her, would matter without my own contribution of:

Two sharpened pencils.

After more than a decade of doing taxes together, we have developed a system. Something that utilizes her talent for working with numbers and complicated tax formulas, and my talent for writing legibly in small boxes. It's a combination that, year after year, has never failed to result in...

You guessed it: A big fat argument.

There are several reasons for this. The first is that, as man of the house, I really have no idea what goes on here. I'm a father of two, which means I'm essentially a pack mule with a mustache. Most of my time is spent moving things from the car to the house, and then back to the car again — often for days at a time. In a lot of cases, decisions are being made while I'm still outside stuffing an inflatable whale into the car.

Even so, it's important for me to at least LOOK like I know what's going on. This requires maintaining a difficult balance between satisfying my natural instincts as a man to be in charge while, at the same time, assuming as little responsibility as possible. After years of practice, I've learned to strike this balance every day except tax day, when I'm reduced to chewing on a pencil and waiting for my wife to call out sum totals.

With that underlying tension already in place, it doesn't help that most instructions in the federal tax booklet read like this:

In order to determine the amount on line 17, please complete the simple, 37-step tax formula found on page 197 of this handbook which, due to budgetary reasons, ends on page 196. If you have any questions, visit the IRS website and join millions of other Americans who are just as confused as we are.

Because my wife likes to be prepared, she went ahead and grabbed one of every tax form available. This meant we had everything we needed should we decide to file as blind, millionaire yak farmers living as part-year residents with our adopted, 65-year-old child. As you might've guessed, we met none of those qualifications this year, which meant choosing between taking the Standard Deduction, or filling out the dreaded Schedule "A" and itemizing our deductions.

I say "dreaded" because, on average, you must complete at least six additional schedules before you can determine, through a progressive series of special tax equations, how much you'll be losing by not taking the Standard Deduction in the first place. This isn't always the case, however, as any blind, millionaire yak farmer can tell you. Regardless, we once again itemized our deductions and, for the first time EVER, realized almost immediately that we were definitely going to go with the Standard Deduction. This not only saved us a lot of time, but allowed us to get back to more important things.

And even though I'm not sure what those things are, I'm pretty sure they include at least one trip to the car.

Men are from NAPA, Women are from Macy's

If you want to observe the difference between men and women at its purest form, study their shopping habits. With the holiday buying season now officially under way, there's no better time to witness this phenomenon for yourself.

Here's a brief study guide to get you started.

Women:

a) Define an outfit as something comprised of at least three pieces of clothing, all of which are interchangeable and flattering.

b) Have researched the best buys and know where there's a sale today.

c) Are undecided about whether or not a drop-waist makes them look fat.

d) Will try on all clothes within arm's reach of the fitting room.

Men:

a) Define an outfit as something comprised of jeans. And maybe a fishing lure.

b) Have researched today's game schedule on ESPN and know they can get to the store and back during halftime.

c) Are undecided about how to answer when their wives ask if a drop-waist makes them look fat.

d) Won't get within arm's reach of the fitting room.

Obviously, the best time to conduct your study is when both men and women are in the store at the same time. This is easy to do if you just follow the Saturday sports schedule and plan your visits during halftime periods throughout the day. The first thing you'll notice is the difference between how men and women enter the department store.

Men don't browse, they buy.

Being a man myself, I can attest to the fact that we enter the store with absolute purpose, and continue walking that way, even if we have know idea where we're going. When we do find the clothing section, there's no wasting time on decisions about color or fabric; if it's denim and has working pockets, we're done shopping.

By comparison, most women enter a department store like archeologists stumbling upon the remains of a lost civilization. After creating a mental grid of the area, they begin the long, slow process of sifting through every rack and every bin of twisted undergarments until, eventually, they conclude there's nothing worth buying.

At which point they move to the next aisle.

For a thorough study of the shopping habits of men and women, you must also include men who accompany their wives shopping. Keep in mind that, in most cases, these men are there by choice, i.e., they've chosen to go shopping over having their wives sleep in mechanic's overalls for the next six months. The easiest way to tell these men apart from those who aren't there with their wives is to look for any man leaning on a shopping cart with the "100-yard stare." This is an unblinking gaze fixed on the exit doors, which, in most cases, are within 100 yards.

It's interesting to note some of the defense mechanisms that have evolved in these men over time. For example, waving at them instantly triggers loss of sight. Next comes deafness. Should you somehow manage to get their attention, these individuals will be unable to speak. Carrying on the experiment past this point isn't recommended unless you are a certified physician. That said, as we enter the holiday, gift-giving season, let's take time to rejoice in the differences between men and women. Let's embrace our diversity, and savor those things that define our genders.

And if possible, let's do it within 100 feet of the exit.

Time to mow again? Learn CPR first

Men, spring is almost here. That means it's time to start preparing for the very real possibility you will soon be neck deep in grass clippings. I made this realization while standing in the kitchen, sipping my morning coffee, and trimming dandelions away from the window screen.

"Do you think the grass is dry enough to mow yet?" my wife asked.

"It really needs one more day of sun," I answered.

"Actually, I think it's supposed to start raining tonight."

I, of course, knew this already, which is why I'd like to submit the following performance to the members of the Motion Picture Academy for their Oscar consideration:

[*Cut to:* Close-up of Ned as he slowly turns away from the grass-covered window and meets his wife's gaze...

"You're not serious, are you?" he says, stopping in mid-sip. He looks back to the window, which has already begun to sprout a new dandelion. Trembling, he sets his coffee down and lifts his gaze toward heaven. With outstretched arms, he whispers between clenched teeth, "Please — just one more day of sunshine" and throws his head back, emitting a deep, primal scream of frustration.]

"Knock it off," my wife said. "I saw you checking the Weather Channel this morning."

Standing in front of our shed thirty minutes later, I realized — like a lot of men — I wasn't prepared for the dreaded "First Mow" of the season. Aside from the fact that our lawn mower was buried beneath several layers of camping equipment and inflatable toys, I had a sneaking suspicion, once I dislodged the mower, that I was going to find what was essentially a hardened glob of grass clippings with a starter handle.

And no gas.

And probably no oil, except for what was oozing out from under it.

Yes, our lawn mower is old. The last time I took it to the shop, a man at the counter (who I'm guessing repaired the first combustion engine) hobbled over, tapped my mower with his cane and said, "Well — That brings back some memories."

This isn't something you want to hear when it refers to an important piece of mechanical equipment you rely on to keep your spouse from wielding a Garden Weasel. While it's true I've considered buying a new mower, I just can't bring myself to spend that much money on something which, for all intents and purposes, I will eventually come to despise. Because of this rationale I found myself straddling the mower in the front yard, yanking on the starter handle and giving what would be the equivalent of CPR to a two-cycle engine with congestive heart failure...

"Spark plug! Starter fluid! Clear!"

Fwopp. Fwopp. Fwopp.

"More starter fluid!"

"We're losing him, doctor!"

"I know that! Clear!"

Fwopp. Fwopp. Fwopp.

"He's hemorrhaging, doctor!"

"Quick, another pint of oil!"

Fwopp. Fwopp. Fwopp.

Sadly, I was forced to give up when the rain moved in earlier than expected, leaving me in the unenviable position of having to tell my wife I wasn't able to mow the lawn again. On the other hand, my performance could provide me with another shot at an Oscar.

Academy members: Please consider my lawn mower for a supporting role.

Inflatable church could have couples bouncing off the walls

The creation of the world's first inflatable church is without question, from a man's perspective, the most exciting matrimonial advancement since the bachelor party because it means the fun no longer has to end the night before the wedding, somewhere in the general vicinity of a commode. That's right, the excitement can continue the next day as the groom, flanked by his best man, bounces to the altar in his tube socks to await his blushing bride.

Because a fellow journalist friend and her sister are very close, and because I know how important it is that everything be perfect, I enthusiastically suggested the idea of an inflatable church for her sister's wedding.

And because she knew I was really trying to help, she smiled and told me I had an inflatable head. (She also added that if I had suggested something like that for my wedding, I would've definitely spent the honeymoon with an inflatable wife.) It became very clear that the inflatable church idea wasn't going to fly with most women, at least not until a smaller, pocket-sized version was made available. Something that could be carried in a handbag and deployed instantly...

"Matt, I think our second date is going pretty well — don't you?"

"Sure. I think you're great."

"Do you really mean that?"

"Absolutely."

"Oh, I'm so happy!"

[PFOOOP!]

"Hey, wait just a MINUTE...!"

I think the problem lies in the notion that, just because a church is made of plastic and can fit into the back of a U-Haul, it somehow won't be taken seriously. I mean, sure — there's a chance someone's high heels could puncture a pew and cause the entire church to deflate in the middle of the ceremony. And yeah, if you're planning to renew your wedding vows in the same church some day, there's a good chance it'll be covered with Monkey-Grip tire patches the next time you see it. But there are still plenty of reasons to consider the idea — beginning with the fact that the church comes with its own inflatable organ.

Since I haven't actually seen this organ, I'm going to assume that it's fully functional and — perhaps more importantly — a musical device. However, if I'm incorrect in this assumption, I CAN assure you that no groomsmen will be volunteering to blow it up.

It's also worthwhile noting that the entire church can be assembled anywhere in just three hours, then dis-assembled in less than two, which, altogether, is still longer than most of Jennifer Lopez's marriages.

But what if you're planning a big wedding?

The inflatable church is 47 feet long, 25 feet wide, and 47 feet high at the steeple. And if that isn't enough room, you can always push on the sides and squeeze a few more chairs in. Try doing that at some fancy-shmancy cathedral with its over-built stone walls.

I, of course, brought all of this to my friend's attention in hopes of getting her to at least consider the idea. She said that she would, as long as I understood that if I suggested the idea to her sister's fiancee, my legs would end up in an inflatable cast.

That's pretty much where our conversation ended.

However, I haven't totally given up on the idea. In fact, I've already reserved an inflatable church for my 10th wedding anniversary in 2018. Consider this your official invitation to what will undoubtedly be a very special and joyous occasion.

That is, once everyone stops staring at the organ.

If the jeans fit, wear them — until your legs go numb

I have a favorite pair of jeans I refuse to give up, and which, over the last few years, my wife has attempted to eradicate on six different occasions. She hates these jeans because, according to her, they are "ripped, frayed and embarrassing." Particularly when I forget to change them before going out somewhere in public, such as our front yard. Her attempts to get rid of my jeans have escalated from them being "lost," to an incident last week in which she claimed my jeans "spontaneously combusted," forcing her to put out the flames with the nearest extinguishing device: A meat cleaver.

She later apologized for hacking my jeans, telling me she reacted instinctively to a dangerous situation. I told her I understood, and that, instinctively, I planned to continue wearing my newly perforated jeans, at least until the remaining threads give way to the force of gravity and I am suddenly de-pantsed.

Probably while raking the yard.

There was a time when my wife actually liked seeing me in these jeans. Whenever I wore them I'd get... *The Look* — an eyebrow raise and quick scan of inventory suggesting the merchandise might be leaving the shelf before I could announce my blue light special.

Now when I put them on all I get is a roll of the eyes suggesting I hold a clearance sale to reduce some of my inventory.

Does that mean I'll stop wearing them?

Of course not.

That's because I'm a man. And as a man, looking good isn't nearly as important as proving I can still fit into the jeans I wore eight years ago, even if getting them on requires a case of cooking spray and an electric winch attached to the bumper of a Chevy 4x4. It doesn't matter that the waist is so tight my spleen is temporarily relocated behind my ears. Or that the contents of my pockets look like they've been vacuum packed.

"Is that a 1964 penny?"

"Yeah."

"How long until the impression on your leg goes away?"

"Depends. One time I had a Susan B. Anthony dollar that lasted a month."

"I hear you. I've still got a bruise from my car key — see?"

"Plymouth Voyager?"

"Wow, you're good!"

This illustrates a fundamental difference between how men and women think. Women by their very nature are theoretical thinkers. For example, just because fitting into the same jeans they wore in their early 30s is now like trying to stuff eight pounds of hamburger into an espresso cup, then, "theoretically," those jeans no longer fit.

(Naturally, there are women who are exceptions to this rule, as anyone who has been in Wal-Mart after 10 p.m. can attest.)

Men, on the other hand, think in terms of practicality, i.e., if we can practically button our jeans without losing all feeling in our legs, then they obviously still fit. It doesn't matter that our mid section is hanging over our belt like an over-proofed dinner roll. What matters is that we are in our jeans, and therefore "practically" in the same physical shape we were during our early 30s. Assuming, of course, that we were shaped like an inverted milk jug.

So, yes, I will continue to wear my "ripped, frayed, embarrassing" and now recently cleaved jeans. In fact, I may even wear them when I get home tonight.

Unless my wife has hidden the cooking spray again.

A woman's ability to remember is only equaled by — Oh heck, I forget!

Thanks to an exciting discovery published by the National Academy of Sciences, we're one step closer to understanding an important, fundamental difference between men and women — which is that women have better memories, particularly when it comes to remembering why they're mad at their husbands. This earth shattering discovery was made by psychology professors at Stony Brook University in New York, the same university that brought us groundbreaking data on the yawning habits of the domesticated yak.

My point being that the “better memory = more time in dog house for men” equation is NOT new information, and ultimately dates back to the very first marital spat: When Eve accused Adam of being insensitive for suggesting she make ribs for dinner.

And here in 2003, things are pretty much the same.

Case in point: After reading last week’s column about how men are essentially better drivers than women because we use the opposite hemisphere of our brain, my wife is STILL mad at me. According to results published by the National Academy of Sciences, this is because memory function in women is highly complex, and includes a direct tie to the emotional center of the brain. By comparison, memory function in men is a lot simpler because, like most brain functions in men, everything is tied directly to the [censored].

This discovery was made through a series of tests involving the ability of men and women to recall details from highly evocative photographs — such as gravestones and people crying. In every case, women’s recollections were 10 to 15 percent better than men’s. Not wanting to be outdone, men in the test group offered their own impressive display of memory skills by recalling the bust size of every waitress at the local *Hooters*. Researchers believe the reason women did better than men on the evocative-image test is because of something called “emotional memory,” which is the ability to associate personal feelings with memories.

[Note: Researchers believe the reason men did better on the *Hooters* test is because of something called “emotional mammary,” which is the ability to associate personal feelings with the bust line of a complete stranger.]

According to assistant professor Turhan Canli, “Emotional memory is the reason women tend to process things a lot more than men.”

Which is just a nice way of saying that if you accidentally recorded an NBA play-off game over your wedding video, don’t count on your wife forgetting about it anytime soon. Especially if YOU forget, and inadvertently watch the game while she's home. If that happens, I'd suggest apologizing, begging for forgiveness, and then taking her out to a nice dinner somewhere that's not even remotely in the same hemisphere as *Hooters* — which brings me to the point I've been trying to make all along, which is...

To be honest, I can't remember where I was going with this, but I'm sure it'll come.

Just as soon as my wife reminds me.

Want to know more about getting a vasectomy? Don't ask a man

There's a scene in the movie *Jaws* where the mayor of Amity Island explains how yelling the word "barracuda" won't get much reaction on a crowded beach. "But if you yell 'shark,' you'll have a panic on your hands..."

Keeping that in mind, you'll have some idea of the reaction you get from most men if you change "shark" to "vasectomy." This was the first word out of my radio this morning. And yes, it caught my attention. Apparently, March is the busiest month for vasectomies — and tomorrow is the busiest day of the year for this procedure.

Maybe it's a result of March Madness compromises reached between husbands and wives, or a subconscious tribute to the start of baseball season. Whatever the reason, when I had mine 10 years ago, it was also in March. The decision had nothing to do with basketball or baseball, and everything to do with weeks of campaigning from my wife.

Because she had a degree in social work, my wife was trained on how to approach sensitive subject matter. That's why I was allowed to discover, with no pressure from her whatsoever, that my new place mat at the dinner table was actually a medical brochure titled:

So, You Want To Have a Vasectomy?

True, we had talked about this subject before. Twice, actually; during the birth of each of our two children. I don't remember the exact conversations. But, on both occasions, I do recall the doctor informing her that, as far as he was concerned, the umbilical cord was the only thing we'd be snipping that day. The topic also came up when we had our dog neutered. Again, because of my my ex-wife's education and training, she avoided pressuring me and took a more subtle approach by calling our dog "Ned" for a week.

After breakfast one morning, during which I watched her repeatedly crack two eggs together and then scramble them — one pair at a time — in a flaming skillet, it became clear that the subject of a vasectomy needed to be addressed. So, after breakfast, we sat down together and discussed the issue like adults.

We went over the information carefully.

We educated ourselves on the mechanics of the procedure.

We weighed the pros and cons.

Then, together, we joined hands and pried my knees apart so I could drive to work.

To help ease my fears, my wife suggested I talk to other men who have had the procedure done. This makes perfect sense of you're a woman. That's because women are educated about their bodies while men, according to a recent study conducted by the American Medical Association, are "complete morons concerning their anatomy." Keep in mind that some have argued the study was inconclusive since researchers openly admitted their interviews with male subjects were "continually being interrupted by laughter and fart sounds."

This isn't to say getting a man to discuss the details of his vasectomy is difficult. What's difficult is getting him to explain it in a way that doesn't scare the pants of of you — which, of course, is his main objective. This tradition has been passed down through the years as an "unofficial" initiation rite in this "unofficial" club to which, officially speaking, no one really wants to be a member. In terms of membership enthusiasm, I'm guessing it runs neck-and-neck with the Hair Club for Men.

On the other hand, there are plenty of valid reasons to have this procedure done, each of which should be listed on a sheet of paper. Bring this list with you on the day of your surgery. That way, when you see the surgical knives and forget who you are, you'll at least have a way of remembering why you are there.

And if you happen to forget your list, don't worry; chances are your wife can recite it for you.

From memory and in the form of a rap song if necessary.

The day of my vasectomy, I just kept telling myself that thousands of these procedures are performed every day. In the are instance that something goes wrong, such as the loss of my manhood, the odds of my survival were very high. Certainly higher than they would be if I tried escaping the doctor's office without getting the procedure done at all.

So to all of you men who will be visiting Dr. Snippit tomorrow, I raise my glass to you; scotch.

On the rocks, of course.

Save water – fix that leaky light switch

The great thing about shows like *Extreme Home Makeover* is that they inspire ideas on how to improve your home. The bad news is that people like me then try to implement these ideas without the benefit of a trained professional. The result is our bathroom, which currently has a commode with hot running water and a wall heater that can only be turned on by unscrewing the third bulb in our vanity mirror.

I'd like to point out it wasn't my idea to take what had been a simple plan to increase the space in our bathroom and turn it into a major remodel. However, after one teeny mistake, my wife insisted on a total makeover — which brings us to our first home improvement tip:

The Importance of Bearing Walls.

You will discover that there are certain walls in your home — possibly even in the bathroom — which should not be removed because, as it turns out, portions of your home will collapse. As important as "bearing walls" are to your home's infrastructure, they aren't marked as such and, as a general rule, look just like other walls in your home. Which is why anyone who accidentally removes one, thereby inadvertently causing the total destruction of an otherwise functional bathroom, should be forgiven for this oversight.

So, let's assume the worst happens, and you find yourself standing in the middle of the downstairs bathroom while surrounded by the upstairs closet. And let's assume your family, in a show of support, still hasn't insisted on hiring a professional. Such as a hit man.

The next step is to rebuild the bathroom — and your dignity — as quickly as possible. To do this, you'll need organization and a basic knowledge of plumbing and electricity. If you don't possess this knowledge, don't worry! You will quickly gain it through practical experience, i.e., connecting the wrong wires and practically electrocuting yourself. Through this process of trial and error you will eventually be able to flush the commode without causing the outlets to spark.

The first step, however, is to clear the area of debris. Depending on the extent of damage to your bathroom, you may be able to do this quickly and easily by shoveling the debris directly through the floor and depositing it under the house. If a hole doesn't exist, feel free to make one. If your spouse catches you, feel free to crawl inside and seal it up behind you.

Once the room has been cleared, it's time to rebuild. Start with the bearing wall. Aside from its structural significance, it will symbolize the emotional healing process you are trying to foster with your family — and help avoid the need for a physical healing process should the bathroom be out of commission for more than 24 hours.

Next comes plumbing and wiring, which, I'd like to point out, should never be done at the same time. Sure, it may be faster and easier to run new wiring through an existing water line. But take it from me: If your pet occasionally drinks out of the commode, it's not worth the risk. The same goes for any other shortcuts that could turn your morning bathroom visit into what looks like an episode of *So You Think You Can Dance?*

That said, I hope this advice has been helpful. Feel free to contact me if you have any questions. I'll be happy to answer them as soon as I fix this leak in the light switch.

Spice up your wedding with a plague of locusts

At this very moment somewhere in The Deep South, a pair of newlyweds is racing past family and friends while being showered with frantically mating cicadas. As you might recall, we used to throw rice. That changed several years ago when environmentally conscious wedding planners tried switching to bird seed. The result was something similar to a Hitchcock movie, with hundreds of couples filing lawsuits after being plucked half naked by packs of frenzied sparrows.

Because of this, here on the progressive West Coast, we've struck a balance between tradition and ecological responsibility by replacing bird seed with low-curd tofu. Ask anyone who's been married here, and they'll tell you weddings are fun, environmentally sound, and, in many ways, a lot like a visit to the monkey cages.

But things are different in the South. Tofu, for example, is still looked upon as ...

Well, *tofu.*

Which is one of the reasons I liked living there. Any supermarket thought to have tofu in it was immediately evacuated, covered in a giant blue tarp, and sprayed. Only after someone from the CDC was able to determine, through extensive testing and analysis, that the substance in question was actually a gestating meat spore — and not tofu — was the general public allowed back inside. When I arrived in Georgia in 1987, many of the Southerners I met were a little suspicious. Some of this was due to my West Coast accent. But mostly, it was because I had been accompanied by a plague of copulating cicadas. You have to understand this phenomenon only happens once every 17 years, which is the only time these locust-like bugs emerge from the ground for their one chance to mate.

In an interesting coincidence, the last time this happened, I had just started dating my ex-wife. Since I have no desire to explore this coincidence any further, I will quickly move on before nature takes its course and, like many cicadas, I'm beaten to death with her shoe.

For those who haven't experienced cicada season, it's easy to imagine if you keep one thing in mind: For six weeks, wherever you go and whatever you do, you will be doing it within the general vicinity of at least 200 cicadas, each of whom will be participating in something generally reserved for late night cable. To make matters worse, thousands of male cicadas will be attempting to attract disinterested females by repeating a series of deafening mating calls, which entomologists, after years of research, have finally translated to mean: "*hey baby hey baby hey baby ...*"

If the cicada is unsuccessful in attracting a female with one approach, it, like any male, will then try something totally different, i.e. the same approach, only louder. This continues until either a) he attracts the attention of a mate, or b) he attracts the attention of my ex-wife and her giant shoe.

Given that we no longer live in The Deep South, male cicadas are safe from my ex-wife this time around.

I, however, am not.

There's a good chance it won't be 17 years before I'm reminded of this. In fact, I'm guessing it will come right after she reads about her "giant" shoe.

And trust me: That deafening sound you hear won't be a cicada mating call.

Self-aware leftovers: The forgotten victims of divorce

There's nothing funny about divorce. At least, not until you have time to gain some perspective and accept the fact that staying up until 2 a.m. reconfiguring the salt and pepper shakers on your dining room table is just part of the healing process, even if you don't happen to watch Martha Stewart.

Just like vacuuming the kitchen tile and mopping the living room carpet.

And getting excited over having extra closet space while at the same time avoiding that space as much as possible.

After a few months, I suddenly turned around and realized I had moved forward. As strange as it sounds, I think it started the day I threw away the last of the leftovers from when my ex-wife and I were still together. Granted, they had been in there for quite a while already. Possibly even as far back as Cinco de Mayo, though I couldn't be sure since the contents appeared to be a member of an unidentified fifth food group.

My point is, as I stood looking at that swollen plastic container of [food editor: please help me], I realized it symbolized much more than my inability, as a single father, to keep my children safe from a biological attack in their own kitchen.

Inside that container was something that had started out with lots of flavor; something good and enjoyable.

Something we had both contributed to.

And over time it had gotten lost somewhere behind everything else; was shuffled around; had things stacked on top of it. It had probably even been checked for freshness a time or two and, regardless of how much it began to turn, had been placed back into the refrigerator until, eventually, I found myself standing there holding it — and knowing it had been going bad for a while.

Naturally, I hesitated to open it. Not just because of what it represented. But also because in the back of mind I knew there was a chance — however slight — that it contained enough bacterium to become self aware. In addition to dealing with this rather delicate emotional moment, the last thing I needed was to find myself fighting off a salsa-based spore creature in my kitchen.

But...

Open it, I did.

There was a burp, and a brief moment of panic until I realized it was just my Tupperwear saying:

It's about time...(burp!) I couldn't hold it much longer..!

While there are plenty of other remnants of our married life together, for some reason this unremarkable, very ordinary (except for its appearance) part of our past seemed especially poignant in that moment.

However, that moment passed.

Specifically, right around the time my son walked in and said, "Dad! What is that SMELL! Geez!"

And with that I held the container upside down and watched my leftovers disappear into the trash can. I then moved the trash onto the back porch.

Then the back yard.

And eventually the curb, on the next block, where it will remain until Monday, when my trash guy will be attacked by a self-aware salsa-based creature.

I'd like to thank all of you for your letters and e-mails over the last several weeks, and for your patience in letting me serve up leftovers while I got back into the swing of things.

It's nice to be back.

Inspirational Holiday Columns That Proved Life Threatening

(Hey, even the NRA fears the National Fruitcake Lovers Society.)

Hold on to your giblets! It's time to prepare that very first Thanksgiving turkey

The countdown has begun. Soon, thousands of newlyweds will be in the kitchen preparing their very first Thanksgiving turkey. As a service to our readers, we felt a responsibility to help educate people about food-borne illness by offering a special holiday feature that we like to call:

Don't lose your giblets this Thanksgiving.

Being a writer, I've naturally spent a good portion of my career working in the food service industry. And like most writers, it was there that I was able practice my craft and eventually acquire something that ALL good writers must have: A Food Handler's card. Because of this, I can stand before you as someone highly qualified to talk turkey.

So let us begin.

Unless you actually live on a turkey farm (in which case you'll be serving ham or nachos or meat loaf or microwaveable pork rinds or ANYTHING but turkey this Thanksgiving), your bird has probably been somewhere in the bottom of the freezer since last January — in most cases, right next to that unlabeled container of something which, in its frozen state, has become completely unrecognizable. This means that you will have to thaw your turkey before cooking it. To estimate how long the thawing process should take, the rule of thumb is 24 hours for every five pounds, which means that if you forgot to pull your bird out ahead of time, you'll be thawing your turkey with a blow torch like the rest of us.

Once it's thawed, reach into the abdominal cavity and remove the giblets, which, apparently, all turkeys conveniently wrap in wax paper and then swallow moments before death. Next, you need to immediately place the giblets into the refrigerator. This will ensure they don't end up on the kitchen floor and, as a result, get thrown away after being mistaken for cat vomit.

If you choose to cook the stuffing inside the turkey, make sure that you don't over stuff the body cavity. This can impede the cooking process and provide a breeding ground for food-borne illness. In addition, the expansion of cooked bread crumbs in a confined space can lead to what culinary experts call "Exploding Turkey" syndrome. Though it's not lethal, it will mean a substantial delay in festivities while everyone waits for you to scrape the stuffing from the ceiling.

Important tip for first-timers: Once the bird has been stuffed, remember to put the legs into a tucked position using twine or a metal clip. This is important because, if you don't, the legs WILL spring up and do the splits at some point during dinner.

Okay, not really.

But if that does happen, you may want to put the turkey back into the oven for a while — assuming you haven't lost your giblets.

Don't forget about the cat when taking down the Christmas tree

For our family, packing up the Christmas decorations is never easy. Not only because it means the official end of the holiday season, but also because it means it's time to pry the cat out of the Christmas tree. What makes this process especially difficult is sap. You see, it's not until after spending the better part of December attached to the mid-section of our tree that our cat realizes she can no longer retract her claws.

A few years ago, this actually resulted in a front page story in the Weekly World News under the headline:

Holiday tree sprouts cat tumor!

It's not like we haven't tried to keep this tragedy from happening. In fact, we've even taken our cat to a pet psychologist, thinking that maybe she suffers from a traumatic experience that is somehow triggered by the site of Christmas trees — such as an unresolved conflict with a strand of tinsel. After six weeks of therapy (equal to eight years in cat time), the only thing the doctor was able to tell us for certain was that our cat had been Shirley MacLaine in a previous life, which, according to him, isn't all that unusual.

In short: He had no explanation for her behavior.

This, of course, led to my own — admittedly less scientific — diagnosis, i.e., our cat is totally crazy. This forced us to take drastic measures this year in hopes of avoiding another appearance in the tabloids. To achieve this, we came up with the idea of spraying our entire tree with WD-40. Initially, this seemed to be the answer as we watched our cat slide down the trunk and into the water bowl. But as we soon discovered, while WD-40 kept our cat out of the tree, it also kept any ornaments from staying on for more than six seconds.

This left us with a handful of desperate ideas, such as moving one of our stereo speakers under the tree and playing "Dogs Barking Jingle Bells" 24 hours a day.

That idea was dropped pretty quickly.

After six barks, to be exact.

We also toyed with the idea of decorating a dogwood tree, the logic being that a cat wouldn't go near a tree with the word "dog" in its name. That suggestion was nixed after my wife pointed out I'd first have to teach our cat to read. What all of this is leading up to is something you've probably already guessed, which is that, once again, the Christmas tree in our living room will remain there until it is completely brown and withered, and the sap has weakened enough that our cat can safely be detached.

In the meantime, we have already begun planning for next year, when we'll try to coax our cat to move high enough on the tree that we can use her as a top ornament.

Accompaniments for deep-fried turkey should include a fire extinguisher

The human brain.

Most of us have one.

For those who don't, there are warning labels.

Unfortunately, these warnings don't appear on actual humans. Instead, they are issued by the Consumer Product Safety Commission, which has the monumental task of thinking up ways stupid people might injure themselves using standard household items. While the commission generally stays ahead of the curve with the help of researchers, lab studies, and a select group of retired circus chimps, from time to time a hot new product is embraced so quickly by the general public that there's simply no time to warn them that actually embracing it could result in serious injury. This past holiday season, according to the safety commission, reports of house fires involving large men submerging whole turkeys into deep fryers has risen dramatically. This prompted the commission to issue a special, multi-paged consumer alert called:

Fryer, Fryer Pants on Fire.

Using this handy combustable pamphlet, I've organized a safety checklist from the American National Standards Institute, which oversees turkey-fryer safety standards, as well as any consumer product that includes the three components of what safety experts call the Triangle of Fire:

1) A heat source.

2) A meat product.

3) An intoxicated male.

This brings us to safety tip number one: *Never leave your turkey unattended.* Studies show that once the initial excitement of watching hot oil has passed, men quickly get bored and wander off in search of the nearest flat-screen TV. So, as a precaution, the standards institute suggests that wives keep an eye on their turkey at all times — or, at the very least, until he's done using the deep fryer.

Tip number two: *Always use turkey fryers outdoors.* Given the opportunity, men will set up their turkey fryer in the living room in order to watch football while cooking. This is dangerous because, should his team score at the wrong moment, there's a good chance the turkey will get spiked into the fryer. And hey, even if you manage to avoid this hazardous situation, there's also your home's resale value to consider — meaning that, should you ever decide to sell, describing your home to a potential buyer as having "three bedrooms, two baths, and a pleasant fried-turkey smell" will, in many cases, end negotiations.

And finally, tip number three: *Don't move fryer while it is in operation.* You should always wait until the oil is completely cooled before moving your fryer.

The only exception to this, of course, is if your wife catches you cooking in the living room.

The Easter Bunny is still getting help from fathers in boxer shorts

Soon, in the wee hours of the morning, something magical will happen in back yards all across America as, one by one, each of them is visited by...

You guessed it!

A half-naked father hiding Easter eggs.

That's right, the same fathers who were stomping on the roof with sleigh bells Christmas Eve will be out in the yard in their boxer shorts, shortly after sunrise, with an arm load of colorful eggs. Their mission? Keep this tradition alive while, at the same time, trying not to step in anything that could elicit a response deemed inappropriate for Easter morning. This generally follows a week of preparation, most of which is spent looking for the latest advancements in egg-dying technology. My parents didn't have to worry about this. When I was a kid there was only one kit available for making Easter eggs. This kit included four colored pills which could be combined to make additional colors or, as I preferred, swallowed whole and used to freak out kids in the rest room at school.

The green pill was particularly effective.

The red pill I tried only once because it gave me nightmares.

As I was growing up, there were a number of advancements in egg-dying technology. For example, the highly-touted "wand" made out of thin copper, which could be used for dipping eggs without making a mess. I know this because the back of the box showed a cartoon family making lots of eggs under the watchful eye of the Easter Bunny who was saying, and I quote:

Look, No Mess!

There were a couple of things that bothered me about this. First, it always looked like the family in the picture was being forced into coloring eggs by a brooding, six-foot-tall rabbit blocking the only exit from the kitchen. Sure, everyone was smiling, but who's to say they weren't just buying time until help arrived? Mysteriously, this family appeared on the back of the box for several years, and then — poof.

Gone.

I was also bothered by the fact that, despite what I'm sure must have been a rigorous testing and design process, the "wand" usually collapsed on itself and dropped the egg directly into the dye the first time you used it. After becoming a parent, I took it upon myself to find out who was responsible for this tradition. As it turns out, Germans introduced it to the Pennsylvania Dutch in the 1700s when, in an eager attempt to share their home land's annual spring celebration, hundreds German children began running around yelling: *Oschter Haws! Oschter Haws!*

Not knowing it was a call for the Easter Bunny, the Dutch children fled, taking their breakfast of boiled eggs with them and inspiring the first Easter egg hunt in the New World. Eventually, the Easter Bunny tradition was embraced by the Dutch who, like the German parents, realized it could be used as leverage against their children.

Three hundred years later, little has changed. Good girls and boys still get a visit from the Easter Bunny, and fathers still stumble outside at first light to hide colored eggs. That said, I'll take this opportunity to apologize to my neighbors in advance of Easter, just in case I step in anything left behind by something other than the Easter Bunny.

Planning your 'Black Friday' shopping? Don't forget Bigfoot

There are times when, as a columnist, I am faced with the difficult decision of choosing between two equally important topics in order to meet my deadline. Then there are times like this when, thanks to years of experience and accidentally consuming a quadruple espresso meant for the person next to me at Starbuck's, I realize both topics can be combined into a single, well-structured piece of journalism.

Which is why, today, we will be talking about how to prepare for holiday shopping with the help of Bigfoot.

As some of you may have heard, a hiker in Utah recently posted video of what appears to be Bigfoot rummaging through the brush.

In addition, some of you may have heard about Thanksgiving.

I don't believe this is a coincidence. Especially when you consider how, year after year, Thanksgiving is followed by Friday — a shopping day so enormously frightening it has become known as "Black Friday." And did I mention the Bigfoot spotted in Utah has black fur? As you can see, the correlations are staggering.

(Note to writing students: This merging of seemingly unrelated topics at high speeds is extremely tricky requiring years of practice, and is a device referred to by journalists and railroad engineers as a "train wreck.")

Now that we have established the irrefutable connection between Bigfoot and holiday shopping on Black Friday (I'm a journalist, so you can trust me when I say we have), I will now explain how, with a little preparation and an oversized SUV or cargo van, you can get all of your holiday shopping done next Friday with the help of Bigfoot. The first step, of course, is to locate and enlist the help of a Bigfoot. This is actually easier than you might think. All you have to do is drive to a heavily wooded area and NOT look for one. This seems to be when most Bigfoot sightings occur, right when the hiker, anthropologist, logger, marijuana grower, *Fox News* reporter, etc., is least expecting it, which is why every video taken of Bigfoot looks like a deleted scene from the Paranormal Witch Project.

Once you have made contact, the next step is to convince Bigfoot to help with your holiday shopping. To do this, offer your help in obtaining something he wants for Mrs. Bigfoot but can't find in the woods — such as an Epilady shaver.

Once you have found Bigfoot and enlisted his help, it's time to go SHOPPING!

Given that Black Friday is the busiest shopping day of the year, with retailers opening before dawn and offering outrageous deals, such as 50 percent off any six-toed socks sold between 5:30 and 5:45 a.m., you'll be glad you brought Bigfoot along to play "wack-a-mole" with anyone who gets in your way. The same goes for sneaky sales people who try the old "bait-and-switch."

For example, let's say the clerk insists that the item on sale for $10 is a cheese spreader, and not the 55-inch flat screen TV in your cart. Simply let Bigfoot do the negotiating by turning the clerk into his own custom Snuggy.

Now imagine the satisfaction of completing all of your holiday shopping in one day as you and Bigfoot breeze through the mall on matching Segways donated by mall security. Needless to say, when it comes to Black Friday shopping, there are many advantages to enlisting the help of Bigfoot.

Plus, I'd suggest staying in touch; he also comes in handy when it comes time for gift returns.

Say what you want, but fruitcake could be our last defense against alien invaders

Recent studies show that mild depression after the holidays is not only common but, in many cases, is the result of FDAD — Fruitcake Disposal Anxiety Disorder. On one hand, your fruitcake was a gift and therefore deserving of some measure of appreciation. On the other hand, it has already become a chew toy for the neighbor's pit bull. This often leads to feelings of anxiety long after the holidays have ended, particularly when you see "Buster," still intoxicated with rum, struggling to dislodge the sugar loaf from his tightly-clenched jaws.

So, as a service to our readers, we assembled a group of psychiatrists to help provide insight into dealing with FDAD. At a cost of more than $200 an hour, we held an informative, three-minute discussion to create the following self-help guide: *I'm OK — You're OK. But Give Me a Fruitcake and I'll Kill You.*

According to our experts, the first step in dealing with this anxiety is understanding where it comes from. To do that, we must go back to the very first fruitcake, which historians agree was baked by Dick Clark in 1609. Subsequently, this same cake was dropped from a tall building each New Year's Eve until 1972, when, after 364 years, it developed a crack and, as a safety precaution, was launched into space. This was done despite protests from scientists, who warned that the loaf could eventually crash back to earth and lead to mass extinction.

Or, at the very least, cause the next several generations of humans to ask, "Is it just me, or does everything STILL smell like #@$% fruitcake?!"

Experts say this has led to a new generation of people who not only distrust fruitcake, but see it as a genuine threat to humanity. For these people, we offer the following four-step guide to controlling their fruitcake anxiety.

Step one: Make a list of your fruitcake's good qualities. The key is to start with what makes fruitcake unique. For example: Its indestructibility. You may not like fruitcake, but you have to respect the fact that cockroaches will be eating it long after humans are being imported to other galaxies on alien party platters.

Step two: Incorporate fruitcake into your daily activities. This is easy once you stop thinking of fruitcake as food. In the same way that Tofurkey is slowly gaining acceptance as an environmentally safe adhesive, fruitcake doesn't seem so bad once you've started using it to block open the garage door. Or as a counterweight on the gas peddle while your car warms up each morning. The point is, if it's good enough to serve as a "bunker buster" for our military, it's good enough to serve as a doorstop in your family's home.

Step three: Consider turning your fruitcake into a treasured heirloom by getting it engraved and then giving it to someone. Just add your name and date, and you can pass this special keepsake on to someone else at the next available birthday party, wedding, house warming, Earth Day celebration, etc.

And finally, if after following these first three steps you're still unable to control your symptoms, go directly to Step four: Investing in a ticket to Mantiou Springs, Colo., for the annual Great Fruitcake Toss. Each January, this event draws hundreds of people from around the world for the sole purpose of showing off their fruitcakes and then catapulting them as far as possible.

Sure, this may sound stupid.

But some day this might be our last defense against invading aliens.

The people have spoken! The world is full of fruitcakes

Every once in a while a column strikes a nerve with readers. These readers then write me to express their displeasure; they are angry, hurt, offended, or breaking in new stationery. Whatever the reason, I appreciate this feedback regardless of the fact that, in many cases, the column they're talking about wasn't mine. So you can imagine my shock at getting unhappy letters from people who (a) read my column and (b) actually like fruitcake.

The letters came in response to the column I wrote about Fruitcake Disposal Anxiety Disorder, which was named in a *New York Times* special investigation as "The fastest-growing mental disorder in the entire world. And we're pretty sure about that," the report concluded. "If not, then it's right up there with 'Fear of Clowns' or something."

After receiving these letters, I looked back over the column and realized that, yes — it was a little insensitive to fruitcake lovers out there. So, in response, I spent time looking into what makes a good fruitcake, compared with the kind of fruitcake the rest of us receive each holiday season. After comparing dozens of recipes and then baking four different fruitcakes of my own, I realized something important — which is that, by using a six-inch bundt cake pan, my daughter now has a full set of tires for her Barbie Jeep.

Again, I'm not saying that there's no such thing as a good fruitcake; I'm just saying that if there's an R-14, all-weather radial bunt pan out there, I'd like to know about it.

I should point out that over 21 million fruitcakes were sold in the U.S. last year, and not one of them was allowed on any flight in or out of Canada. That's because fruitcakes have been added to the list of banned carry-on items on all Canadian flights. This is due to the X-ray machine's inability to penetrate fruitcake, therefore making it impossible for screeners — or even Superman — to verify if they're safe.

"Well, look at that! A fruitcake from Lex Luthor. How thoughtful!"

"Be careful, Superman."

"Relax, Lois. What danger could there be in...WAIT! THOSE AREN'T CANDIED GUAVAS!"

Admittedly, there is a huge difference between what passes as fruitcake here in the U.S., and what the English refer to as "plum" cake. While the English version is said to be extremely moist and flavorful due to its high rum content, American fruitcake is known — like many U.S. food products — for its durability. This is particularly true of commercial fruitcakes, which are primarily used for keeping decorative tins from getting bent during shipping.

Lesley Hatcher of Panama City, Fla., who wrote in promising to change my mind about fruitcake by shipping me a homemade sample next year, is obviously very passionate about fruitcake. Frighteningly, she's not alone. As a member of the Society for the Protection and Preservation of Fruitcake (www. Fruitcakesociety .org), she is "one of thousands" who are "spreading the gospel about fruitcake."

(Note: After looking long and hard, I'm happy to report there's no reference in either testament to The Gospel According to Fruitcake.)

According to Lesley, the fastest way to get someone to stop making jokes about fruitcake is to give them a piece. I'm not sure if that's supposed to change their mind or keep them from speaking, but whatever the case, I promise to keep an open mind until next year.

Who knows? I may end up eating my words. Then again, I may end up with a spare for my daughter's Jeep.

Okay, maybe fruitcake doesn't threaten humanity

Journalism can be a dangerous profession, even for those of us who never actually leave our desk unless a "situation" develops, such as the sudden and unprovoked arrival of free donuts. On several occasions, I have found myself in harm's way as a dozen employees stampeded into the break room (which, according to the fire marshal, has a "maximum occupancy level of two, as long as no one is using the commode"). It is at those times, while being crushed between fellow employees grappling for the last maple bar, that I am reminded of just how dangerous my job can be.

But it doesn't end there.

No.

Not for those of us with the courage to SPEAK OUT against what is wrong with the world. Or, in my case, what is wrong with fruitcake. As you may remember (and judging by the number of fruitcakes that have been appearing on my desk, at my home, or through the window of my car, many of you do), it was last year around this time that I drew the wrath of fruitcake lovers everywhere after suggesting that untold numbers of people (source: Dan Rather) suffer from Fruitcake Disposal Anxiety Disorder.

To refresh your memory, FDAD occurs when the recipient of said fruitcake has feelings of anxiety over how to dispose of their gift in a way that is (a) respectful, without (b) inadvertently raising the terrorist threat level. I say this because, unlike its English counterpart, which is said to be moist and delicious, American fruitcake is known — like many U.S. food products — for its durability. This is especially true of commercially produced fruitcakes, which are primarily used to keep decorative tins from getting bent during shipping.

My flagrant disregard for fruitcake rubbed a lot of people the wrong way, particularly those who were already on edge after waking up from the holidays in a rum-induced fog. I was besieged with e-mails and letters from readers like Lesley Hatcher of

Panama City, Fla., and Dale and Yvonne Pretzer of Florence, Ore., who promised to change my mind about fruitcake by sending me homemade samples this year.

I had no reason to suspect this would actually happen, and that I would receive enough fruitcake to finish the retaining wall in my back yard. If I had, I would've also flagrantly disregarded beef tenderloin, and any Scotch over 30 years old.

But a promise is a promise. I said I would sample everything with an open mind and, in the event of a sudden fruitcake epiphany, seek immediate medical attention. After which, I would issue a formal apology to the fruitcake lovers of the world.

Just as soon as doctors had me stabilized.

Due to the volume of fruitcake I have been consuming, this process has taken longer than expected since I've spent most of the last few weeks hung over and picking candied fruit from my teeth. However, I'm willing to admit I may have overstated things when I called fruitcake a "threat to humanity." The same goes for what I said about launching fruitcakes into space as a defense against alien invaders. The truth is, I may have to renounce my title as "Ned Hickson: The Fruitcake Grinch," as given to me by the Pretzers. I'm not saying I'll be joining the Society for the Preservation of Fruitcake any time soon. Only that I'd be willing to put myself in harm's way should we experience an unprovoked fruitcake attack again next year.

Which brings us to our next topic: My flagrant disregard for live-shipped Maine lobster...

Men: time is running out if you want to avoid being a love dunce

As a public service to men everywhere, I am hereby issuing the following announcement: Valentine's Day is *tomorrow!* If you are married, have a girlfriend or, for reasons of your own, feel a need to continue the charade of dating a Swedish airline stewardess who is always out of town, it's time to start planning something romantic. For those of you in the latter category, this will be easy since the only person you have to worry about pleasing is yourself.

And, yes — I plan to clarify that last statement immediately.

What I mean is that every male currently in a relationship with an actual living female could, by Feb. 15, all be dating the same fictitious Swedish airline stewardess should they fail to impress their Valentines. As a result, men everywhere are panicking because we know that impressing the women in our lives isn't easy. We realize that you are complicated creatures who need more than a physical connection when it comes to romance; you also need an emotional outlet in order to feel satisfied.

We, on the other hand, just need an outlet located near the television. Metaphorically speaking, even if romance was a TV channel, and suddenly every station on the planet went out except for that one, it still wouldn't make any difference because, let's face it: Men would curl up in a fetal position and require regular changing.

It's not that we don't want to be romantic. We just have a hard time expressing our emotions and allowing ourselves to become THAT vulnerable again so soon after the Super Bowl. However, we realize how important this is and will try anyway because we care.

Sure — fear does play a small part, but mostly it's because we care. For this reason, I'd like to offer a few romantic tips that men can use this Valentine's Day.

Tip number one is to bring flowers to your Valentine. This seems pretty obvious. However, I should point out that, even if you don't remember them until Feb. 15, the gesture will still be appreciated by your Valentine since she can just bring them to your funeral.

Tip number two is to cook her a romantic dinner. That said, keep in mind that dinner by candlelight is always romantic; dinner by flaming-chicken light, however, is not. So if you can't cook, don't. Sure, she may be impressed with your take-charge attitude as you "stop, drop and roll" with a blazing chicken thigh, but more than likely the mood will fade once you both realize...

Well, you're on the floor with a flaming chicken.

And my final tip: If you plan a surprise getaway in which you whisk your Valentine away for the weekend, make sure you carefully pack everything she will need. Because no matter how nice the hotel is, no matter how incredible the view, and no matter how wonderful dinner and dancing might be, none of it will matter if you forget to pack any actual clothing.

To ensure you remember everything, I have developed the following fool-proof packing technique: Dump everything from the closet, dresser and bathroom into Hefty bags, even of some of the items appear to be components to the Mars Rover. She will appreciate the gesture.

But feel free to leave out the flaming chicken thigh.

If at first you don't succeed, I'll meet you at customer service

It was 12 years ago this week I found myself standing in line with approximately 800 other husbands (conservative estimate) who, like me, had been sent to return the Christmas gift they had gotten their wives. I distinctly remember this for a number of reasons. First, because it's rare to see so many men standing in line for something that isn't leading to a sporting event, urinal or more beer. Not necessarily in that order.

Secondly, I remember it because the loudspeaker, which was positioned directly over my head, played the same Christmas song 16 times. This was over the course of an hour, by the end of which I was making up lyrics I can't print here. What I can tell you is that my son will never, EVER be allowed to have a drum.

However, the main reason I remember this so well is due to sheer coincidence, i.e., coincidently, every man standing in line with me was returning an Epilady Shaver. Each conversation with the customer service person went something like this:

"Can I help you?"

"I'd like to return this."

"Is there something wrong with it?"

"Yes, my wife can't use it without throwing it at me."

"It looks like it's been damaged. Is this the way it came?"

"No, that happened when it landed in the driveway. My wife has a good arm but not much aim."

(Uncomfortable pause.)

"I'm serious. She chased me. Naked. I don't think I'd be alive if she hadn't slipped on the linoleum. I'm just glad the dog was there to break her fall."

"Sir, unfortunately I can't give you a refund because of the damage. All I can do is give you a store credit, which you can use to get her something else."

"Good grief!"

This is the typical male reaction when it comes to gift buying for their wives, particularly in this case, when the stakes have been raised exponentially by the "make-up gift" factor. For example, let's say a man gives his wife a robe that is too big. Exponentially speaking, we're talking about a factor of one because, in spite of the sizing error, his wife had been made to feel petite. Therefore, he can simply exchange the robe for a smaller one. Looking at the opposite end of the spectrum, let's say the robe in question is too small. Exponentially speaking, we're talking about a factor of 50, which is the number of times he will be rat-tail whipped with his wife's robe before she has exhausted herself enough for him to yank it away.

As I stood in line that day, it was obvious that every man was attempting to calculate the exponential "make-up" factor for a gift that had come from the heart and left through the bathroom window. It was also obvious that most of us had forgotten every mathematical equation we'd learned since the seventh grade, which could explain why several men broke from the line and disappeared into the business supply section.

I, however, was not one of those men.

I'd like to say it was because I managed to calculate the "make-up" factor in my head and, through my mathematical prowess, determined the exponential number to be...

Well, a big one.

Possibly involving something algebraic.

But, no. The reason I didn't race for a calculating device is because, by that time, my brain had been lulled into submission by a drum-beat pattern. When I got to the customer service counter, our conversation went something like this:

"How can I help you, sir?"

"Rum-ba-ba-bum."

"Are you returning that Epilady?"

"Rum-ba-ba-BUM."

"Sir, it looks damaged. All I can give you is an in-store credit. Is that OK?"

"Rum-ba-ba...oh God..."

So men, as you return that special gift this week, remember the "make-up" factor and exchange your wife's gift accordingly. It probably wouldn't hurt to bring a calculator

Mother's Day cards have no rhymes for 'episiotomy'

Soon, it will be Mother's Day. For many of you, it means sending a flowery card that says all the wonderful things you'd say if only you had a thesaurus and someone from Hallmark breathing down your neck.

The truth is, the meaning of Mother's Day has been lost over the years thanks to stupid greeting cards filled with heartfelt phrases like:

If your love was an ocean, you would've drowned me as a child.

Or,

When I think of love, I think of you. Because of this, you have no grandchildren.

Or,

With every smile, I remember a special moment that will never ever be forgotten — Happy belated Mother's Day!

The true meaning of Mother's Day, as any mother will tell you, has absolutely nothing to do with flowery cards or fond memories — and everything to do with sacrifice. That's right. You want to let Mom know you really care? Forget about comparing her to "a beautiful rose laden with thorns of caring," and remember all the stuff she endured for you even before you HAD a memory. If you're not sure where to begin, I have two words for you:

Breast Pump.

True, not every mother utilized this torture device, but the mere thought that she could have is reason enough to be grateful. If you don't believe me, go right now to the nearest full-service car wash, attach an industrial car vacuum nozzle to one of your mammilla, push the "on" button, and keep it there until your chest resembles a deflated balloon animal. Then switch sides. Repeat this process three times a day for at least six months, WITHOUT the aid of alcohol.

Remember that breast pumping came after nine months of losing control over most of her bodily functions, including — but not limited to — food cravings. These cravings came as a direct result of YOUR needs inside the womb, even though, in many cases, those needs could gag a contestant on *Dumpster Diver*. But she did it anyway, in spite of the fact that, as you were developing and shaping, so was she: Developing swollen feet the size of couch cushions, and taking the shape of a giant Weeble capable of destroying Tokyo.

Keep in mind that during this process, she was still merrily preparing for your arrival by hanging borders, assembling mobiles, making trips to the doctor, all while visiting the bathroom once every three minutes.

Then finally, to show your appreciation upon arriving into the world, you treat her to an episiotomy. Chances are, you won't find any of this in a greeting card. Mainly because there are very few phrases that rhyme with "episiotomy."

Although The things you taught-a me since your episiotomy has potential.

That's why I'm mentioning it here, so that hopefully, someone, somewhere, will read this and offer me a job at Hallmark.

Okay, that's only part of the reason. The main reason is to say "Thank You" to all you wonderful mothers out there, especially those who are celebrating their very first Mother's Day this year.

You know who you are.

And if you don't, try turning down that breast pump a notch or two.

No pumpkin-carving experience is complete without a near-fatal knife wound

Carving a jack-o-lantern used to require little more than a pumpkin, an oversized kitchen knife, and a tourniquet. It was a simple matter of plunging a 10-inch French knife into the gourd of your choice and creating a triangle-eyed, square-toothed masterpiece of horror. In those days, the trickiest thing about making your jack-o-lantern was deciding on how to light the candle.

Option one: Light candle, then attempt to lower it into the pumpkin without catching your sleeve on fire.

Option two: Put the candle inside the pumpkin first. Then attempt to light it without catching your sleeve on fire.

Option three: Accept the inevitable and just light yourself on fire, then go find a candle.

After a quick trip to the emergency room for stitches and some light skin grafting, you could return home and set your jack-o-lantern on the porch, where it would remain until gravity and molecular breakdown eventually caused it to collapse in on itself like the birth of a new star — appropriately enough, usually around Christmas time.

But somewhere along the way, things have gotten complicated. The 10-inch French knife — once the pumpkin-carver's tool of choice — has been replaced by kits that include sophisticated, high-precision instruments that, aside from creating fancy Halloween scenes on your pumpkin, can also be used, if necessary, to perform an emergency triple-bypass. The first time I saw one of these kits was a few years ago on *Good Morning America*, when Martha Stewart was re-creating the flying monkey scene from *The Wizard of Oz* on the face of an 800-pound pumpkin. After scooping out the insides with a back-hoe (which she had forged herself out of recycled Mason jar lids), Stewart demonstrated how anyone could sculpt their own gourd into a Halloween Mecca by first creating a simple pattern using common household items, such as a dry-erase marker, overhead projector, and $300,000 movie still.

In spite of this newfound knowledge, I kept with tradition because it's hard to imagine any Halloween without a near-fatal knife wound to reminisce about.

...Until this year, when my children quietly took me aside and told me our pumpkins always look ... how did they put it? Oh yeah.

Really stupid.

Being a father dedicated to his children's happiness, I of course told them that I appreciated and respected their honesty. After which I told them Halloween had actually been cancelled this year, and that we would be proceeding directly to Arbor Day. That's assuming that Santa and the Easter Bunny were still missing.

I didn't really say that! Ha! Ha!

Okay — so I did.

The important thing is that my children have learned to laugh

HEARTILY whenever their therapist brings the subject up.

As you've probably guessed, I gave in and bought a fancy carving kit this year. The first thing I discovered about these kits is that, once spread out, the assortment of tools bares a striking resemblance to an operating tray on *ER*; lots of shiny things that look sharp but appear to serve no obvious purpose. Next, there are the instructions, which describe how the tools can be used to create any of the following *As Seen on TV!* images:

1) Witch riding broom across moon.
2) Black cat with hair standing on end.
3) Bat sitting on tombstone.
4) Martha Stewart.

Included in the kit are four patterns, along with a list of the really cool patterns which, naturally, are sold separately. Knowing how important this was to my children, I was willing to make one final trip to the store in order to obtain the blueprints to our ultimate pumpkin masterpiece: Martha Stewart hitting bat with tombstone. Of course, by the time you read this, we will have already completed our jack-o-lantern. I promise to share the details with you.

Just as soon as I put these flames out.

Your decomposing pumpkin could threaten mankind

I left the house this morning and made an important realization: What I had assumed was a fleece-lined, bright orange sweatshirt laying crumpled on the front steps was actually NOT a garment at all.

It was our jack-o-lantern.

This realization was made while attempting to pick it up. Though my intention was to give my children a stern lecture on taking care of their clothing, I decided instead to scream uncontrollably after grabbing a handful of pumpkin mucus. Somehow, our pumpkin's aging process had accelerated, causing it to collapse in on itself and sprout white fur — literally — overnight. This isn't an isolated incident. Anyone who hasn't disposed of their jack-o-lantern by now has witnessed this process, which we can all agree defies the natural laws of physics. One morning, your pumpkin's face is triangle-eyed and gap-toothed as normal. The next morning, it is Buddy Hackett.

Should the process be allowed to continue, there's a chance your pumpkin will actually collapse so far in on itself it will create its own gravitational pull and eventually threaten the space-time continuum. If, while poking at the remains with a stick, you suddenly find yourself leading a pack of ape-like people into battle to obtain fire, it may already be too late. (Though there's no hard evidence to prove it, this phenomena might explain the '60s.) To avoid a cataclysmic event ushering in the return of bell-bottom pants, you have a responsibility to the rest of us to dispose of your gourd immediately, even if it means scraping it up with a shovel and transporting it to a government facility.

However, for those of you who remember to dispose of your pumpkin before it contains enough organic matter to become self-aware, you have another option, which is to drive to Milton, Delaware for the annual Punkin' Chunkin' World Championships. There, you will find the kind of excitement one can only get from jettisoning a large gourd as far as possible without the aid of rocket fuel.

The annual event, which has taken place each year since 1986, got started the way a lot of sporting competitions do: by having two men argue over who can throw something the farthest.

In this case, an anvil.

Fortunately, fate (most likely, in the form of a pulled groin muscle) intervened, and "Punkin Chunkin" was born. In a nutshell, participants use catapults, air cannons and oversized slingshots to hurl large pumpkins over great distances. Last year, Bruce Bradford's winning toss set a new world's record but, tragically, took the life of an Amish man during a barn raising in nearby Pennsylvania.

The good news is, "Punkin Chunkin" is catching on across the U.S. Soon, you may not have to drive as far as Delaware to chunk your punkin! The bad news is, because of growing popularity, you could, at this very moment, be standing in a "Punkin Chunkin" drop zone. This is similar to standing in a golf course drop zone, except, in this case, no one will be yelling "FORE!" before you get hammered with a 10-pound gourd traveling in excess of 60 mph.

Just to be safe, I would avoid going outside until the competition officially ends this weekend. Assuming, of course, there isn't a sudden shift in the space-time continuum. In the event that happens and I find myself wearing checkered bell-bottoms, I ask that you please direct me to the nearest "Punkin Chunkin" drop zone.

Santa Summit prompts Greenland 'No-Fly Zone'

What makes e-mail great is that it's so darned easy to use. For example: If you come across something that absolutely HAS TO BE SEEN by everyone you know — like say a picture of a cat doing chin-ups — you can simply click a button and send it to 100 people. Or in the case of my favorite aunt who still hasn't mastered this process, you can send that very same knee-slapping picture to one person — such as your favorite nephew — 100 times. The reason I bring this up is because, if not for e-mail, I sincerely doubt someone from Midland, Mich., would've gone to the trouble of sending me a photo of 176 Santas standing on the deck of a fishing boat off the coast of Greenland (and YES, this is primarily the kind of e-mail I get).

I should mention that we were one of 50 newspapers that received the photo, which was part of an announcement letting people know that classes at the Charles W. Howard Santa Claus School had come to an end.

Now, opening my e-mail at 5:45 in the morning to find a pack of wild Santas waving champagne glasses at me from the bow of a fishing boat was enough to make me re-start my computer AND swear-off watching any more claymation Christmas cartoons after 9 p.m. However, it wasn't enough to keep me from visiting the school's website in order to find out the connection between Michigan, 176 wild Santas, and what must've been the strangest cruise ship experience this side of Orlando.

What I discovered was that the photo was taken during the first-ever Santa Summit in Northern Greenland, where men and women from 13 different countries — including the U.S. — came together to exchange ideas, drink too much, and get stuck in the chimneys of local villagers. This would explain why all 176 Santas were apparently confined to a large fishing boat and taken out to sea. It also explains why Greenland, a peace-loving country that has no military of its own and proudly proclaims it has never waged war on anyone, recently passed a resolution allowing persons dressed as Santa to be attacked by snow dogs and/or harpooned on sight.

No questions asked.

Given that all three of my questions had been answered, the safe thing to do would have been to delete the photo and get back to work. But as we all know, the Internet can be a dangerous place, particularly for those who are impressionable, unsupervised, and not facing a deadline. As a result, I discovered some interesting mathematical equations about Santa's yearly trip around the world.

To begin with, Santa actually has 31 hours to work with on Christmas Eve, thanks to the different time zones and the rotation of the earth. Considering that Santa is able to deliver an estimated 91.8 million presents in that amount of time, I really have no business whining about going to Wal-Mart and having my dozen or so presents wrapped for me while I sit across the street drinking coffee at Starbuck's. In addition, for Santa to make all of his stops by Christmas morning, he must fly at speeds in excess of 650 miles per second — or roughly 3,000 times the speed of light.

Given that the air resistance would be similar to a space craft re-entering the earth's atmosphere, we can safely assume that Rudolf and the rest of Santa's reindeer would burst into flames and cause a sonic boom loud enough to knock the top ornament off of every Christmas tree on the planet. Santa, meanwhile, would be pinned to the back of his sleigh by a gravitational force about 17,500 times stronger than Earth's gravity.

Of course, this is all just speculation.

Odds are, he might not make it past Greenland.

Before you buy that Christmas gift,ask Mr. Knowitall

Since the introduction of our new Consumer Products investigator a few weeks ago, many of you have written in to Mr. Knowitall seeking advice about holiday gift-giving. For those of you who might not be familiar with Mr. Knowitall, I should explain that, in addition to being our resident historian, he is also our economist, consumer products expert, food critic, movie reviewer, foreign affairs consultant, science correspondent, and vending machine repairman.

Not necessarily in that order.

We chose him because of his vast knowledge on a variety of subjects, and because, conveniently, he happens to be here every Wednesday to re-fill the Cheetos. I know this doesn't necessarily make him an expert, but he says he is — and, being a professional journalist, that's good enough for me. Before we begin, I should explain that due to the enormous volume of mail we received, letters will be answered through a lottery-style process. Which means that, until he wins the lottery, Mr. Knowitall will continue to answer your letters.

So let us begin.

Dear Mr. Knowitall: Do those electronic muscle stimulators really help trim fat and tone muscles?

— Really hope so in Reedsport

Dear Really: As you know, the principle behind the device is the utilization of a continuous sequence of small shocks that stimulates muscle activity, similar to your body's own natural electrical impulses. An easy way to think of it is to visualize a car and its battery. Now visualize the car, the battery — and a pair of jumper cables clamped to your buttocks as someone starts the engine. While there's no scientific proof this will trim fat and build muscle, studies show that most people find themselves stimulated enough to go to the gym after one session.

So, in answer to your question: Yes, it does work, but indirectly.

Dear Mr. Knowitall: I'm looking at getting my husband something to help with his snoring. Any suggestions?

— Yawning in Yachats

Dear Yawning: I'll tell you there are a lot of products out there that claim to end snoring problems, and most of these products are 100 percent effective. And though they may look and cost differently, these devices all rely on the same two principles, which are:

• Fit into someone's nostrils

• Be really uncomfortable

This combination is proven effective because it:

• Keeps snorers from sleeping

My advice is to try rolling him on his side. If that doesn't work, try rolling him the other way. If *that* doesn't work, keep rolling until you hear a big thud. Repeat this until he's too frightened to sleep.

Dear Mr. Knowitall: I'm thinking of getting my wife some of that spray that helps remove body hair. Is it safe?
— Harry in Florence

Dear Harry: Not for you, it isn't.

Dear Mr. Knowitall: I'd like to get my wife a personal protection device for Christmas. I heard about something on the internet that's a combination pepper-spray gun, flash light and whistle. Any idea where to find it?
— Wondering in Waldport

Dear Wondering: It's called the Pepper Escort defense kit and you can find it at www.pepperescort.com/description.html. It was invented by Dan McClarin out of concern for his daughters, who are apparently very attractive and very good at multi-tasking. The gun shoots a steady stream of pepper spray, which causes burning of the eyes and throat, constriction of the nasal passages, and inhibited breathing. Aimed in the opposite direction, the gun can be equally effective against an attacker. In addition, you can also blow your whistle and shine the flashlight in his eyes.

Yawning in Yachats, if you're still reading, this is one option I hadn't thought about...

Men: Help your wives avoid jail by returning those stupid gifts you got them

Many years ago, I bought my wife an Epilady shaver for Christmas. Because it was a sleek, modern, electrical device costing over $50, there was no reason to suspect it would feel like someone had just ripped the hair out of her legs using Super Glue and a roll of duct tape. While I'm sure I'd gotten her gifts she didn't really like, she's always accepted them. But in this case, as she chased me through the house completely naked and swiping at my scalp with her new Epilady, two things came to mind:

1) She really hates this gift,
and
2) I shouldn't have gotten her the cordless model.

Now, before I get an angry letter from Park Products, Inc., I should clarify that this was a long time ago, and I'm sure the latest model is a vast improvement over the one my wife hurled through our bathroom window. My point is this: Men, if you've gotten your wife a really stupid Christmas gift, it's not too late to save yourselves. Even if it means dropping the newspaper right NOW and wrestling your wife's gift away from her.

She may be shocked.

She may get her feelings hurt.

But trust me, it's better than what'll happen if she unwraps her present and finds a purse that looks like a coconut. As cool as it may have seemed when you bought it, chances are it will go totally unnoticed by the people who matter most — such as detectives searching for the weapon used in your murder...

"I know this is difficult, ma'am, but did your husband own a cannon ball or something similar that could've been used against him?"

"Hmmm. Not that I know of. Would you care for a mint?"

"Say, that's a cool coconut purse."

"It was a gift from my husband. [Pretending to cry] It was the last thing he ever gave me..."

"Well, he obviously had good taste — OUCH!"

"I'm sorry. Did I close it on your finger?"

The first step in defusing this situation is acceptance; as men, we must accept the fact that we are — by our very nature — total gift-giving morons. We simply do not understand the complexities of choosing a woman's gift. Heck, we barely understand the complexities of choosing the correct hand towel in the bathroom. How can we be expected to walk into a department store, spend 5 to 10 minutes scrutinizing hundreds of gift options, and emerge with anything other than a coconut purse?

Furthermore, it's when denying this fact to ourselves that we really get into trouble. This usually occurs when attempting to be creative with our gift buying by—how else?—trying to think like a woman. This is a bit like Donald Rumsfeld trying to be Britney Spears. Even if he learns the moves and memorizes the songs, once the wrapping's off, no one is going to be happy.

So men, take it from someone who has experienced, first hand, what it's like to have portions of your hair ripped out by an angry wife wielding a cordless shaver: If you think you've unwittingly purchased a stupid gift for the woman you love, you must do whatever it takes to make sure she never finds it.

If it's already too late, then I'm truly sorry.

But chances are, no one is ever going to find you.

It's time separate Thanksgiving fact from fiction with the help of Mr. Knowitall

It's been 382 years since that first Thanksgiving, when the Pilgrims and Wampanoag Indians sat down together in celebration and, much like the Americans of today, made a solemn vow not to eat more than your standard bull elk. We know this because of a passage recently discovered in the diary of Pilgrim Edward Winslow, who described the first Thanksgiving like this:

Our harvest be large so that we might rejoice! Our plates and bellies be full to swelling! We have feasted on meats and gathered crops, and pies of sweet fruit!

Aye, I say! I think it be time to vomit!

— Edward Winslow, Dec. 13, 1621

In spite of this kind of irrefutable historic documentation, many myths still exist about one of our most celebrated holidays. For example: Did anyone actually eat the Indian corn, or was it just used as a decoration?

As a special tribute to Thanksgiving, we asked our resident historian, Mr. Knowitall, to help separate fact from fiction about this important holiday. For the last several weeks, we encouraged readers to send in their own Thanksgiving questions and, as a result, were inundated with literally dozens of empty mail bags.

That was as of yesterday.

Amazingly enough, our postal person showed up this morning with a truckload of mail from people all around the country! That's right! In fact, there were so many letters that we were forced to utilize a highly complex selection process requiring dozens of volunteers, an empty office, and one wild squirrel. I know it sounds unbelievable.

But I'm on deadline right now, so you'll just have to take my word for it.

Before we get started, for those of you who might not be familiar with Mr. Knowitall, I should explain that, in addition to being our resident historian, he is also our economist, consumer products expert, food critic, movie reviewer, foreign affairs consultant, science correspondent, and vending machine repairman.

We chose him because of his vast knowledge on a variety of subjects, and because, conveniently, he happens to be here every Wednesday to re-fill the Cheetos. I know this doesn't necessarily make him an expert, but he says he is — and, being a professional journalist, I believe him.

That said, let us begin.

Dear Mr. Knowitall: Is it true that the Pilgrims made popcorn on the first Thanksgiving?

Mr. Knowitall: Yes and no. By the end of the celebration, the Wampanoags noticed that no one had eaten any of the Indian corn they brought. When asked about this, each of the 56 Pilgrims said they'd somehow overlooked it. Not wanting to insult their guests, Miles Standish then offered to hand out the corn, but "accidentally" dropped the bushel into a fire pit. The result was the beginning of popcorn and the end of the first Thanksgiving.

Dear Mr. Knowitall: Why is there no traditional Thanksgiving song?

Mr. Knowitall: Because Weird Al Yankovic hasn't written one yet.

Dear Mr. Knowitall: What's the best way to prepare a turkey?

Mr. Knowitall: That's a tough question. Everyone has their own preference. Personally, I think it's best to avoid eye contact. Just call it into the kitchen and don't let it know what's coming. The same goes for your guests if you happen to be serving Tofurkey; if you want them to stay, it's best not to let them know what's coming.

Unfortunately, that's all we have time for today. I'd like to thank Mr. Knowitall for sharing his wisdom and helping to clarify some of the history behind Thanksgiving. In addition, I'd also like to tell him I'm sorry—

But we're out of Cheetos again.

Fireworks restrictions take excitement out of having facial hair

First, the good news. According to the National Council on Fireworks Safety, fireworks-related injuries have dropped by 75 percent in the last decade. The bad news, as anyone over the age of 30 can tell you, is that today's fireworks are about as exciting to watch as a pile of smoldering pencil shavings.

For example: It used to be that "sparklers" actually sparkled. They showered the air with tiny crackling embers so bright you could see them through your eyelids. The bravest kids would spin them like propellers, knowing full well their eyebrows would grow back by mid summer.

My kids don't believe me when I tell them this. That's because, each July Fourth, they are handed "sparklers" that are basically sticks of incense that smell like sulfur. No crackle. No shower of sparks. Just a momentary flame as the paper wick ignites, then — upon reaching its climactic flash point — fizzles into a puff of flatulent-smelling smoke.

Note: In the event you happen to purchase a defective sparkler, and find yourself the unwitting victim of actual spark-spitting action, DO NOT PANIC. Call the NCFS hotline immediately so your rogue sparkler can be safely deposited in a special, undisclosed location three miles beneath the Mojave Desert. If there's no time to drive to the desert because, say, you live in Michigan, you will be instructed on how to disarm the sparkler yourself. This will mean transporting it to an unpopulated area and, utilizing protective gear and the most extreme caution, dipping it into a glass of water.

Several times if necessary.

Those of you who live in Alabama or Tennessee have no idea what I'm talking about. That's because you have real fireworks. The kind that childhood memories (and a good portion of our nation's first-strike capabilities) are made of. In addition, the only real restrictions you have are as follows:

1) If a skyrocket is longer than your boat trailer, it must be flagged during transport.

2) You must, by law, inform neighbors when using any fireworks that require a dynamite plunger.

3) Though there is no limit to the number of M-80s you can join together with a single fuse, the Department of Homeland Security warns it can't be held responsible should your area, as a precautionary measure, be swept with heat-seeking missiles.

4) If you have studded tires, you must remove them. This has nothing to do with fireworks; it's just a friendly reminder from the folks at the Highway Department.

And lastly,

5) Any and all skyrockets capable of leaving southern air space must be pointed north.

The fact is, even though I whine about having wimpy fireworks here in Oregon, at least we have them. In Georgia, they are illegal. This means watching public fireworks displays or, as many Georgians do, going outside and facing Alabama. Even though these displays are beautiful, it's still not the same as being knocked unconscious by a runaway ground flower.

Being as I lived in Atlanta for six years, I can tell you illegal fireworks do make their way across the Alabama border. This, of course, is a huge problem.

Especially if your boat trailer isn't big enough.

Stop the presses...

That's right; you've reached the last page of this book.

This leaves you with two options. The first is to fall to your knees in a heap while beating your fists against the ground in agony. This will likely draw a few stares, depending on where you are at this moment. For example, if you are a teacher at a daycare center, it will probably go unnoticed. On the other hand, if you happen to be an airline stewardess on a transcontinental flight, it could raise a few eyebrows. Especially if you are encountering turbulence. The second option is to sit quietly while I thank you for reading this book. As I mentioned, this book has been a long time in the making. Granted, it's mostly because I'm a procrastinator — which is something I plan to change.

Soon.

Until then, I want to take this opportunity to extend a handshake and appreciative nod for your purchasing and reading this book. Particularly if you aren't actually related to me. If you happen to be a regular reader of my column — or even if you suffer from irregularity — I owe you a tremendous thanks. In all seriousness, this book wouldn't have been possible without you; without your support; without your encouragement and participation.

For all those things I am truly grateful.

And for those of you who are just now getting here, it's good to have you.

But I still expect a written excuse from one of your parents...

CPSIA information can be obtained at www.ICGtesting.com
Printed in the USA
LVOW04s0515260115

424330LV00001B/1/P

9 780989 260831